Journey to the Land of the Inca

OUR ERRAND FROM THE LORD

Richard Berry Whitaker

Journey to the Land of the Inca
OUR ERRAND FROM THE LORD
Richard Berry Whitaker

© 2017 Richard Berry Whitaker. All rights reserved.

No part of this publication may be reproduced or transmitted in any form or by any means, mechanical or electronic, including photocopying and recording, or by any information storage and retrieval system, without permission in writing from author or publisher (except by a reviewer, who may quote brief passages in a review).

Disclaimer: The Publisher and the Author make no representations or warranties with respect to the accuracy or completeness of the contents of this work and specifically disclaim all warranties, including without limitation warranties of fitness for a particular purpose. No warranty may be created or extended by sales or promotional materials. The advice and strategies contained herein may not be suitable for every situation. This work is sold with the understanding that the Publisher is not engaged in rendering legal, accounting, or other professional services. If professional assistance is required, the services of a competent professional person should be sought. Neither the Publisher nor the Author shall be liable for damages arising here from.

ISBN-13: 978-1533408402
ISBN-10: 1533408408
© 2017 1st Edition
Cover Photo: Machu Picchu, South America. Author Unknown, Public Domain.
Type-Editing & Cover Design by:
Michael Barlow (contact@michaelbarlow.info)
Additional Editing by Judith Naegle (judithnaegle55@hotmail.com)

CONTENTS

Ecuador Quito
Mission Employment Resource Center
2000-2001

The Adventure Begins 3
The Senior Missionary Training Center 9
Shafted! 13
Cesar Cacuango 19
Men in Black 23
Our First Trip to Guayaquil 25
A Comedy of Errors! 35
A Road Trip to Otavalo 45
A Trip to Manta 63
Cheryle Subject of a Police Search! 81
Served Rat on a Platter 85
Locked Out of Our Apartment with Dinner on the Stove ... 87
A Conman Scams the Church 91
A Special Christmas 105
Cheryle Falls in a Stairwell 109
Maintain the Fire in Your Gut and Passion in Your Soul! .. 111

Allegations of Disobedience 117

The Volcanoes of Ecuador 123

Our Departure from Ecuador 133

Our Lives Spared 141

Ecuador Quito Mission
Perpetual Education Fund
2007-2009

Time to Serve Again and a Change of Assignment 149

The Journey Begins.. 155

The Work Begins... 161

A Trip to Otavalo 167

A Special Family 171

The Parking Lot Bandit 175

Serving on a Fractured Ankle 179

Are You A Whitaker? 185

A Belligerent Cop Fails the Attitude Test 189

Confronted by a Deranged Woman 197

Evil Walks the Streets 201

An Attempt to Murder Two Senior Missionaries 203

A Difficult Assignment Comes to an End 207

South America Northwest Area
Perpetual Education Fund - Special Project
2009-2011

Evil Tries to Thwart a Special Assignment 213

The Adventure Begins..217

Finding an Apartment..221

On to Interpol! 231

Elder René Loli and Our Trip up the Amazon River.........239

Our Return to the Cities of the Amazon 267

Medications Held for Ransom 273

Our Efforts Acknowledged by the First Presidency............277

Machu Picchu..281

Terror in a Taxi 291

Cheryle Blows a Fuse! 295

Peru's Answer to the French Guillotine..............................299

Do Not Defile the House of the Lord 301

Required to Return to United States 307

Fiestas in Lima 313

Should We Rob the Silver Haired Gringo?.......................319

Travel Home and Divine Intervention 325

Reporting to the Brethren 331

Uruguay Montevideo Mission Leadership Support 2012-2013

Amid Chaos and Catastrophes 337

Cheryle's Near Fatal Fall 345

Finding an Apartment 351

Travel into the Interior 353

Our Apartment Burglarized 357

The Work..361

Bikers as our New Neighbors...367

Cheryle is Assaulted and Robbed 373

The Meek Shall Inherit the Earth......................................379

Invasion of the Insect Hordes!...383

Life is Hard in Uruguay 387

Pickin' and Grinnin' with Some Very Drunk Neighbor's..393

The Beginning of the End...397

Departing Uruguay..401

Ecuador Quito Mission
Employment Resource Center
2000-2001

The Adventure Begins

The adventure begins. Let me start by describing the manner in which we received our first mission call.

My missionary service began after my call as a Ward Mission Leader in June 1992. The call came while Cheryle and I were members of the Morning Sun Ward. After that, all of my time, means and talents were dedicated to the building of the kingdom through my involvement in missionary work. That included the time spent as a Ward Mission Leader, second counselor in the Sunrise Stake Mission Presidency serving with Don Nesbitt and Neil Dutson, and my five years in the Nevada Las Vegas Mission serving in three mission presidencies as the first counselor to President's Ross McEachran, Robert H. McKee and Warren G. Tate.

I was serving with Warren Tate, and nearing the end of my fifth year in the mission, when he received a telephone call which he told me about when we were traveling to a meeting. He said, "I received an interesting telephone call today. Elder Pinegar wants to know if you and Cheryle would be willing to submit your mission papers."

"I don't think there would be a problem," I answered.

"There are a couple of hitches."

"What are they?" I asked.

"First, he asked that the paperwork be completed in the next ten days and secondly, that they be sent directly to his desk, attention to him and not to the Missionary Department."

So, that is how a remarkable adventure began.

We completed the papers within the ten day period, which included the medical and dental appointments, and sent them directly to Elder Pinegar. However, I failed to realize that one word on the back of my personal information sheet would impact the entire process dramatically. And what was the word? Spanish!

On the back of the missionary form, I was prompted to put my two years of high school Spanish, as well as the two years of Spanish at Los Angeles Valley College. That, combined with the Spanish used on the streets of Los Angeles and during my five years as a counselor in the Nevada Las Vegas Mission, would have a dramatic impact on our call.

Whatever Elder Pinegar had in mind, never materialized. Instead of an English speaking assignment, our call was for a Spanish speaking mission. Originally, it was to the Employment Resource Center, Caracas, Venezuela; however, three weeks after we received our first assignment, we received an e-mail from Elder Cartmill, the Area Welfare Agent for the South America North Area who advised us that the assignment had been changed from Caracas, Venezuela to Quito, Ecuador. This e-mail was later followed by a letter from President Hinckley making the change official.

So, there it was! We were going to Quito, Ecuador to work in the Employment Resource Center. Our directions were to report to the Mission Training Center on June 27. Pondering on the magnitude of the assignment, I was comforted when the Spirit whispered, "Richard, learn the language, and love the people. You will be fine."

Although we both were excited, the roller coaster ride had yet to begin. That would occur in the Senior Mission Training Center. However, before the Mission Training Center (MTC), one other interesting item of note occurred.

The Friday afternoon before our farewell which was held on June 18, Bob McKee and I sat in our kitchen talking about the experience Cheryle and I would soon have. When the topic of language came up, Bob said, "You don't need to spend any time in the MTC being taught Spanish. You know Spanish. You and Cheryle will do fine without that."

He then picked up the telephone, and while I sat and watched, he called Lloyd Owen in the Missionary Department. Before I knew it, McKee was telling Lloyd, "The Whitaker's don't need any Spanish classes in the MTC. Just get them into the field." And that is exactly what happened.

McKee's telephone call and the recommendation by Lloyd Owen, eliminated any Spanish language training in Provo and ensured our timely arrival in Ecuador. Again, it's not what you know, but who you know!

If asked, I would like to have eliminated the entire Senior MTC experience, however, I was grateful that all we had to stay was thirteen days, not six weeks. So again, because of Robert H. McKee, we were blessed!

Prior to the mission, Cheryle and I visited the McKee's in Houston. During our visit, I knew that I was sick, but I said nothing. However, on the plane flight back home, the pain in my stomach became excruciating, and as I began to vomit blood, I knew there was a problem, but believed, as I had on other similar occasions, it would clear itself up. I was mistaken. It didn't clear up.

The day after we arrived home, I was unable to get out of bed. As I lay in the bed unable to move, I heard a sweet voice whisper, "Richard, you are dying. You must get to a doctor immediately."

I have learned always to listen to that still, small voice, so when Cheryle returned home, I told her that I was to get to the doctor immediately. She didn't realize the severity of the illness at the time, but soon would.

Cheryle called Dr. Joe Hardy's office, and I went in on an emergency basis. Once there, a new young doctor named Lisa Haworth looked at me and realized that there was a severe problem. She recommended immediate admittance to the hospital where I remained for a week with severe bleeding ulcers. In the hospital, I was given four units of blood.

Because of the number of transfusions, all the veins in my hands and arms collapsed. That caused not only pain, but complicated the transfusion process. I remember the nurses putting the needles in my arms, and when they could not find a useable vein, they began to poke the veins in the top of my hands. Again, they had difficulty and finally were required to call the senior nurse. She stuck the needle into the top of my right hand and then moved it around in an effort to hit a vein. Over and over she moved the needle around. While the nurses watched my face, tears ran down my cheeks because of the excruciating pain, but during all of their prodding, I never said a word. Eventually, they located a vein and the transfusions started.

After a week in the hospital, I was released; then came some outpatient surgery to close the bleeding ulcers. More discomfort. All of this occurred six weeks before Cheryle and I left for Ecuador. Few, except Bob McKee and the Tate's knew about this ordeal. No one from Salt Lake or the Missionary Department was advised, for as far as I was concerned, we had been called by the Lord to serve, and we were going to fulfill that commitment. I had endured pain all my life, so this was not a new or unique experience.

The Senior Missionary Training Center

The Senior MTC was interesting and not an experience I would want to repeat. We arrived on July 1, 2000. Our facility was located in what was once a small motor lodge. It had rooms built many years ago when such places were fashionable. In the main building was a small dining area, a conference room and a kitchen. Within the facility proper were a number of former motel rooms which were converted into small classrooms. Because the description fit perfectly, I referred to our residency as "The Bates Motel" from the film, *Psycho* by Alfred Hitchcock.

Our employment group consisted of three couples. The Palmer's, who were from Texas, the Taylor's from Nova Scotia, Canada, and the Whitaker's from Las Vegas, Nevada.

While in the MTC, we received an e-mail from Elder and Sister Cartmill asking if we wanted to purchase their goggles and gas masks which they used when one of the local volcano's erupted. Of course we would! It seemed that if you didn't have goggles and masks, you could not see and if the ash entered your lungs, infection set in. So we sent them a check, not knowing if we would ever need the masks, but, as I was taught by my great-grandmother Nana, "An ounce of prevention is worth a pound of cure."

While Cheryle enjoyed the MTC experience, I found it less than fulfilling. The accommodations were old and outdated, and the Employment training ill-conceived and poorly presented. When one of the instructors began throwing candy across a full room of priesthood leaders and their wives for correct answers to questions, I had had enough.

The instructor looked at me and said, "It appears that Elder Whitaker has a problem with my teaching techniques. Do you Elder?"

I realized that I should have remained silent, but I didn't.

"I have just spent five years in a full-time mission assignment in which I not only was treated as an adult, but also taught by using the scriptures. You have failed on both counts."

The room was deathly silent.

The teacher was a very large man, and his face erupted in bright red while his eyes disappeared. Trembling, he made a comment under his breath and continued. I opened my scriptures and read. This would not be our last confrontation.

It was then that I stopped going to the employment classes and instead went to the Brigham Young University library and studied my Spanish. My faithful companion represented us at all employment functions until the last day.

When the final day of training arrived, I waited until the last hour and then walked in, sat down in a large overstuffed chair and told myself that I was not going to say a word, or at least, that was what I had planned.

No sooner had I sat down, the same instructor from the candy throwing incident stormed over to where I was seated, stood in front of me and assumed an aggressive stance with hands on hips and voice raised.

"Elder Whitaker, if you do not want to serve in the Employment area, we can have it changed!"

Calmly, and very quietly, I responded. "Do us both a favor and just walk away."

Again, as in the candy throwing incident, his face became bright red, his body began to tremble with anger, but unlike the candy incident, he now began to yell.

"I can have your assignment changed!" he bellowed. "If you are not happy, I will have it changed!"

As he stood, face flushed and body shaking, I sat expressionless. "Just walk away," I repeated.

With those words, he stormed off.

I later learned that he called a General Authority and told him that, "Elder Whitaker was going to destroy the

Employment Program in the South America North Area." Nothing would be farther from the truth.

Shafted!

Our apartment was located on the top floor of an eighteen floor apartment building; Apartment 18c to be exact. The view of the city was spectacular and the furnishings, although modest, met our needs. We were content with the living arrangement of two bedrooms, a kitchen, bathroom, and maid's quarters off the kitchen and to top it off, the apartment was fully furnished. The rent was a reasonable $450.00 a month in US dollars. In the basement of the building was a modern grocery store, much the same as Smith's that is found in the United States, as well as a number of small stores and a barber shop. The second floor also had shops. Our building had two elevators because of building occupancy.

We had been in country five days when catastrophe struck. On Thursday, July 20, at about 6:00 p.m., Fanny, our landlady and owner of the apartment knocked on our door and told us that she wanted to move the queen sized mattress from the Cartmill's apartment on the tenth floor to our apartment located on the eighteenth floor. Since the Cartmill's had returned to the United States and their bed was larger than the double in our apartment, we agreed. When I asked who was going to move the mattress, Fanny looked at me, smiled and said, "You and your esposa!"

Taking the elevator to the tenth floor, we walked into the Cartmill's apartment and saw the queen sized mattress we needed to move. Struggling, Cheryle and I flipped the mattress off the bed, and while it buckled and swayed, we slowly slid it through the apartment door. The next obstacle was the elevator. While I pulled, Cheryle pushed it along the heavily polished hardwood floor. Arriving at the elevator, the thought crossed my mind: *Was it going to fit? It has to,* I thought. *They got it up here in this elevator!*

It took considerable effort, but I finally was able to cram the mattress into the elevator. With barely enough room to stand, both Cheryle and I had to flatten ourselves against opposing walls.

"Take a deep breath, hold it and then pray that this thing gets us to the eighteenth floor," I said laughing.

Cheryle did not find the humor in my comment and from the other side of the mattress there was only silence.

I hit the button for 18. The elevator shook, then began its upward climb while I clicked off the floor numbers in my mind.

Upon reaching the eighteenth floor, the elevator jerked to a stop and the doors slid open. Squeezing to the door, I saw that the distance from the elevator to our front door was only about thirty feet. *This will be a breeze,* I thought.

Cheryle stepped from the elevator and stood in front of the doors. "Now what?" she asked.

"Why don't you take the keys, open the front door, and then throw the keys back to me. Then we'll slide the mattress across the floor and into the apartment. Once done, we will go back downstairs for the bedding."

Cheryle did exactly as requested. She opened the door, left it ajar and then with a hefty throw, tossed the keys onto the freshly polished, hardwood floor.

As I watched from behind the mattress, time slowed down spiraling everything into slow motion. As the keys sped toward me on the polished floor, I tried to free my right foot from its prison, however it was stuck between the mattress and the inside elevator wall. I jerked on the mattress, but it would not budge. Closer came the keys. Then I looked down. The keys were headed directly for the space between the hardwood floor and the elevator.

"No!" I yelled, but it was too late. With the smoothness of a hockey puck gliding past the goalie and into the net, the keys and their chrome ring slid rapidly across the floor and disappeared into the black abyss of the crevice that led into the elevator shaft! In the blink of an eye, they were gone!

At first I was angry. Angry at Cheryle, then angry at my stupidity. But that soon passed and a calmer mind prevailed.

"Do you happen to have your spare key? I asked.

"No, it's locked in the apartment."

"Wonderful."

So there we stood. The mattress blocked the elevator door; the apartment was locked with the spare key inside, and the television was on.

"What about the kitchen, any food on the stove?"

"I don't think so," Cheryle answered with a degree of hesitation in her voice.

Dejected, she walked over to the elevator, and after helping me dislodge the mattress and place it against the wall in the hallway, she began to cry. Then we began to pray.

In Quito, Ecuador, the businesses do not stay open at night, so finding a locksmith was out, even if we could find one at home, we would not have been able to communicate the problem.

I stood with the mattress while Cheryle went downstairs to Fanny's apartment to see if she had a key to our apartment. She did not, however she did have two large key rings that each contained approximately two hundred old keys. With concern on her face, she handed the rings to Cheryle. "Have your husband try these, maybe one will work."

Sitting on the floor outside the apartment door, I tried each key. None worked. Frustrated, I went downstairs and asked Fanny to accompany me to the basement. I stood there as she explained to one of our security guards the problem, and asked him to check the basement floor in elevator shaft number one. Since we had two elevators in the building, and the keys fell down shaft number one, it was thought that number one would be the place to look. I returned to the 18th floor as the guard continued his search.

Standing outside the apartment door, we prayed for a miracle. There we were, five days in a foreign country with limited language skills; locked out of our apartment; no money; the television on and possibly something cooking on the stove that could burn down the entire eighteenth floor before the fire department arrived. To add to the dilemma, it was getting late, we were exhausted and would not have a place to sleep unless we dragged the mattress back to the tenth floor and threw it on the floor of the Cartmill's empty apartment. Seeing we had no option, and not wanting to struggle a second time with the mattress, we decided to go to the Cartmill's apartment and wait it out, even if it required sleeping on the floor.

Once inside, we sat down on the couch and numbly looked at each other. There were no words that could describe our frustration, but we each knew that silently our prayers for resolution of the situation would continue. And they did.

About ten minutes passed when there was a knock at the door. There stood Fanny, a huge grin on her face and in her right hand she held our keys!

She went on to explain that one of the security guards had found the keys in the basement. Incredibly, they had fallen eighteen floors—a trip of over one hundred and eighty feet—down the elevator shaft, missed all wiring and metal reinforcing beams and popped out onto the floor of the parking garage.

Gratefully, we took the keys, thanked Fanny for her assistance and went back to our apartment knowing that prayers were answered, especially when the pleading came from two senior missionaries who were in dire need of divine assistance.

Cesar Cacuango

We reported to the Ecuador, Quito Employment Center on August 7, 2000 for our first day. Things got off to a quick start. Cheryle was asked by the Regional Employment Director, Hermano Cesar Cacuango to coordinate the front desk responsibilities which included answering the phone, welcoming visitors and registering those who wanted to take the employment training called the Curtis Course. She also was given the responsibility of scheduling those with previous appointments, as well as screening those seeking a referral card that acted as a letter of recommendation. And that was what she was given her first day!

Since there was no place for me to sit in the cramped two room office which measured six feet by seven feet and was already occupied by six men, I went outside, sat on a concrete wall, opened my computer and studied my Spanish.

I knew of Hermano Cacuango before we arrived in Quito. He had served as a bishop, stake president, regional representative to the Twelve, mission president, and had been an employee of the church for twenty-three years.

While in the Senior Mission Training Center, I was approached by one of the instructors in the Employment Resource Training program and "warned" that I should be cautious in my relationship with a native Ecuadorian leader in Quito named Cesar Cacuango. Remarkably, this instructor was the same man who later would contact a General Authority and advise him that "Elder Whitaker would destroy the employment program in Ecuador."

When we arrived in Quito, another senior missionary issued the same "warning." After the second warning, the red flags were hoisted, but not as they pertained to Cacuango. I was more concerned about the two men whom I believed were not only less than objective, but also highly judgmental. I learned long ago that those who were criticized and disliked, I usually worked with quite well. I also have learned not to prejudge, but find out for myself if I can work with a man or not. This was especially true in this situation, especially since the first warning came from a man for whom I had very little respect. He was loud, boisterous, confrontational, argumentative, and he used these personality traits to cover what was an apparent feeling of insecurity.

On the other hand, the senior missionary, although a very nice man, had spent his entire life sequestered on a college campus before his mission and had yet to understand fully the real world. His was a far different environment from mine. So, as far as Cacuango was concerned, I left discernment to the Spirit, and I slowly plotted a course that would tell me whether he could be trusted or not.

During a four month period of having daily contact with Cacuango—traveling with him, sitting in meetings, having deep, spiritual conversations—I was able honestly to say that he was one of the finest men I had the pleasure to work with and to know. I believe that these warnings were false, hurtful, and disseminated erroneous information. Contrary to the warnings, I found a man dedicated to the Lord.

I am grateful for the ability to rely on the Spirit and to evaluate each individual, for had I walked into this assignment with a chip on my shoulder having prejudged a magnificent man, I would have robbed myself of a wonderful friendship.

Unfortunately, my assessment of this man, and my love for him as a brother in the gospel was not shared by some who had the ability to make decisions that would impact not only Cacuango, but also the employment program.

Not long after our arrival in Quito, it was rumored that some in Salt Lake were not happy with his performance, and he was to be replaced. As time passed and I had the opportunity to work with the man, I realized that my assessment of his capabilities and that of his superiors differed, and all I could do was make my recommendation and then allow the decision to come from those with authority. This they did, and I was notified by Daryl Nancollas, the Director of Temporal Affairs for the Area, that Hermano Cacuango soon would be replaced and the brethren desired that I assume his responsibilities for the Quito region until a replacement could be hired. Their decision to replace

Cacuango with another paid church employee proved disastrous.

It was the beginning of October, 2000 and I was standing in the confines of the small employment office when I received the call from Nancollas.

"How are you doing?" I asked.

"Fine, and you?" he responded.

"I'm fine."

"Well, you were, until I called! Elder, I have some good news and some bad news. Which would you like first?"

"Give me the bad news first. I know, I'm being fired and Cheryle and I are being sent home, right?"

"Well, no. The termination of Cacuango hit Salt Lake. It got to the Welfare Committee and the Brethren. They have decided to move the Regional Employment Office to Guayaquil. The brethren have approved you as the new Director of Employment for Quito. With that in mind, what do you think about transferring to Guayaquil?

"I would rather stay in Quito," was my response.

So, there it was! Cacuango was out, and I was in. The trials were just beginning.

Men in Black

From the beginning of our arrival in Quito, we watched as men dressed in black suits waited in front of our apartment building for a high priority resident. They stood dutifully next to a black SUV, wore dark sunglasses and waited until a woman left our building accompanied by two additional security personnel. I later found out that she was a ranking member of the Ecuadorian government and a resident of our building. But it gets better.

One day our doorbell rang. When I opened the door, there stood two "Men in Black" asking for a Spanish family. I didn't recognize the men from any I had seen out front, but when I told the one asking the questions that no one lived here by that name, he quickly looked inside, apologized up and down for disturbing me, and off they walked. During this brief conversation, the second guy stood off to the side, and upon hearing my "No," he immediately started to walk away.

Later that evening, we heard shouting come from the end of our hallway accompanied by a violent banging noise. I ran to our door, threw it open, stepped into the well-lit hallway and saw a number of men, some in police uniforms, others in black suits, standing at the end of the hall in front of an apartment door. More loud bangs erupted as a battering ram splintered the thick wooden door.

There was more shouting and I heard the words, "Policia, Policia!" That announcement was followed by a crashing sound as wood splintered sending the door flying off its hinges and sliding across the apartment floor.

"What in heaven's name is going on?" Cheryle asked.

"Just some spring cleaning," I answered as I closed our door.

We later learned that the policia were Federal Narcotics Agents. It seems the guy at the end of the hall, also a foreigner, was selling drugs. What led to this drug dealer's downfall was the fact that he was married to the sister of one of the drug enforcement officers. It appears that love wasn't that grand, and not wanting to go to jail, she snitched him off to her brother.

Our First Trip to Guayaquil

Our first trip to Guayaquil began with a bang! I arose at 5:30 a.m. and once up, realized that I had not turned on the hot water. We were told by the Cartmill's that to save money, it had to be turned on at 4:30 a.m. We did this for two weeks and then decided our sleep was worth the additional ten dollars a month.

Consequently, the water was cold and the preliminaries for the day were fast and furious.

I was scheduled to meet Hermano Cacuango in front of our apartment complex at 7:00 a.m.

I was there at 6: 55 and at 7:00 a.m., he drove up. He jumped out of his car and asked,

"Where is your companion?"

"Upstairs, in bed," I said.

"Oh," he said, "she was scheduled to go also. I have her tickets." Then he realized that he had forgotten to tell me this.

I jumped out of the car, ran to the elevator and hurried upstairs. As I turned the key and opened the door, I was calling to Cheryle, "It's a Chinese fire drill. Get dressed. You're going to Guayaquil!"

Cheryle jumped out of bed, and if you can believe it, she was dressed, hair done, makeup on and purse in hand in nine minutes! By 7:10 a.m., we were in the car and headed for the airport! That had to be a record!

The internal flights in Ecuador are interesting. There are no pre-seating arrangements, nor are there reservations. After entering the terminal, everyone gets in a very long line and eventually gets to one of the ticket counters. There were three open today, and it only took us about twenty minutes before we were at the front. After receiving our boarding passes which were stapled to our tickets, we were ushered into a pre-boarding area with all of the other passengers.

While we sat in the pre-boarding area, Hermano Cacuango told Cheryle and me that he and his wife wanted to take us to Otavalo, which is a city north of Quito inhabited by some of the staunchest members of the church having Lamanite blood coursing through their veins. They were also wonderful artisans and world renowned for their Indian folk dancing. We set the date for Saturday, September 9.

Again, there were no seat assignments on internal flights. When they announced over the intercom in a garbled fuzzy Spanish that they were boarding, everyone jumped up and like a herd of stampeding buffalo, rushed to get into a single file line. This line was five to six people wide and entered from two different directions, one from the left and the other from the right. The downside was that only three at a time could elbow their way through the doors leading out to the plane. Once we had pushed and elbowed our way through the exterior door and quickly flashed our boarding pass to an airline employee, we hurriedly made our way to the plane.

The boarding process reminded me of the old days in high school when we were required to run for classes and if we didn't get to the classroom on time, we didn't get a seat. It wasn't much different heading for the plane.

Once on the tarmac, some of the passengers hurried to the front of the plane where a steel boarding ladder was placed, while others ran to the back of the plane where another ladder allowed entry through the tail.

Cheryle, Hermano Cacuango and I walked along the tarmac heading to the boarding ladder located at the front of the plane. When I was about fifteen feet shy of the rusted metal ladder, I looked into the cockpit and began to laugh, for seated behind the controls was our pilot, older than Methuselah and wearing eye glasses that had lenses as thick as the bottom of coke bottles! Then I glanced at the airplane's tires. They were nearly bald. All I could do was shake my head, say a quick prayer and start up the ladder.

Upon entering the plane, I heard Hermano Cacuango say to Cheryle and me, "It's everyman for himself! Get any seat you can as soon as you can, or you might not find one!"

And he was right. It did not take one long to figure out that when flying in South America, you never plan on sitting with the person you travel with. Cacuango wasn't joking. It really was every man for himself!

I stepped into the cabin behind Cheryle and without giving it much thought, grabbed the first seat I saw. Cheryle stepped back and glared at me. "Find the first seat you can!" I shouted.

The glare intensified and she pushed her way down the corridor until another empty seat materialized. She sat down between two passengers, and when I glanced back in her direction, her eyes were daggers. If looks could kill, my mission assignment would have ended on that plane.

Because of this, she didn't speak to me for two days! To say she was angry would be a mild understatement.

Where Cacuango ended up was anybody's guess, but he got on the plane in Quito and got off in Guayaquil.

The air above Quito was turbulent, but the flight wasn't that bad. Before the flight we were told to try and get window seats so we could see the volcanoes. Fat chance! We were lucky just to get seats, let alone seats by the window!

Once in the air, I was able to catch glimpses of the countryside. The land was covered by mountains, flooded plains and deep valleys. On our approach to Guayaquil, we passed over enormous homes situated on the banks of a river. One of the homes had a swimming pool in the back yard, and all of them were surrounded by high walls. Their opulence, size and walls reminded me of the type built by the Colombian drug barons.

We landed in Guayaquil, and after bouncing a couple of times, Captain Jet pulled into the airport proper. As quickly as possible, everyone exited the plane. We found a taxi and made our way to the Guayaquil Employment Center.

At the Center, Hermano Cacuango presented training to four of the young men who would present the material to the stake presidents in Guayaquil. For training purposes, a role play situation was used. The first presentation was made using Hermano Cacuango's Laptop computer. The four brethren represented the stake presidency. Then following Cacuango's presentation, the director of the center was required to make the presentation as he would do with the stake presidencies. Finally, we had an evaluation. This was all in Spanish and Cheryle and I were expected to participate in the evaluation process, which we did, or at least we gave it a good try. Following the presentation, we all went to lunch at a KFC where Cheryle and I bought lunch for the group.

After lunch, Hermano Cacuango interviewed the four employment center personnel while Cheryle and I talked to a number of full-time missionaries who were at the chapel for a zone conference.

Then we traveled to an appointment that had been scheduled with one of the major businesses in the city. In attendance were Cheryle, Hermano Cacuango, me and two of the four Employment Center employees. The meeting went well, and because there were not enough chairs, the general manager of the company and I both stood. All others were seated. I was impressed that both Cheryle and I understood much of what was said. The language was coming, slowly but surely.

Following the meeting, we had some free time, so Hermano Cacuango asked if we would like to go see the Guayaquil Temple. Cheryle and I jumped at the chance. The ride to the temple was interesting. Cacuango sat in the front seat next to the taxi driver, and as we got going, he asked the driver what he knew about the Mormon Church. With that, the nonmember taxi driver, who appeared to know more about the Mormon Church than we anticipated, broke into a grin and began to give Hermano Cacuango the first missionary discussion not missing a doctrine or principle.

When Cacuango asked the driver how he knew so much about the church, he explained that for fares, he tried to find missionaries wearing missionary tags. Once they were in his cab, they never failed to ask him what he knew about the Mormon Church. When he answered with his standard answer of "Nothing," the discussions began. Both Cheryle and I found this to be so amusing, that we sat in the back seat and chuckled all the way to the temple!

The Guayaquil Temple was lovely and much larger than we expected. It was about the size of the Las Vegas Temple. The exterior was made of beautiful gray rock that appeared to be granite. As we approached the front gate, it was apparent that Hermano Cacuango was well known by the temple personnel.

We were greeted warmly at the security gate which was manned by an armed security guard. Entering, we walked the grounds. Even though the temple was dedicated in August 1999, the landscaping still was being completed. Apparently, they had encountered problems with the contractors. I soon would understand what that experience was like.

Across from the temple was a beautiful apartment complex that was used to house patrons who traveled great distances to attend the temple. After touring the grounds, we went into the temple foyer. The foyer did not have carpeting, but beautiful flooring made of green marble imported from Brazil. The front desk also was made of the same marble accompanied with beautiful dark mahogany wood highlighting the area behind the desk.

We sat in the foyer and waited for the temple recorder who was a personal friend of Cacuango's. While we were seated, a number of patrons said hello to Hermano Cacuango. We were there for about thirty minutes reveling in the Spirit of the Lord which was apparent from our first stepping onto the grounds. Even though there exists deep economic depression, and the city had far more graffiti than Quito, and the people are extremely poor compared to the standard of living in the United States, the Spirit of the Lord was there.

We saw many humble, loving Saints come and go. It was wonderful to watch as Lamanite sisters, who did not know Cheryle, came up and greeted her warmly with a big abrazo (hug) and kiss on the cheek. What a blessing it was to feel the power of the Spirit so tremendously and so far from home. After visiting the temple, we walked to the main street and hailed a cab. Now that was a ride we would never forget!

The taxi, which was a converted small Toyota station wagon, pulled up and parked. The yellow paint looked like it had been applied with a spray can, and in the back window just behind our heads was a revolving red light! It felt like we were riding in a travelling house of ill repute rather than a taxi.

The clown driving was worse than any of the drivers we had in Quito. I told Cheryle that he had to have been trained in Kamikaze driving tactics in Mexico City! On more than one occasion, we went from the far left lane to the far right lane. No signal, no hesitation, just a quick crossing of three lanes, and to add to the excitement, each time he slammed on the brakes, the red light behind our head would begin a whine like a police siren while spinning wildly!

Before we knew it, we were on the street headed for the airport! Suddenly, he was three lanes away from the turn!

Never fear! A quick snap of the wheel and we quickly crossed three lanes of traffic to find ourselves headed into the rear of a parked car. No problem! Just squeeze the traffic on the left into the curb and whip by the parked car, with at least a half an inch to spare. For Cheryle, this was a real white knuckle flight.

As the brakes locked, the taxi slid to a stop. Behind our heads, the siren blasted and the red light spun. Without hesitation, the three of us bailed out of the suicide roadster and raced for the terminal. Behind us, tires squealed as a plume of smoke erupted from underneath the taxi that last was seen with its out of control driver weaving in and out of the airport traffic headed east.

The Guayaquil Airport did not differ much from the Quito Airport except the line was shorter and the seats in the waiting area were softer. However, the process was the same mad dash for the door once the announcement came over the loud speaker. Once inside the plane, as before, the three of us were separated, each grabbing the first available seat. The seat I found was again in the middle, between two men.

We took off on schedule, unlike our departure from Quito which had been fifteen minutes late. On each side of me, passengers read newspapers. I sat quietly hoping that before landing, the man on the window side would put the paper down, so I could get a glimpse of the terrain. As we approached Quito, he did set the paper down which provided me a brief view of the country below where I saw a beautiful snowcapped volcano jutting its enormous cone through the clouds. It was Cotopaxi! Then, in the distance, another and then another. There is a splendor and raw power expressed in even the dormant shells of these majestic volcanoes; such an awesome sight to see these wonders of nature towering in their grandeur above the cloud level upon which the airplane seemed to rest like a toy on a white fluffy blanket. During the flight, Cheryle sat next to a young lady who attended MIT and had traveled the world. They had a wonderful conversation, so Cheryle really enjoyed the flight back.

The landing was interesting. We looped around and made our approach. The air was turbulent and bumpy. As we started down, the plane shook a few times and then touched down. We bounced and then suddenly the pilot locked the brakes. I have never been on a flight where the brakes were locked so hard. The plane lurched, shuttered and quickly slowed down. We were safely on the ground and home!

I told Hermano Cacuango to go home. Cheryle and I would take a taxi to the apartment. He was thankful for that. It would have required him to add another half an hour to his day, and I could tell he was tired. We arrived home at about 6:15 p.m., exhausted, but grateful for a wonderful day.

A Comedy of Errors!

When Cheryle and I walked over to the church offices at lunch time, we were told that we had a package at the post office. We were elated! Finally we would put the postal system to the test.

From the beginning, I realized that the process might be more difficult than expected, because when I looked at the slip of paper that contained the name of the post office, the hand-writing was illegible. We had no idea where to go!

Taking the paper upstairs to the regional offices, I asked Sandra, the personal secretary for Daryl Nancollas if she could help. Quickly, she deciphered the writing and made a telephone call to verify the location. With that information, we were out the door.

I flagged down a taxi, gave him the address and we were off. When we arrived at the post office, we were told that we needed to return tomorrow morning. I didn't understand exactly why, but I got the jest of the conversation so we left.

Back at our office, Danny Mino, one of our employees, called the post office and was told that we had arrived after the time when International packages were available, so, tomorrow before 2:00 p.m., we should try it again.

After Danny's phone call, and with Hermano Cucango's blessing, I began to rearrange the office. Now everyone should be pleased that I waited nearly six weeks before recommending any changes. It didn't take long to move two computers, re-connect them, move file cabinets, small desks and chairs. In about two hours the job was done and it was far more functional than before.

Cheryle and I left the office, and walked next door to a copy store where we picked up some Xerox copies Cheryle had made. These were of a food storage pamphlet written in Spanish that I found in the closet during cleaning. Cheryle had copies made for the Sisters who would attend the presentation she scheduled for Saturday afternoon.

The next morning Cheryle and I went directly to the office and after letting everyone know that we were going to the post office to get our package, we left.

I don't ever want to hear anyone complain about the postal system in the United States. Even on its worst day, it could not match the experience we had that morning. I am not really complaining about it, and in reality—something few of you will believe—I had more patience throughout the entire experience than did Cheryle. Hard to believe? It is true. Here is the scenario of what we experienced just to pick up a package at la Oficina de Correo, Quito.

Leaving the office, we flagged down a taxi and were off to the post office for the second day in a row. As we drove, we talked to the taxi driver. He told us he had been in Quito for five months and didn't like the city. He was from the country and this was a difficult transition for a country boy.

As the conversation continued, it became apparent that the young man didn't know where he was going. He was lost! After circling the wagons for a period of time, we spotted a parked cab. Our driver pulled over and asked directions. Fortunately, the other driver knew where the post office was located and helped out by giving us the exact directions. It really was rather funny as Cheryle and I were making an attempt to converse in Spanish while the lost taxi driver tried to figure out where we were so he could ask in what direction to proceed. Surprisingly, our conversation didn't seem to add to his confusion!

At last, we pulled up to the post office. Anxiously, we both bailed out, paid the driver and entered the building.

The invoice for the package was in Cheryle's name and we knew that we had to have passport information, etc., so Cheryle was the one in line with me right next to her.

We went first to window #1 where Cheryle presented her passport, her Ecuadorian identification card and the post office invoice we were given. The clerk looked at the identification, had Cheryle sign the invoice and then told us that we needed a Xerox copy of the identification so it could be attached to the invoice. He told us we could get copies down the street. So, out the door we went and down the street to a small hole in the wall "tienda de copias." We found the storefront and Cheryle handed her identification to a young man standing behind a rickety wooden counter. He quickly made us five copies. The cost was ten cents. We were on a roll!

Back to the post office we walked and again up to window #1. At window #1, we were told to attach the Xerox copy to our invoice. When this was done, we were directed to step to window #2, which was across the office. We went to window #2, presented our invoice to the woman behind the window. She stamped the invoice and affixed a stamp which indicated that we had paid the correct fee. We were charged seventy-five cents for this effort and then sent back to window #1. Back at window number #1, a different clerk took the invoice that now had been signed by Cheryle and stamped by the clerk. The new clerk took the paperwork, turned around and walked to the rear of the office where the storage room was located. Opening a large door, she stepped into the room. After a few minutes, she returned carrying a package. The package was no bigger than a shoe box, and we still had no idea what it contained.

To my astonishment, she did not bring it to our window, but walked to an adjacent office, and as I watched through a glass partition, she placed it on a table. She then returned and told us we needed to go to the adjacent office where our package was located. While Cheryle grew more irritated, I began to laugh. The situation had become so ridiculous that it was funny.

Taking some deep breaths, we reminded each other that we were guests in the country and we needed to be patient.

Easier said than done, I thought.

Slowly we walked the ten feet to the adjacent office that contained our package. When we stepped up to the window, we were met by another employee. He told us something in machine-gun Spanish that went over both of our heads. When we told him we didn't understand, he slowed down and told us we owed six dollars tax on the box and we would need to go to the Filabanco which was located across town at Avenida Amazonas and Avenida Unidas in order to pay our fee. He showed us the copy of a receipt that we needed to get from the bank, have it filled out and then bring him back the stamped copies. Cheryle's face became red, and I again laughed, not at her but the situation. Out the door we went, again to try and find a taxi.

After fifteen minutes of walking the neighborhood, one finally drove up. To hail a taxi required great skill and dexterity of foot, somewhat like a bullfighter in the ring. I was getting pretty good at stepping into traffic and using the proper Ecuadorian hand gestures that stopped taxis. When one stopped, we climbed in, gave the driver his directions and started for the other end of the city.

The journey to the bank lasted nearly forty-five minutes. During the ride, we made the best of the situation and took in the wonders of the city. When we arrived in the general area of the bank, we drove around the long block a couple of times, and with a break in traffic, the driver let us off in the middle of the street and drove away.

So much for asking him to wait, I thought.

Dodging the heavy traffic, we crossed the busy street and hurried into the bank. Both Cheryle and I actually had gotten pretty good at the fine art of dodging traffic, jaywalking and making our way across busy main streets without becoming Ecuadorian road kill.

The bank reminded me of a Bank of America in the states, except in this bank, the guard was wearing a flak vest and had a fully automatic machine gun under his right arm. We asked him where we could get the correct receipt. He walked over to the information counter, got us a receipt and then directed us to window #1. Sounds familiar, right!

Here we go again, I thought.

We waited patiently in line until a roaming employee was available and Cheryle was able to ask her a few questions about filling out the required paperwork. Confident that all was now on track, we stepped up to the next available teller. She looked at our papers and quietly said. "You are in the wrong line." She directed us to the main line which was to our right. We looked to our right and saw that the main line had about sixty people in it and serpentined around the bank. Having no choice, we stepped into the other line.

If I have failed to mention it before, Elder Whitaker hates crowds and waiting in line.

We stood patiently, shuffled a few feet, stood and shuffled a few more. This continued for nearly an hour before we reached the front of the line. All this for one small package and a six dollar fee!

Three tellers worked the customer service stations. That's right…three tellers for a bank crowded with at least one hundred and fifty people. Eventually a light went on and we were signaled to approach the next available teller. Stepping up to the window, Cheryle gave the teller her paperwork and paid the required six dollar's. When the teller put the paper into the computer to stamp it, the paper jammed. She turned the machine off, took the receipt out and started over. It jammed again. Patiently, she smiled, made a comment and tried the third time. It worked! With the receipt in hand, we got our change and walked back out to the street to hail another taxi to take us back to the post office.

We walked around the corner and were fortunate to find a taxi who had just dropped off a fare. As the fare stepped out, we jumped in. Cheryle showed the cabby the address of the post office and off we went, back across the city. This time the driver knew his way and we got to the post office without incident.

Most streets in Quito are one-way, so to travel to one location, usually requires that you travel some very circuitous routes. No straight shots. Once we arrived at the post office, the driver asked if he should wait.

"Yes, please," I responded.

Into the post office we walked and back to the window behind which we could see our package still sitting on the desk. Cheryle presented the receipt and invoice to the same man who had told us to go to the bank. He checked everything over and I asked him if it was all correct?

"Yes," he said.

Another employee then told us step around the partition and grab our package. When I did this, two employees again inspected the package and paperwork. When each was comfortable that all was in order, I was told to proceed to a counter across the aisle where we needed to sign a ledger. I placed the package on the counter where a woman looked at it, then removed a custom's invoice from the side of the box, then filled out some information which she entered into a large eight inch thick ledger book, and then asked Cheryle to sign her name and again place her passport number in the ledger. Once Cheryle did this, the package was ours. Four hours had now passed.

With package in hand, we hurriedly left the post office, glad to have our first package and aware that we just had passed an enormous test: securing a package in South America! I was grateful that the taxi driver still was waiting across the street. Jumping into the cab, we directed him to the Robles office building. The four hour post office experience took the entire morning, and all for a package the size of a shoe box that contained nothing more important than candy and some office supplies!

A Road Trip to Otavalo

It was a beautiful, fairly clear Saturday. From the window of the spare bedroom that I used as an office, I could look to the south and see a volcanic mountain peak still capped with snow. We were preparing for our trip to Otavalo with the Cucango's, and were excited about the opportunity to see more of this beautiful land.

We spent twelve hours with Hermano and Sister Cacuango and their daughter traveling north through miles and miles of the Andes Mountains. What a memorable day!

The experience began at 8:00 a.m. when they picked us up. Cheryle asked me to go back upstairs to get the backpack for her which she purchased a week ago. When I returned, she shared with me the following observation.

While waiting for me, she happened to look across the street where an older woman was standing with a young boy. They both were Indians, and the older woman was carrying a small pail. Slowly, she shuffled over to a faucet that belonged to one of the office buildings and turned it on filling the pail with water. Then she and the young boy walked to the street where she proceeded to wash her hair and the hair of the child. Unfortunately the water coming from that tap was highly contaminated.

A ROAD TRIP TO OTAVALO

After leaving the city, we drove northeast through the first set of mountains that separated Quito from the valley of Cumbaya and the other major cities north of Quito.

On a number of occasions, I have related the conditions of the roads in Ecuador and the driving skills of the people. Today we experienced more. The drive reminded me of "Mr. Toad's Wild Ride" in the early days of Disneyland!

First, there was no speed limit. One might, on a very rare occasion, see a speed limit sign posting the speed around a curve, but in reality, the sign meant absolutely nothing. The police didn't patrol the streets outside the city, and they didn't write tickets in the city. The rule of thumb for driving in the country and in the mountains was to drive as fast as you could for as long as you were able, passing as needed and when you desired. Safety had nothing to do with it.

On the topic of passing, cars passed cars on the mountain roads whether going up or traveling down. They passed whether or not the road was straight or curved. It didn't matter if one found a rare double solid yellow line, or not. You passed if and when you could. If you didn't, you might end up being run off the road and into one of the deep drainage ditches.

The cruising speed for maneuvering through the mountain passes was about seventy-five miles an hour, and that included the busses. While the driver snapped the steering wheel back and forth, and the tires squealed and slid, the passengers, most of whom were Catholic, could be seen crossing themselves and praying for deliverance while uttering additional words of supplication. I was confident that their prayers also included pleas seeking protection so that the brakes did not fail, the vehicle didn't fly off a cliff and the car or bus didn't hit a pole or meet another vehicle head-on while passing.

Next are the large deep pot holes. You might be interested to know they averaged between four to twenty-four inches deep and were abundantly scattered all over the road. They too, were no respecter of persons. On one occasion, we watched as the car in front of us hit a sizeable hole which caused the driver to lose control, which sent the car fishtailing into the dirt. Fortunately, the driver was able to regain control of the torpedo-like projectile before it rolled or crashed head-on into oncoming traffic. Once again in control, our Ecuatoriano answer to NASCAR put the pedal to the metal and continued to race down the road never thinking about slowing down.

Then were the busses that passed on straightaways and curves while racing side by side. Incredible as it seemed, they actually raced side by side through the high mountain passes vying and jockeying for position no different than two race horses screaming down the straight-away toward the finish line at Belmont or Santa Anita.

This action continued up hill and down. It didn't take long to figure out that the drivers justified their irresponsible and erratic driving by honking their horn. Somehow that made sense to them, even though the echoes in and through the mountains and deep canyons could not be heard around the corners. The blaring "honk, honk, honk and beep, beep, beep, gave the appearance to the terrified passengers that the driver was in complete control.

So, the key for driving in the Andes of Ecuador was to lean constantly on the horn while your foot was slammed on the accelerator pedal. The winner was the car or bus with the biggest engine and the driver with the greatest death wish. So now you have a picture of the drive we were taking on that Saturday.

Oh, I forgot one thing. The driver needed to have memorized where the "chipas"—speed bumps across the road that are unlike any in the United States—are located. Another term for them in Ecuador was "lying down policemen." If one of those little buggers was hit at seventy-five miles an hour, the driver most likely could kiss the car and his life good-bye, because hitting one of these at high speed usually launched the vehicle into Ecuadorian space in such a manner that found it crashing somewhere at the bottom of a deep cliff.

Now that I have set the scene, I will continue to describe some of the remarkable things we experienced.

As we drove north and through the small towns, I was impacted by the poverty. It truly was unbelievable. Construction and the building of houses was like nothing we had seen before. Houses were built of anything and everything, including adobe brick, cinder block, wood, cement, trees, leaves and tin. The roofs can be tile, tin, or thatched and woven banana leaves.

Large buildings were built much the same as homes, unless they were built of adobe brick. They usually would place stucco-like material over the brick which sealed the brick and allowed it to be painted.

More often than not you would see the first floor partially completed, then they began to work up. There is no such thing as putting reinforced steel in-between the cinder blocks. The brick homes and all wooden buildings had little to no reinforcing steel.

If the house was brick or cinderblock, all that held things together was the cement or concrete. The homes were built in much the same fashion as our old fashioned barn raising in the United States. Friends and neighbors all got together. The person who wanted the house, bought the beer, and the project began. On it went throughout the day, week, or the month. The cement was poured, the bricks were thrown one on top of the other, and the workers were lubricated and kept happy with beer. You can imagine the slant and tilt that some of the people ended up with, not to forget the collapsing of the home when it rained hard or an earthquake struck.

If someone wanted a second or third floor, and that was common, the process was somewhat altered. After completing the first floor, they built a flat roof made of wood. This served not only as the roof to the first floor but also the flooring for the second floor. It was a floor that would support the many round timbers they used for support.

These support poles were about four inches in circumference and approximately twelve feet long and resembled a smaller version of the logs used by the pioneers to build their log cabins. They placed the poles, about one hundred in number, under the floor to support it and keep it up while they built the second floor. As they built, you saw a first floor totally encompassed by at least a hundred wooden poles. All this was done just to hold the second floor up while they built. If they wanted a third floor, they did the same thing on the second floor that they did on the first. It was quite remarkable to see. The poles actually were able to support the cinderblocks that made the exterior walls.

Nothing was wasted. We saw them build an office building and watched as they put large I-beams across to connect the sides. But there was a problem. The I-beams were not long enough to go from one side of the building to the other. They were about eight feet short. To remedy the problem they took two by fours and used them to extend the

I-beams and make them the right length. Then they wrapped the two by fours to the steel I-beams with some bailing wire and continued on. It appeared that they understood that necessity was the mother of invention.

It was easy to see that there were no stringent building codes in place in Ecuador. We especially saw the lack of building codes as we traveled out of the cities and into the rural areas. I seriously doubted that they had building inspectors, and the results were disastrous when earthquakes or volcanoes made their presence known.

Well, enough on the building defects, back to the adventure.

As we traveled through the countryside, we saw the volcano Cotopaxi with its peak still heavily shrouded in snow. On we drove until we came to a small rest stop that was basically a spot for tourists to get a bite to eat and use the restrooms. On the topic of restrooms, they are not a major part of life in the Ecuadorian countryside. We watched during the day as busses pulled over and cars stopped at various roadside locations to allow passengers to disembark and use the side of the road as a bathroom facility. If one is shy, modest, or has a case of weak kidneys, they better choose another place to visit, especially if they plan on traveling long distances and touring Ecuador. I do not recommend traveling by bus in any part of South America, for if the drivers don't kill you, the bandits who regularly stop the tourist busses and rob the passenger's, will.

On the way to the mountain, we left one state of Ecuador and entered another. We were stopped by police who checked the driver's identification. We got through this and found traffic slowing again. Then to our disbelief, we saw a young boy sitting in a chair in the middle of the fast moving highway. He was right smack dab in the middle of the fast lane. Next to him was his mother begging for money by stepping into traffic attempting to stop the cars that sped past.

Unbelievably, neither the mother nor the son were killed by the cars, but who knows how long their luck lasted.

The next stop was at the top of a beautiful pass which not only had a small rest stop and café, but also an area where we could stand and look out over the valley and lake below. Cheryle took some pictures to capture not only the magnificence of the Andes and the incredibly beautiful country of Ecuador, but also some llamas grazing nearby.

We drove on to the bottom of the valley to the rustic Puerto Largo Lodge which sat directly on the lake. The lodge housed a beautiful restaurant, an inviting dock, and charming wood cabins behind the main building. The cabins could be rented out for the night, or longer periods of time and all of them, whether on the first or second floor had a magnificent view of the lake. We walked around this picture-perfect area for a while, and then Hermano Cacuango rented a row boat in order to take his daughter out onto the lake.

When they left for their boat ride, I continued to explore. Not much time passed and I heard them call, "Ricardo." They wanted me to help row! If I had wanted to row a boat across an Andean lake, I would have rented the boat, but since it was a charming setting, I climbed into the boat and grabbed an oar. I felt a little like Jean Val Jean in *Les Miserable* during the time he was shackled to the oars in the slave ship; and I probably rowed about as well.

Hermano Cacuango took one oar and I took the other and with his daughter sitting in the back of the boat, off we went. I think we made more distance going in circles than in a straight line, but it was fun. The scene of us rowing must have looked like something out of a Laurel and Hardy movie. In an effort to keep us from continually going in circles, I put an oar into the water and used this as a rudder to straighten us out. After about fifteen minutes of this, we decided to head back to the small wooden dock. I suspect that all aboard were thankful to be safely on solid ground again! I know I was.

Upon leaving Puerto Largo, we drove to the city of Otavalo, a very strong area for the church. It is inhabited by one of the indigenous peoples of Ecuador.

The streets of Otavalo were narrow and bustling with activity centered in and around the central market. This market is where the Otavalan Indians brought their goods each Saturday. The streets were closed, and stretched for blocks in all directions. Thousands of Indians set up booths to sell anything and everything.

In the market we saw a mix of Indians, European tourists and Ecuatorianos, but in all that mass of humanity, and even throughout the entire day, I saw only one blonde: Cheryle. Needless to say, she really stood out. Heads turned, and it was obvious we were not native Ecuatorianos. Norteamericanos simply did not travel to Ecuador, mostly because the State Department continued to have a safety advisory recommending that Americans not visit the country, thus the only tourists seen were from Europe.

As we wandered through the miles of booths, Cheryle found a beautiful table cloth. The price started at $34.00 which included the cloth and twelve matching handmade napkins. I started to barter with the woman and made a bid of $28.00. She then went to $33.00. I countered at $29.00. We agreed at $30.00. Cheryle was thrilled because in the United States, it would have been three times that amount.

The colors, sights and sounds were incredible. Families made and sold the items. Small children, tightly wrapped in blankets were carried on their mother's backs while others curled up and slept underneath the booths and stands. Unfortunately, when tourists were present, so were the thieves. Although I wandered and enjoyed the experience, I never forgot where I was and that danger was ever present.

At a later time during the year, Daryl Nancollas, the Director of Temporal Affairs took his in-laws to Otavalo where the husband was robbed, or in our terms, his pocket was picked. The wallet was deftly removed in a smooth maneuver, but Daryl saw the theft, and in Spanish started to yell wildly which brought the entire community down on the female thief. She immediately dropped the wallet and claimed she had no knowledge of the theft, but since she was caught red handed, she was taken away by the policia.

In the streets of the market, we also found beggars. Men, woman and children all dressed in rags and carrying cups that were shaken up and down in a motion that appeared patented. After having watched the activities of the beggars in the city and now in Otavalo, I am convinced that they are unionized and trained in the same schools, dressed by the same seamstress and taught to speak in the same tone of voice. It was incredible. They even looked like they had the same father. The men and women were often old, had no teeth and were filthy. Many times, small children, also filthy and dressed in rags, would have a brother or sister strapped to their back with a cloth which was the custom amongst the Indians. They too had a cup or bowl in hand which was used as they begged for money.

Cheryle made another small purchase in Otavalo at the market. She found some beautiful earrings and bought two sets.

Upon leaving the market, we drove farther north toward the cities of Cotacachi—known for its leather products—and Ibarra—known for its wood artisans. Before traveling to Ibarra, we stopped for lunch. Cheryle and I both had found that eating our large meal in the middle of the day between noon and 2:00 p.m. did wonders for my stomach.

After driving for about twenty minutes, Hermano Cacuango made a turn into a long tree lined drive that extended for at least a quarter of a mile and ended in front of an old style Spanish hacienda that had been built by the Spaniards. The hacienda was now a restaurant with facilities for banquets and other activities. The estate was enormous. Large buildings with red tile roofs formed the traditional massive box shaped structure which had smaller fingerlike buildings shooting off in different directions. They were used as stables and quarters for the early Indian slaves who ran the hacienda under the tyrannical rule of the owner.

Huge trees were everywhere. They were planted hundreds of years ago when the hacienda was first constructed. It reminded Cheryle and me of the very old Spanish homes and massive estates seen in the old movies and television, but this was not television. This was both real and surreal.

We parked the car and walked up beautiful old steps that led us through the wooden front doors and into the hacienda. After entering through the large and spacious rooms that made up the entry, we walked to the rear where the restaurant was located.

Hallways led from the sides of the main entrance and when one continued forward, they entered the patio that had been converted to a dining and entertainment area. The patio was surrounded on all four sides by a covered veranda. As we looked at the areas under the veranda, we could see the original family Chapel and other special rooms designed for use by the family. Placed in the patio were round tables with umbrellas, and under the large veranda that surrounded the patio were placed additional long banquet type tables with long benches and chairs.

The floor to the patio was old cobblestone. We were seated at a circular table in the back which afforded us a clear view of the front entrance and patio. A young waiter took our orders and then the place began to fill rapidly with other patrons. Suddenly, Hermano Cacuango broke into a smile and stood, as did Hermana Cacuango. Coming through the large doors into the patio area was Hermano Cucango's sister-in-law! She, a nonmember as are his family member's, was visiting with a large group from Colombia. Introductions were made and she then excused herself and went to the veranda area to be with the others in her party.

As the appetizers were served, we watched seven men, all musicians, prepare and set up for the afternoon entertainment. They had a lead guitarist, tenor guitar, bass guitar, bass drum, and three men who played a variety of different percussion and native instruments, including flutes. They began to play and sing native music from Ecuador, Bolivia and Paraguay. It was exquisite.

Personally, I enjoyed this music far more than the Mexican music often heard in the United States. The group played and sang while we dined, and after about fifteen minutes, we noticed that costumed dancers were standing on the steps just below the entrance to the patio.

Suddenly the musical group broke into native Ecuatoriano music and the folk dancers entered. The dancers, five boys and five girls were all young ranging in age from twelve to twenty-two. They entertained for an hour dancing a number of different native dances, each of which told a story, and each of which required different costumes and different folk dance steps. The colors of the costumes were identical to those seen in National Geographic when they did layouts on South America. Bright reds, greens and blues were accompanied by native Indian costumes and headgear. It was magnificent.

During lunch, Hermano Cacuango mentioned that we, along with he and his wife, had been invited to visit the jungle located on the Colombian border. The area is part of the Amazon jungle and has a lodge which is visited by many European tourists. Hermano Cacuango told us that since we were scheduled to have a visitor from Salt Lake, it would be necessary to tell those issuing the invitation that the four of us would make the trip at some date in the future. However, as it turned out, we were never able to make that trip. With the increase in terrorist activities directed toward Americans by Colombian guerrillas, that part of South America would not have been the ideal place to travel.

Before we realized it, we had taken a two hour lunch, which was common for this South America, but uncommon for Whitaker.

After the entertainment ended, the bill came. For the five of us, five full meals including appetizers, drinks and wonderful entertainment, the bill came to $45.00. I paid this gladly and we were again on our way.

From the hacienda we traveled to Ibarra where we parked the car and walked the streets looking into the many tiendas, or stores that lined the streets. Cheryle made another find and another purchase. In one store she found a small, ten piece, wooden, hand carved Nativity set. We asked the price: $19.00. We told the young lady behind the counter that we were going to look further and if she had the best deal we would return, which is exactly what we did after walking the town. It was a pretty good deal.

Cheryle bought the set, had each piece individually wrapped and gave the girl a twenty dollar bill. The clerk didn't have the dollar change, so she excused herself and left the store to get some change. Now this will show the difference in mentality between those in the city and those in the country. Here we stood in a store full of wooden hand carved pieces of every size and price. Cheryle had her bag, and granted the girl had our twenty dollar bill, but we had her merchandise and her store at our disposal. Yet, with complete trust, she left, went down the street to get change and returned. She never doubted that all was well, and we weren't even wearing our missionary tags. We were dressed in casual clothes with no reference whatsoever to the church, just two norteamericanos, and two Ecuatorianos. I guess we looked honest.

Cheryle was thrilled with her buy, for we later saw the same set for five dollars more, and that is how Cheryle began her collection of Nativity scenes.

Leaving the store, we returned to the car and drove up the street to the city park where we parked and began exploring again.

We entered one store and I immediately saw a number of beautiful hardwood canes sitting in a large container. One was especially pretty with a round wooden ball for the handle. It reminded me of the old police baton I carried on the streets of Los Angeles, or the type of cane Bat Masterson would have carried as he strolled the towns of the old west. The price was three dollars. That was my purchase for the day.

We left Ibarra and headed back south toward Cotacachi. Oh, lest I forget, in Ibarra, Cheryle made another find. As I said before, the city is known for its leather work. In one of the many stores we visited, she found a beautiful black leather handmade purse for $16.00.

As we walked the streets, I saw something that even tore at the heartstrings of this hardened street cop. Sitting across the street on the curb was a young boy about ten years old. In front of him were two small wooden crutches. It was obvious that they had been made at home since they were very crude and roughly hewn. They were the type that one would envision being used by Tiny Tim in Dickens famous story, *The Christmas Carol.*

As we passed by him, the boy suddenly jumped up, one tattered trouser leg hung close to the ground, the other was ripped and torn just below the knee where the other leg had been severed. With only one leg, I realized that this was one young boy who, if he remained in this small town under these conditions, would never have much of a life. His lot in life as it now stood was to be consigned to the streets, being required to beg from dawn to dusk in an effort to survive. In the United States the problem would have been readily solved and a normal life lived, but in South America, in Ecuador and under the extreme poverty, there was little hope for him.

Leaving the city, we started home. Along the way, we continued to see the large bodies of pigs and sides of beef hanging in the patio areas of some homes.

The drive home was as hair raising as the drive north, except now the sun was setting and darkness closing in. I will say that Hermano Cacuango did a pretty good job at maneuvering in and out of the cars, buses and potholes! He surely would not have a problem in the world earning his Kamikaze Taxi Driver's License!

Cheryle and I sat in the back seat of the small station wagon, and marveled at the fact that we were serving in South America and traveling in the Andes Mountains! It still seemed incredible.

We arrived home about 7:30 p.m. and although exhausted, we were thankful for a wonderful day, and eternally grateful for the precious friends we had found in the Cacuango's. They went out of their way to be of help and assistance to Cheryle and me. For them and many other wonderful Ecuatorianos, we will be eternally indebted.

A Trip to Manta

It was 3:38 a.m. when suddenly both Cheryle and I awoke with start to find that we were in the middle of an earthquake! The entire room was moving. The doors were swinging and groaning; the wooden doors to the closets were creaking and bending. My first concern was the building was rocking and we were eighteen floors up.

I could picture in my mind the brick buildings around us without any reinforced steel. The earthquake was not a sudden cracking whip like movement as experienced in California, but a slow, rolling motion that lasted nearly twenty seconds. Then suddenly, as is the practice with earthquakes, it was over. I was grateful that we were still on the eighteenth floor and not sitting in a heap at street level. We later found out that the quake was centered in a city about four hundred miles southwest of us and measured a 5.4 magnitude. That was Tuesday night.

Wednesday afternoon we left for Manta.

The weather that week had been stormy and it rained every afternoon. Before leaving for the coast, Hermano Cacuango and I visited another employer for the purpose of firming up their relationship with the employment center. Once we finally were able to see the chief of personnel, Dr. Fanny Ortiz, I was a little taken back at how very young she was.

It was interesting that during our time in her office, she talked a great deal about the church and then told us how she wanted to learn English. She also asked me the difference between Americans and Ecuatorianos. I answered the question as best I could while remembering I was a guest in their country and how wonderfully we had been treated.

She was pleased with the response as was Hermano Cacuango. Our meeting ended and we returned to the office. We needed to fine tune the presentation for that night which would be presented to the stake presidency and the other volunteers in the Manta Employment Center.

At 3:30 in the afternoon, Hermano Cacuango, Cheryle and I grabbed a taxi and made our way to the Quito airport. Fortunately we had airline reservations which put us on the plane, but we knew when the flight was called, it still would be every man for himself.

The boarding process was the same craziness as before. Fortunately, we were with Hermano Cacuango because the announcement came over the loudspeaker garbled and almost inaudible. We had no idea what was being said, so we took our direction from him. When he got up, we got up and proceeded to make a mad dash for the door, where the line leading to the plane was four abreast. Each passenger's ticket was rapidly checked and permission given to enter the concourse. Once on the concourse, we were required to walk between two yellow lines that eventually lead to the stairwell leading into the plane.

I found the first available overhead, opened it up, and deposited the goods. Again, Cheryle and I were separated and she thought the flight a bit turbulent which didn't help things out. I didn't find it rough in the least, but she told me that one man seated near her tightly gripped the seat in front of him for the entire thirty minute flight to the point that his knuckles were white and beads of perspiration were seen rolling down his face. And the man on the other side of her never said a word, but just kept crossing himself! Both men were real confidence boosters!

Eventually, we landed safely in a city named Puerto Viejo. The airport was small with only one runway. The military patrols at the airport were in combat fatigues, carried M-16 automatic weapons, and had dogs. Walking through the small airport we were besieged by boys wanting to shine our shoes, women selling Lotto tickets and taxi drivers all wheeling and dealing for fares.

As we approached the door, one driver got Hermano Cacuango's attention and gave him a price of eight dollars for the thirty minute ride to Manta. Stepping through the doors, the driver took it down to seven dollars. And as we walked out the door, another cabbie stepped up and said, "Six." Six it was. And then the first cabbie said, "I would have done it for six!" Too late, pal. Bartering is a way of life in Ecuador.

We got into the taxi and off we went. On the thirty minute drive from the airport to Manta, we saw some of the greatest poverty we had seen. Many of the inhabitants of the country lived in this condition. We saw homes on stilts built high above the ground because of flooding; homes constructed of wood scrapes, and some thatched together while others were made of homemade bricks. Many didn't have windows or doors. None had sanitation facilities. The yards were dirt. The floors in the homes were also dirt.

Laundry was hung on lines strung from anything that would hold the line. The roads were typical of Ecuador: rough and pitted with potholes. Trash and garbage was thrown next to the side of the road and often eaten by the farm animals that were tied to a post or stake which allowed them to graze.

As we traveled closer to the coast, I noticed that banana trees were in every yard and field. And when I rolled down the car window, the smell of smoke filled my nostrils. The people constantly were burning off land in order to plant more crops. This was an ongoing process.

In the yards children were running and playing with sticks, balls, and cans. No matter where we went, we found that young children were the same, unless at a very young age, they were sent to the streets by their parents to learn the art of begging and hustling foreigners and tourists.

As we sped through the country side, it didn't take long to realize that the two lane road on which we were traveling had suddenly become a four lane road without any expansion. The width of the road had not changed. We now simply had two cars, or a car and a bus, or even a car and a truck on the same, single road, occupying the same lane, and all traveled as fast as they could, acting as though they didn't have a care in the world.

In the taxi, the fleas, thinking that I was a fast food take out, had a field day. I was eaten alive, while Cheryle and Hermano Cacuango had nary a nibble. It was as though they weren't even there. It appeared that I was the main course and desert, and this only took about thirty minutes!

We arrived at our hotel at 6:30 p.m. and had our first meeting at 6:45. The name of the hotel was the Cabanas Calbandras. We have pictures, but basically it was a number of beach type cabanas that were three stories high. We were on the third floor. After hurriedly checking in and dropping off the overnight bag, we were out the door and on our way.

Because of the time restraint, we decided not to walk to the stake center, but take a taxi. We hailed a cab and got in. On entering, I wondered why the music was so loud, but it didn't take long to figure it out. The blaring music hid the loud thumping noise that was coming from the undercarriage in the vicinity of the transmission. The banging was the worst I had ever heard in a car. It sounded like someone was keeping time to the music with a sledge hammer, all directly under our feet.

Then, I noticed that hanging from the rear view mirror was a very, very large crucifix. That's right; the taxi actually had a rear view mirror! After seeing the crucifix and listening to the sledge hammer like pounding underneath my feet, I was thankful that we were only traveling a short distance.

At the stake center we were met by the stake president. The building was locked up so we waited about ten minutes for a counselor in the presidency to arrive with the keys.

Our first meeting was with the stake president, his counselor, and executive secretary. All in all, it was a very young stake presidency. The room we met in was a bishop's office. We had a table, nothing like what we had in the states, and metal folding chairs. Linoleum tile was on the floor. A file cabinet sat in the corner and pictures of the First Presidency were on the wall immediately behind the bishop's chair. They were very humble surroundings.

The stake president presided and also conducted the meeting. For the opening hymn the president took two very well used and torn hymn books from on top of the filing cabinet, blew the dust off the covers, and then handed them to us. Amazingly, without a piano the singing wasn't half bad.

The training was presented by Hermano Cacuango. The only problem was that because of the heat, we had to leave the door open. This allowed everyone passing to look in, see the stake president they all loved and respected, and say hello.

Since the door failed to provide adequate ventilation we opened a window. The only problem with that was that we were located right next to a major street and the trucks that passed were noisy. That was coupled with the honking of horns and pedestrian traffic laughing and talking on the sidewalk just outside the window. The interesting thing was that although it drove me nuts, it didn't appear to bother the other brethren in the room. As far as they were concerned, they could have been in the Celestial Room of the Guayaquil Temple.

Hermano Cacuango provided excellent training and at the end of this meeting we adjourned to go upstairs and meet again with the stake presidency, but now the employment volunteers were also asked to join us.

We sat on metal folding chairs, and as in the first meeting, the stake president presided. After Hermano Cacuango introduced himself, it was my turn. I did so, stumbling over a few verb conjugations, but to those in the room it didn't matter. When I made a mistake, they vocally corrected me, and I made the necessary corrections and we moved on. It is interesting that these wonderful people were just grateful that Cheryle and I were there. They didn't think anything about our mistakes and were thrilled that we were trying.

As the meeting progressed, a Sister brought us bottled water. They treat missionaries and leaders very well, especially when they have traveled great distances to provide them training.

I had to chuckle to myself, for during the two hour training meeting, one individual monopolized much of the time. He was asking some pertinent questions, but cutting into the time provided for others to learn. Again, I can't stress the tremendous patience these people have for each other. It is not in their makeup to cut someone off or tell another person that time is running out. For the most part, the others just sat and listened, as did Hermano Cacuango.

When the training ended, the stake president chose for the closing hymn, "Because I Have Been Given Much," and then asked Cheryle to offer the benediction. Cheryle did well getting through that particular hymn, and then did fine with the prayer.

As we were leaving the building, they offered us a tuna sandwich and drink. None of us had eaten since breakfast, so the food was welcomed. My greatest concern wasn't the tuna, or the bread, or the carbonated drink. My concern came when I looked down into the cup after drinking the drink and noticed the ice cubes floating around. I never will know if the ice cubes were made with pure water or water that contained millions of parasites. Only time would tell!

Following the training, we walked back to our rooms and Hermano Cacuango asked if we would like to take a walk and get something to eat. I didn't mind the walk, but eating at 9:30 p.m. was not in the routine. Cheryle said she would pass because her knee was bothering her. So it was Cacuango and I.

A comment on our travel: The travel had been very hard on Cheryle. To go from 10,000 feet to sea level in thirty minutes, and then be enveloped by the humidity was hard on her system. It didn't bother me, but she had a rough two days. Where I enjoy walking the streets and seeing what is going on, day or night, she was very uncomfortable with the city of Manta, whether day or night. Frankly, she thought it dirty and didn't like it.

Cacuango and I went off into the night. As we walked down the main street, we saw only two other norteamericanos.

Now you need to capture the picture. We were walking along the boardwalk of the beach. Lined up on the inside of the sidewalk were about fifteen small food and drink stands. Some had chairs out front, some had stools, some sold food and some sold alcohol, primarily beer. Then interlaced up and down the sidewalk were the others involved in various capitalistic pursuits. As late as it was, kids were still shining shoes; old and young were selling candy, cigarettes, and small novelties for the tourists, but that wasn't what made the scene so exciting.

The excitement came because each small stand had a boom-box; and each boom-box not only was turned up as high as the volume could go, each boom-box was tuned to a different station or playing a different CD or tape! That's right, you've now got the picture. Fifteen different pieces of music blasting at 150 decibels! It was truly something to see and hear!

We walked about a mile, and then Hermano Cacuango found the bar-b-que stand he was looking for. He placed his order, and dinner was served. That was about 10:30 p.m. We sat and talked for about forty-five minutes while he ate. When he finished his late night snack, we started back to the hotel.

On our way back, I saw a very old man with his small stand open. Although it was night, he had a small umbrella open above the wooden portable stand. Across his back he had slung a sawed off, twelve gauge shotgun. It was a single shot with a chrome barrel, and it was being held on his back with a piece of rope that found one end tied to the barrel and the other end tied to the stock.

There was no need to hire any security. He carried all the protection he needed and it was in plain view. The only problem would be the weapons accessibility. Should a problem occur, this old man would be dead before he could even think of trying to swing the shotgun around in front.

The sights, sounds and smells of Latin America are very different from those experienced in the United States. In some areas you get a mix of food cooking, trash burning, urine reeking from the sidewalks and trash rotting, but even with all this and the poverty, the people are wonderful.

When I got back to the room, Cheryle was in bed, still not feeling well. I had to laugh at the pillows. It appeared that they had taken concrete building blocks and slipped them into pillow cases. They were that hard. Cheryle had earlier killed a mosquito in the room and I thought, *well, this is all I need. What the fleas left, the mosquitoes will feast on,* but I didn't get bitten during the night, and had I been, I would have known it, because sleep for both of us really never came.

Before I go further, let me share with you the prerequisites for owning or driving a cab in Manta.

First, the car must have four tires. The less tread, the better. That allowed for a smooth slide around corners. The less traction the better. Then the car must be painted yellow. How this is done was not important. Paint brush, spray can, probably even a rag soaked in yellow paint would do the job, or so it appeared. Now once you had the tires on the cab and it was yellow, you needed two headlights, preferably, glass. Whether or not they worked didn't matter. Many cabs only had one dim light. That was not a problem, for in Manta, not unlike Quito, the police didn't write traffic tickets. So often you saw only one headlight working. Sometimes, two. Often none. That just meant the driver followed the car in front of him more closely so he could run in the other cars lights.

Now some might ask about the ability to accelerate or decelerate. No problem. If you can drive faster than the pedestrians can walk, you are in business. And as long as any portion of the minuscule braking system you have will grab before you hit and cream a tourist or another cab, that will pass for brakes.

You also needed a front passenger seat which should be bolted down, but then again it might not be, and also a back seat. The front seat needed a seat belt, but it didn't need to work. Once the unsuspecting fare climbed in and sat back, you took off as rapidly as you could.

And what about the passengers in the back seat? Well, each cab had at least eight to nine speakers which were located directly behind the back seat. This was done for a number of reasons. First, the loud music blocked the failing engine and transmission noise that might clue the unwary passengers that they made a mistake. The loud music also drowned out the screams of the terrified passengers in the backseat when the driver passed oncoming traffic narrowly missing a head on collision.

And last, but not least, each cab must had its resident fleas. And these, for the most part, occupied the rear seat and floorboard area.

So, there you have it: the taxi system in Manta, a system that provided at least one taxi for every foreigner who entered the city.

Another wonder found in Ecuador not found elsewhere are the traffic signs. However, don't let the placement of a sign confuse you, for in Ecuador, signs have absolutely no meaning. People here don't stop and take the time to read the signs even if they are posted. They don't read traffic and speed limit signs, nor do they bother to read the signs giving directions or asking you to keep off the grass.

If you want to make a point, e.g., you want to keep people off the grass or away from the trees or bushes, you place some posts deep into the ground and then surround the area with barbed wire. The meaner and nastier the barbed wire the better, but even that didn't always work. On occasion, I saw where some ingenious soul had taken the wire and laced it over the piece above, thus allowing them to slip in and onto the grass for a nap under the trees!

Thursday morning, while Hermano Cacuango conducted more training, Cheryle and I took a walk down to the beach. While we were walking, we were approached by one man who appeared to be a security officer. After a brief conversation, I bid him good-bye and we continued. The beach at Manta is very clean and has very small waves even though the wind blows.

We walked past some larger stands that sold food and drinks. Upon walking to the end of the boardwalk, we found ourselves in front of the National Police Station. We were the only ones on the entire boardwalk dressed in Sunday clothes, so needless to say, we stood out, and when we stopped in front of the police headquarters, one policeman came out and asked if everything was all right and if we were having any problems. We told him no and continued our walk. It was during this time that Cheryle again felt ill, so we went back to the room and waited for Hermano Cacuango to return. While Cheryle went to the room to rest, I sat near the pool for about an hour, made notes and reflected on the experience of visiting Manta.

At noon, Hermano Cacuango returned and we went to lunch. We found a very nice restaurant and had what I considered a good meal. We first had a shrimp like soup or cocktail with chips and hot salsa sauce. In the United States we use corn chips with the salsa. In Ecuador they use thin pieces of roasted bananas. Different, but good. However, Cheryle still liked the corn chips.

Lunch was so much food that I didn't eat again for nearly twenty-four hours. While the meal didn't bother me, it did Cheryle. After lunch we went back to the hotel, sat near the pool and awaited the arrival of the taxi driver who had originally taken us from Puerto Viejo to Manta the day before. At 4:00 p.m. he was there, and off we went for an uneventful ride back to the airport.

Along the way we again saw the great poverty many of the people lived in. On the outskirts of Puerto Viejo was a large circus, much like the old Ringling Brothers Barnum and Bailey Circus found in the United States many years ago. It had the large tent and all that went along with it.

When we arrived at the airport, we again were barraged by shoe shine boys and Lotto ticket sellers. As quickly as possible we made our way inside the terminal, past the vendors, and found seats. At one point, a woman sat down next to me with Lotto tickets in hand. I have become so accustomed to telling them no, that immediately I said "No thank you," but she kept talking. Funny thing was that she wasn't trying to sell me any tickets; she just wanted us to know that she was a new member of the church and loved to see and talk to missionaries! She, Cheryle, Hermano Cacuango and I talked for a few minutes, and then with a smile on her face, she left to go sell more Lotto tickets!

We waited for about forty-five minutes and then we were called to board. As I passed the plane, I noticed that the front two right side tires were not in real good condition. The inside tire was completely bald. With that I prayed that it would withstand the take off in Puerto Viejo and impact of landing in Quito. For if the tire blew, I doubted that the second tire was in good enough shape to handle the impact and weight, which would have meant that we would then be sliding along on a wing creating a situation that would in all probability be disastrous.

Fortunately, we got off the ground safely, yet it was different from any take-off I had ever experienced. Normally, the plane taxis to the end of the runway, slowly turns and once facing in the direction of take-off, the pilot revs the engine to build up the rpm's, releases the brakes and then starts down the runway.

That was not the case with this jet jockey. As we approached the turn in the runway, the pilot accelerated so that the plane was really moving when we came to the curve. It appeared that he wanted to make the turn already flying and thought that 50-60 mph would do just that! As we rounded the curve, greater acceleration was experienced and the moment we started to straighten out, we were feeling the G-forces as we were pushed deeper into our seats. Then, before I knew it, the tires left the ground and we were airborne.

The flight had its rough spots, but nothing like the banking maneuvers the pilot made. If I hadn't seen all the flight attendants in the passenger cabin, I would have sworn that one of them was at the controls!

On two occasions the pilot banked the plane dramatically and we descended rapidly. Once this was accomplished, we began our approach. It wasn't the long, smooth approach as one would expect. Instead, we literally dropped into the Quito airport and onto the runway. Never before had I ever asked for protection on any plane flight like I did on this one. Concerned about the tires on the aircraft, the turbulence and the sudden drop onto the runway, I did request some additional assistance, which we received.

Once the plane came to a stop and the door opened, Cheryle and I both were grateful for our safe return to Quito. We were thankful to be home, to be back at 10,000 feet and to smell the rain in the air.

Cheryle Subject of a Police Search!

The day was overcast with the normal threat of rain. Clouds hung heavily above the city of Quito and since Cheryle needed to mail a package no larger than a small shoebox to the United States, she felt motivated to stop at the small neighborhood post office while I walked to work. Little did she know that as she stepped from our apartment and onto the street, she was destined to have another one of the many strange experiences that helped to make our five years in South America truly a remarkable journey.

Fastidiously, Cheryle wrapped the contents of the box which included some small Christmas ornaments and trinkets for family members. She used brown wrapping paper, scotch tape and then tied the box from one end to the other with string. The box was nothing special, but because of the postal restrictions in Ecuador, wrapping was important. Then, in strict adherence to the Customs regulations, she filled out the appropriate paperwork and affixed it to the box.

As she entered the post office, she took her place in line, noticing that in one corner of the room was what appeared to be a plain-clothes police officer who it appeared was there to assist the paid security guard that faithfully stood at the front door scrutinizing with great care all who entered.

The line moved slowly and before she reached the window, she felt a presence standing to her immediate left.

Then suddenly from beside her the man she saw earlier in the corner of the room stepped in front of her and flashed his badge. "Policia Señora, may I see that package?"

"Of course," Cheryle responded somewhat startled.

As the police officer took the package, he asked Cheryle for her passport and Ecuadorian identification. Guess what? Cheryle decided to go to the post office today without any identification. Something that one never did whether you lived in or traveled to a foreign country. Especially in Latin America. She had nada! Nothing!

Well, without identification, her missionary name tag pulled no weight especially in light of the fact that a number of people in line were now watching the scene with wide eyed curiosity.

The police official now realized that the norteamericana had no identification and many were watching him. He also saw that the package was about the right size to send illegal items. So, with the professionalism that comes from conducting laborious searches as a career, he took out his small pen knife and began to cut the wrapping paper off the package.

Wisely, Cheryle just stood there and responded to his questions when asked.

"What is in the package?" asked the policeman.

Cheryle told him exactly what it was, but that didn't inhibit his cutting away the brown wrapping paper and opening the box. Once he had it opened, he removed each item and examined it meticulously. Now the show was on.

The officer was now putting on a wonderful show for all in line. With pen knife in hand, he prodded and picked, eventually bringing the item close to his nose to determine whether or not there was the possible odor of any narcotic. Finding exactly what Cheryle had declared was in the package, he put it back in the box and thanked her.

Then, another man stepped forward and began to rewrap the package in an official way that only an employee of the Quito Postal Service could or would do. Once it was wrapped, Cheryle stepped to the window and paid the postage fee. As she turned to leave and literally was walking out the front door, the man who rewrapped the package chased her down and told her that there was an additional fee for the wrapping job he had done. Angered, humiliated and now broke, Cheryle fished out some change from her coat pockets and returned to the Employment Center.

Served Rat on a Platter

I had been attempting for three weeks to get the FAX machine in our office repaired. It appeared that we were going to make it four.

On one beautiful afternoon, Cheryle and I took Daryl and Nanci Nancollas out to lunch. We had planned this outing a week in advanced and selected one of the "Finer" restaurants in Quito, named La Ronda. President Robert Whetten of the South America North Area Presidency recommended it, so we thought that we would give it a try.

In Whetten's opinion, it was a five star gig. The ambiance was wonderful. I ordered pork ribs, and what an experience that turned out to be. I couldn't cut through the skin with the knife, and the meat had a very gamey flavor that tasted like a cross between liver and small wildfowl. It was absolutely horrible, but I decided that I was in Ecuador, so.....I added as much onion and other spices as I could and tried to eat. Nothing helped. The ribs were much smaller than they should have been for pork and the piece more resembled a small rodent rather than pieces of pork. I should have gotten the hint when my plate was served and staring up at me were two dark beady eyes and two long teeth.

As I sat there, I honestly thought about our daughter Shannyn who served her mission in Costa Rica, and her husband Greg who served in Venezuela. I can imagine that they also tasted some pretty interesting things. So I ate most of it, that was until the onions and spices ran out. Then I was done! It was hideous.

It is amazing how spoiled one gets when accustomed to the restaurants and food in the states. Yet, the time with the Nancollas' made the afternoon most enjoyable. Back in the office when I shared this experience with my staff, they laughed and told me, "Elder Whitaker, if it wasn't pork ribs, it was rat. The two are sometimes interchanged!"

Needless-to-say, we never again revisited that five star restaurant!

Locked Out of Our Apartment with Dinner on the Stove

It was Sunday and the day began with a bang. Cheryle and I walked out the door, and when I went to double lock the top lock, the tumblers broke. So, there we were, standing outside our apartment, the bottom of the door was locked, the Sunday dinner was cooking on the stove, and we couldn't get back into the apartment.

Now this time, it wasn't that we lost the keys down an elevator shaft; we had the keys. The only problem was the top security lock on the front door was now in a locked position and the tumblers were broken, leaving the door permanently locked! So, there we stood.

I asked Cheryle to go down to Fanny's apartment before she left for the day, and tell her we had a problem. So off Cheryle went while I tried everything I could to get the tumblers just to slip back a little which would let me open the door; but it was in vain. The key just kept turning and turning, making perfect three hundred and sixty degree circles. No catching, no unlocking, no friction. Nothing. Just a smooth spin.

Not long after Cheryle left, she returned with Fanny. With the situation in Cheryle and Fanny's hands, and realizing that Sacrament meeting had long ago started, I went over to the office to complete the needed preparations for tomorrow morning. I was in the office about an hour and a half when the front door opened. "You won't believe what happened," said Cheryle. "You left and Fanny decided that she was going to call the Bomberos. That's right. The Fire Department!"

So Cheryle and Fanny went downstairs and waited for the fire department to arrive. Fortunately, they didn't send one of the large fire trucks, only one of the smaller units. The firemen exited the truck and Fanny panicked. In their hands they had crowbars and everything else needed to pry, ax or batter down a door. I guess that when Fanny called them, she told them there was food on the stove and the place was in jeopardy of going up in smoke! So on arrival, they tromped to the eighteenth floor ready to destroy anything in their way, but Fanny had a different idea.

"Just lower the fireman over the side of the building and have him open the big window," Fanny recommended.

Over the side was a drop off at least one hundred and eighty feet, straight down! Not the normal walk in the park for an Ecuatoriano fireman.

Well, they got to our apartment building door, and after realizing where we were located, the smallest fireman "volunteered" to try and slip onto a ledge just outside our kitchen window, slide open the window and crawl in. Here is the setup.

As you stand at our front door, just to the left was a large sliding glass kitchen window. If you could open this window, you could enter the kitchen. But if you missed, the drop was eighteen floors. Balancing on the ledge, once you opened the window, you ran directly into a concrete planter that was about two feet wide. The planter ended just to the side and below our kitchen window. Fortunately, none of the windows in Ecuador, at least in our apartment, were capable of being securely closed or locked so there was never a real problem of actually being, "locked out." Especially if you didn't mind climbing out on a narrow ledge eighteen floors up, stretching and then climbing through a very small window. And that is what this bombero did.

His buddies rigged him with a life line which was attached around his waist. As he eased out onto the ledge, they held the other end of the rope. The small 5'2" inch fireman crawled out onto the planter, and with all the strength he could muster; he stretched to his body's extreme and managed to slide the large kitchen window open. Only one problem: located in front of the window was a shelving unit. The same you can buy at Home Depot. You attach the sides to the wall, and then attach the shelves. The space between the shelves: about ten inches, and you cannot remove the shelves. They are securely attached. So, once the window was open the fireman made like Houdini. In what Cheryle described as a very awkward and contorted position, still hanging out in never-never land eighteen floors up, this guy wiggled and maneuvered into the small window opening. Then, making like a snake, he slithered into the kitchen, over the shelves, and dropped to the floor. The next concern?

LOCKED OUT OF OUR APARTMENT
WITH DINNER ON THE STOVE

Now that he was inside and the lock tumblers were broken, would he be able to open the deadbolt? Yelling through the locked door, he voiced the concern. Undaunted, using the key that we keep at the door, he slid the key into the lock, turned it sharply, and guess what? It opened! Fanny thanked the men and left. Cheryle, grateful for the death defying performance wanted to give them something. Fanny, wanted nothing to do with it. Finally she told Cheryle, "Give them five dollars."

"But there were four firemen," said Cheryle. So, Cheryle, after ensuring that she could get back in, got a ten dollar bill and went down stairs and gave it to the fireman. Now some would say, well, they get paid for doing their job. Yes, but in Ecuador, they are paid very little. And considering what it was worth to us in the long run, we both felt that the ten dollars was well spent.

Eventually, Fanny got the top deadbolt repaired, but before doing so, she found the least expensive locksmith around; a little man who had a small stand on the corner of Seis de Diciembre and Colon and he worked off a small wooden stand and made keys and repaired locks. In all reality, he did a pretty good job replacing the broken tumblers and tightening up the whole mechanism. Our only question was: Would it hold out for another eleven months? We would see.

A Conman Scams the Church

This next experience I will preface with a brief explanation. The Area Welfare Agent in the Quito Region was a man whom I shall call Elder Boyd. He and his wife were both in their mid-sixties serving their first mission, and when they exited the plane upon their arrival in Quito, both Cheryle and I commented that we had never seen anyone shake from fear as violently as did Sister Boyd.

Elder Boyd was a very sweet man who absolutely never opened his mouth. I was confident that he had a voice, but his wife never gave him a chance to use it. He came across as the original Casper Milquetoast. In all situations and on every occasion, whether in the Welfare Office, on the street, or at church, she would speak for him, and constantly gave him directions telling him what to do, how to do it and when it should be done. Yet try like she might, he still was the Area Welfare Agent.

Sister Boyd spoke a spattering of Spanish, but in the first six weeks they were in Quito, I never heard her husband utter a word of Spanish. The minute he opened his mouth to speak, she interrupted and spoke for him. When he was asked to pray in priesthood, he prayed in English.

On the organization chart, he was my supervisor. Now with that explanation, I will share an experience.

It was a Tuesday. Elder Boyd called and asked if I would come to the Robles Building for a meeting that concerned my office and a banking organization called CFN, which was the Ecuadorian Federal Financial Agency used in the past by the church to fund small business loans, and to fund training for church members. They were paid very well for their services.

I arranged my schedule to accommodate Elder Boyd, and when the day of the meeting came, he called and canceled. Since I was trained that we never cancel a church meeting except in the case of a dire emergency or serious conflict, I was a little annoyed when I discovered that the meeting was canceled because Sister Boyd decided she wanted to go shopping.

Wednesday, Elder Boyd called Cheryle and asked for another time. I had her call him back and tell him that 3:00 p.m. the next day would be fine.

As is my routine developed over many years, I always arrived at a meeting or appointment early. Not to do so was rude and reflected that in your opinion, your time was more important than the other person's. While I was early, the Boyd's were always late.

On the day of the meeting, I entered a small conference room, sat down and waited. At 3:15, Elder and Sister Boyd arrived. They were accompanied by Jorge Lopez who was hired by the church as an independent contracting attorney and represented the church in some inconsequential legal issues. I had dealt with Lopez on prior occasions and did not feel that he had the best interests of the church at the forefront of his decisions.

After we were all seated, Elder Boyd looked at Lopez for direction. Lopez told him it was his meeting. Sister Boyd then ordered her husband to offer a prayer.

"That's what we were taught in Salt Lake by Brother Flood," she said.

Sheepishly, Elder Boyd stood and offered a prayer.

Lopez then laid some papers in front of me on the table. He said that these were the plans that the Guayaquil Employment Office employees had developed for a special employment program. As he read the plan, it began to sound very familiar. He outlined the process that would allow for the implementation and controlling of this new and innovative program and stressed that the program never before had been used in the church. He closed his presentation by reiterating that the program was an excellent way to meet the needs of the church members while hiring and using returned missionaries to teach the skills needed to identify and secure gainful employment. He focused on the fact that CFN would handle the funds used to pay the returned missionaries for classes taught and administrative functions directed.

While he and the Boyd's lauded the innovative nature of the plan, I sat dumbstruck. This was the exact program Cesar Cacuango had developed and implemented for the Quito office including the use and payment of returned missionaries for involvement in various aspects of the program, and it was the same program he developed and presented to the folks in Guayaquil before his termination. It was this program that had been approved by Salt Lake and it was the same program I supervised in Quito, but for some reason, now that Cacuango was no longer in church employ, the Employment Resource Center Employees in Guayaquil decided to claim it as their brainchild. I was livid. A side note: It was while I used this program, which had been approved by Salt Lake, that a church administrator in South America wrote me a terse letter of condemnation stating that because of my use of the church headquarters approved program, I was dishonest, a liar and robbing God. Daryl Nancollas received the same condemnation, but since the writer of the correspondence and Nancollas were on the same organizational level and had a business relationship, he was later sent an apology while I never heard a word.

At the conclusion of the presentation by Lopez, the Boyd's were all smiles. All that was missing was the brass band and dancing girls. Sister Boyd congratulated Lopez for such an innovative approach to a serious problem, and turning her attention to me said, "Now Elder Whitaker, we want you to implement the same in Quito, and we expect it to be done immediately!"

I said nothing, just stared unblinking into her eyes. It was obvious that the Boyd's and this inept attorney had not spent much time with an assertive North American church administrator, especially not one cut from the cloth of a Whitaker.

Still standing, Lopez continued, speaking to me condescendingly while lauding the efforts of the Guayaquil employment team. He went on to show me the timeline they developed which was for November and December. He explained what they were doing, the organization, and money from CFN, personnel needed, how they were going to work with the stakes, etc. "This is how we want it and what we want from you!", he said as his face darkened to a blood red firehouse hue.

As he rambled on, I sat quietly. His rambling, combined with my silence began to make Elder Boyd uncomfortable, for when I turned and faced him, he looked away, a sure sign that he knew the presentation should not have been made by Lopez and Sister Boyd, but by him.

After hearing enough of his canned dialogue, in a soft but assertive voice, I asked, "Please explain to me why you are rushing into this before the Director from Guayaquil and the Employment Specialists are hired? What is the hurry especially in light of the past problems with CFN, our lack of personnel, and the upcoming Christmas holidays? Why not take the time to plan adequately and organize the project so it successfully can be directed, coordinated and controlled?"

When I finished, silence filled the room. Then the Spirit gave me the strongest impression that something was not as it should be with the role CFN was playing in this program. I knew something was very wrong. I recalled that in the past, some of the returned missionaries assisting in my office shared with me that when they were living in Guayaquil, they were approached by representatives of the church associated with CFN and offered jobs to teach and help administer a special employment program. They accepted and had accumulated over eighty hours of time, for which they were never paid. When the Spirit brought this to my mind, I knew we had a problem.

I looked around the room. Lopez sat in silence. Elder Boyd likewise was silent. They didn't have an answer, but Sister Boyd did.

Realizing that things were not going as she desired, Sister Boyd decided it was time for her to take over the meeting. She began by parroting the words of Lopez, and rambled on for about five minutes before I calmly turned to her and politely said, "Sister Boyd, your husband presides at this meeting and I would like to hear from the priesthood first. After his remarks, we can all share our opinions. Elder Boyd, you are my priesthood leader and I would like to hear from you." My words were spoken softly and delivered without malice.

Before I could finish, Sister Boyd became absolutely irate. She began to shake violently and was visibly flustered. Her English became garbled as she nervously rearranged the items on the desk and in her lap. Apparently she never before had been told that the priesthood presided and should be heard from first. *"Let he who has the keys to speak, speak."* This principle seemed foreign to Sister Boyd. Visibly agitated and in a voice laced with anger, she began to argue with me. Again, very calmly and in a subdued voice, I explained to her that I wanted to hear from her husband first.

She was now out of control. The trembling increased as did the volume of her voice. She now was screaming at me. Looking her directly in the eyes, I said, "Sister Boyd, I have never taken *priesthood direction* from the Relief Society and I will not start now. Your husband is my priesthood leader, and he presides at this meeting. I want to hear from him first. After he speaks, we then can discuss the matter further, each sharing their opinion. Elder Boyd, please give me your input on this matter." Elder Boyd looked to his wife for direction. None came. Just a face bathed in fury.

Angrily she turned her chair in my direction and shouted, "I knew that men were chauvinistic in Ecuador, but I didn't think it was the same in the United States. My heart is going pitter patter. I'm going to leave!"

"Sister Boyd," I said, "I love and appreciate you, but...,"

"Oh, no you don't," she screamed. "Oh, no you don't!"

And with that, she jumped out of her seat, grabbed her notebook, and while still yelling, bolted from the room. Elder Boyd just sat there and said absolutely nothing. Not a word. Not a change of expression. Stoic. Emotionless. He just continued to sit in his chair and watch as if he were somewhere else and oblivious to what was going on around him. The poor man had checked out.

A look of panic crossed Lopez's face.

"I don't feel a good spirit in this meeting," he said. "I think that we should all leave and do this another time."

He, too, was trembling and shaking. It was apparent that these people not only did not understand the priesthood, but they never had anyone say so few words in such a direct manner. With Lopez's comment, I looked him directly in the eyes and said, "We are here brethren to discuss an issue. We don't cancel or walk out of meetings in the church. Now let's just sit here and finish what we came to do!"

And so with Elder Boyd stone cold silent, Lopez's hands shaking and his voice quivering, we pounded out what appeared to be a sensible plan close to the reason for which we met. We came to a consensus that we needed to secure additional information and then meet after the Christmas Holidays.

When I shared the following incident with both norteamericano and ecuatoriano priesthood leaders, they all agreed that the firmness was definitely needed, but in the future I might consider softening the manner of presenting my concerns. While I thought that I did well on the softness, it appeared that if one did not agree with some, they were thought to be too aggressive and blunt. When I heard this assessment, I decided to rework my future presentations.

Upon leaving the meeting, my first telephone call was to Daryl Nancollas. He was one of the finest priesthood administrators and organizational minds I knew. I told him that the old detective in me sensed something was wrong, and the Spirit verified that impression. Daryl shared my concerns and told me he would look into it. He also asked me to patch things up with Elder and Sister Boyd. I agreed to do so, knowing it would not be easy.

A few weeks following this debacle, the Colon Ward Christmas party was scheduled. The starting time was 7:00 p.m., but knowing the different level of punctuality here as compared to the states, Cheryle and I decided to arrive fashionably late.

When we arrived at the chapel at twenty after, not only had the party not started, but the preparations still were ongoing, and ward members were few in number. I glanced into the cultural hall where I was told there would be a piano and microphone. I had been asked to provide some entertainment, but neither was there. To get a piano into the cultural hall would have required it to be moved from the chapel, and I knew that was not going to happen, so my participation for the evening was taken care of.

Looking down the hall, I saw Elder and Sister Boyd walk in. *No better time than the present to begin the healing process,* I thought. So I walked down the hall to greet them. First I approached Sister Boyd, extended my hand and said, "Good evening, Sister Boyd.

It was a moment that electrified that old colloquial saying, "If looks could kill, I would have been dead." Sister Boyd stood frozen, a hateful, stoic expression emanated from her countenance as she glared at me. I waited with extended hand, but she refused to shake it. The loathing and hatred that emanated from her countenance was exactly the same that I had seen during the most difficult of the president's interviews I conducted while serving in the Nevada Las Vegas Mission Presidency. Her face was distorted, the image dark and odious. It was something to behold, especially coming from a full-time senior missionary. Looking into her insufferable countenance I said, "Excuse me for bothering you," and I turned to greet her husband. Extending my hand to him, I said, "Good evening, Elder Boyd." As he extended his hand, his wife abruptly turned and marched down the hallway. Another first. I had never had a member of the church, even those with whom I had differences of opinion, ever express such abhorrence and animosity; nor had I ever had either a male or female member of the church refuse to shake my hand.

Later, I had a conversation with Nancollas in his office and he said, "Elder Whitaker, it is not what you said, but how you said it." I reflected back on the incident, and although my demeanor was businesslike, I did not believe it to be offensive; however, I was given good counsel and chose to do everything in my power to soften my approach.

Weeks passed and I received an invitation to have lunch with Daryl. As I walked into his beautiful office, I had to laugh. Here were opulent black leather chairs and a very large desk, such a contrast to the small corner of a flea ridden office where I sat on a chair that required a telephone book on the seat because the small table was too high, and all the chairs in the office were too low.

As we sat and talked, I mentioned to him that I needed a chair that didn't require me to put a phone book on the seat. He couldn't believe I had to use a phone book to get the proper height. With a smile on his face and twinkle in his eyes, I was told that the problem would be resolved.

We spent two hours together talking and sharing many experiences. When we returned to the Robles building, we stood out front and talked some more.

He told me that after my meeting with Lopez and the Boyd's, he instigated an investigation into CFN and their relationship with the church, especially the Employment Program.

It appeared that my feelings about CFN and some of the primary players in the scenario were correct. Following a thorough investigation, it was determined that the man who was pushing so hard for the church again to get involved was receiving financial kickbacks from the training institution and many of the people who were paid to administer and conduct the training. Many of these kickbacks came from the funds promised to a number of returned missionaries who were hired to teach, but never paid. The money designated to be paid to the returned missionaries was withheld under the guise of a number of excuses and instead was given to this man and a select few of his crooked friends. In the end, the church was being bilked out of their funds and the returned missionaries scammed of their paychecks. So fraud was committed against the church and the returned missionaries were the victims of an elaborate grand theft scheme. The entire setup was rotten from the top down.

Nancollas had a big smile on his face as he shared that bit of news with me. I knew something was wrong and unfortunately it required a pretty tough stance in one meeting to get the point across. Had this not been done, the church and members in Ecuador again would have entered into an arrangement that not only would have proven bad for them, but also disastrous for Nancollas who would have been held responsible for the decision and possibly fired. He told me he was grateful for the way I handled the situation using my investigative background and also was grateful for the fact that I listened to the Spirit. "And I will forgive you for your toughness," he said laughing.

So, even though some felt that my ways of doing things were a little too straight forward and no-nonsense, those who would have suffered were appreciative. Again, the old street cop instincts came through.

I felt bad for Cheryle. Because of the Sister Boyd incident, she was as nasty to Cheryle as she was to me, and anyone who knows Cheryle, realizes that she constantly goes out of her way to be sweet and kind to everyone, including those who are truly nasty to her, as was Sister Boyd. Try as Cheryle might, the situation only worsened, so much so that several weeks later when the North American Sisters in Quito met for their monthly lunch, Cheryle opted not to go. She did not want the affair ruined by anything that Sister Boyd might do or say, nor did she want to continue to humiliate herself by being the recipient of the woman's hateful attitude. The sad thing was that those who attended these luncheons would have loved to have Cheryle's company coupled with her very loving and kind spirit.

The Wednesday following the luncheon, an interesting thing occurred while we were in the office. As I sat at my computer looking out the window at the long driveway that provided entrance to the Church Educational System facility, I noticed Sister Boyd walking down the driveway toward the Institute building and our office. We knew that she had had a very rough time of it, not only because of her feelings toward Cheryle and me, but also because she had been diagnosed with a severe case of facial skin cancer that was so pronounced it required a painful treatment. She was confined to their apartment for nearly six weeks awaiting the disappearance of the many ugly puss-filled blisters which covered her face. They were a result of the cancer treatment.

Earlier in the week, Cheryle had written Sister Boyd a Get Well card and delivered it to their apartment. Sunday, I asked Elder Boyd how his wife was doing and told him she was in our prayers. With that, I forgot about it and moved on, that was until I saw her walking down the driveway toward our office.

Our small, temporary office was crowded. Suddenly, and in all the confusion, I realized that Sister Boyd had walked into the office and was standing talking to Cheryle. She thanked Cheryle for her kindness and even spoke hesitatingly and somewhat fearfully to me. I wished her well and told her to take care of herself. And although it was apparent that I scared her tremendously, it took great courage to do what she did. I later told Cheryle that the Lord has many ways to humble each of us, some ways being more difficult than others. Hers was severe.

A Special Christmas

For Christmas, Cheryle and I picked out some of the street people that we saw and talked to on a regular basis. We gave each of them a Christmas card with a five dollar bill inside. None of those to whom we gave a card, ever asked, begged or solicited anything from us. They only smiled warmly as we approached and greeted us each day with a warm, "Buenos días."

Many who received a card were very poor and considered to be on the bottom of the social and economic level. A few even would be considered poverty stricken. They lived day to day and struggled to stay alive. They were ignored by most and were forced to live in their own world.

I shared with you the response of our weathered old parking lot attendant who directed the parking of cars in the market parking lot, and who was grateful for whatever tips he received. The next time I saw him, he shuffled up to me and gave me a big hug. Cheryle was wishing she had the camera. Each day this kind hearted little man greeted me warmly as he removed his beat up gray police hat, then he would salute me as though I were a General in the Ecuadorian Army, and he would finish with a bow.

Another recipient of our special Christmas Gift was a little woman named Maria who worked outside our building cleaning and sweeping the sidewalks, tile floors and doing basic cleanup work using only a small dustpan and a tattered old broom. She stood no more than four-feet ten and couldn't be more than forty years old. She was slight in build, and was missing her top and bottom front teeth. Her daily uniform, which she faithfully wore, was a dirty blue smock wrapped around her tiny body and topped with an old blue baseball cap. Diligently she worked, but earned nor more than twenty-five cents an hour.

On the day before Christmas when Cheryle and I searched for Maria to give her the card, we couldn't find her. Cheryle went to the laundry located on the third floor of our building and mentioned to the ladies in the laundry that she was looking for Maria.

"We'll send her up to your apartment, that will be better," Cheryle was told. About thirty minutes passed and there was a light knock at our door. When Cheryle opened the door, there was Maria. Cheryle handed her the card and wished her a Merry Christmas. Tears filled Maria's little eyes as she reached warmly around Cheryle's waist and gave her a loving hug.

"This is the only card I have received this Christmas. Thank you, Señora."

Christmas Day came and went, and the next day we were back at work.

We didn't see Maria Tuesday or Wednesday, but Thursday morning as we left the building, we saw her outside cleaning. As usual, she was dressed in her old blue smock and dirty baseball cap, and was holding her broom and dust pan. When we walked out, both Cheryle and I bid her good-morning. Stopping what she was doing, she hurried up to us, shook my hand and then stepped in front of Cheryle.

Looking up into Cheryle's face, she hesitated. Tears filled her eyes as she threw her arms around Cheryle and while giving her a hug said, "Señora, thank you."

Cheryle's eyes filled with tears. "You're welcome Maria," she said softly. "You're welcome."

As we walked up the narrow street toward Amazonas Blvd, we were both grateful that under the direction of the Spirit, we were able to do something that to us appeared to be a small gesture, but to a daughter of God, it meant so very much.

Cheryle Falls in a Stairwell

The first ten days of the New Year were difficult, and it was topped off as Cheryle and I returned home from work. Since we lived on the top floor of an eighteen floor high-rise apartment building, it sometimes was fun to walk the eighteen floors from the bottom to top. The stairwell we used was concrete and dimly lit. At times, it was completely dark, and we had to inch our way up until we reached a single light bulb that cast an eerie shadow through the dimly lit prison like pox marked walls.

We found that it was not our legs that proved to be a challenge, but for Cheryle it was the altitude. It was interesting that the 10,000 foot altitude at which we lived had no effect on me, and when I was alone, I could take the climb nonstop.

On this particular day, Cheryle said she wanted to walk a portion with me. We had the guard open the locked door leading to the dark interior corridor and concrete steps. After we turned on the single dangling bulb, we started up. At the third floor, it became very dark again. I walked past the light switch saying, "There's light above." Suddenly, I heard a loud thump and turned to see Cheryle lying on the concrete floor. She had tripped on a step and fallen. I didn't realize that she had hit her head and the side of her face on the concrete. It should have been worse, but I have no doubt that someone else was in that darkened stairwell was providing additional protection. Fortunately, she was not hurt too badly, just very shaken. This wasn't her week.

The fall, the stress of the office, doctor's appointments and not knowing if her cancer had returned took its toll on both of us. Emotionally, we both were frazzled, and when we were alone, it showed to some degree. After a couple of very difficult days, things returned to normal. Amazingly, Cheryle only had a slight cut to the inside of her lip and small discoloration to the outside of the top lip from the fall.

Needless to say, she took the elevator after that, but I continued to walk the eighteen floors. I wanted to be able to run all eighteen floors, but I needed my oxygen capacity to increase. I figured if I could do that without the increasing hip pain, I should be able to go back to distance running in the future. Something I missed greatly.

Maintain the Fire in Your Gut and Passion in Your Soul!

These had been some very trying days. Then came Tuesday. In comparison, the difference between Monday and Tuesday were as stark as night and day. The physical discomfort had not been reduced, but the experience in the morning that awaited me, gave a hearty stamp of approval on all we had done. It all but eliminated the hours of frustration with some church employees in Bogota. I was seated in my office running some statistics when I heard, "Hermano Whitaker, Hermano Whitaker?"

Suddenly, Julio Cabeza de Vaca, the Regional Manager from Ecuador, with the biggest grin, stepped from behind the divider. He was accompanied by two brethren from Salt Lake who introduced themselves as Richard Ebert and Gustavo Espinosa. Ebert was the new Welfare Manager over the Employment and PEF sections for the church and was taking the place of Tim Sloan, who was going to be the new mission president in Quito. As I shook hands with Espinoza, a former US Marine from Salt Lake, he said, "We've heard a lot about you Elder Whitaker."

"Good, I hope?"

"Excellent," he replied.

MAINTAIN THE FIRE IN YOUR GUT
AND PASSION IN YOUR SOUL!

Stepping into an office adjacent to mine, the brethren told us that from the standpoint of effectiveness and efficiency, our office was the number one Employment Resource Center (ERC) office in the church. It was documented by statistics maintained in Salt Lake City. Then in the doorway, I saw Carlos Fernandez, the Area Welfare Manager who was stationed in Bogota. The Area PEF manager, Saul Vargas reported to Brother Fernandez. After a warm hug and some kind words from Carlos, Brother Ebert spoke.

"We want to meet with you, Elder.'

"Any time," I responded.

"Give us a few minutes, and then we'll get back to you."

They walked from the office leaving Patricio grinning and Cheryle smiling.

After ten minutes, Patricio Alvarez and I were summoned to meet the group in the conference room.

While I am not going into details about the meeting, I will say that I had the opportunity to answer honestly some very straightforward questions. It was apparent to me that none of the brethren in the room had ever sat in front of a priesthood leader who was so truthful, straight forward and direct with his observations and recommendations. That fact was confirmed when, as we were leaving, the two brethren told me they never had expected such honesty and candor, and since they were new in their callings, they were more than appreciative of not only the observations, but also the very candid recommendations that pertained to our program, the importance of Priesthood Correlation with the stakes and wards, correlation with the employment side of the house, and the nonexistent support and training we had received from the PEF office in Bogota. The situation was so bad, that two senior couples who worked under the direction of that office and experienced dreadfully poor relationships with the supervisors, stated they will not plan to serve another mission and wanted to leave as soon as possible. I shared with the group that sad commentary and made it clear that because of the lack of direction given by the PEF office in Bogota, if I were told by another couple they had been assigned to the Bogota office of PEF, I would tell them to get their assignment changed. It was harsh, but no senior couple should be required to endure 18 to 24 months of incompetence, nor should they decide to cut their mission short, which was done in one case because paid church managers treated them so poorly.

I realize that some might think I was harsh, and maybe I was, but in that directness, I was neither condemning nor complaining. I just was stating the hard, cold facts. It was information based upon my personal conversations with the parties involved, and not hearsay.

MAINTAIN THE FIRE IN YOUR GUT
AND PASSION IN YOUR SOUL!

When the brethren asked their first question, I told them that I was very honest and direct. "That's why we have made you our first stop," said Brother Ebert.

I told them that behind closed doors, if they asked, I would answer. If they found this offensive, we should forego the meeting. They opted to stay.

At the end of the meeting, I was thanked for my honesty, candor and the remarkable work coming out of our office. Carlos Fernandez also requested a copy of the PowerPoint presentation we had developed and presented to nine stakes in Guayaquil. It was powerful and had an immediate impact. I told him one was sent to his office in care of Saul Vargas. He smiled and asked for another copy. Three additional stakes had been scheduled for July, and there were those who wanted me to accompany Efrén Espinosa for the presentations. Personally, with my ankle which I broke, I could take it or leave it.

Regarding the presentations, not only were we receiving telephone calls from stake presidents requesting additional copies of the report for their stakes, we also were receiving personal visits by other stake presidents.

Carlos Fernandez knew I was not happy at the manner in which senior missionaries were treated by employees in his office. As he was leaving, he said "We will make some changes in Bogota." He also told me he would be back in July and planned on having dinner with us.

Two days after our meeting I received two e-mails from Salt Lake again reinforcing their gratitude for my honesty and stating, "Maintain the passion."

On another occasion, I was in a meeting with Hermano Cevallos. The normal work week ended with me having lunch on Friday with Frank Cevallos, the new Regional Manager for Ecuador. I took Frank to the Hilton Colon for lunch; then he asked to see our new offices, so after lunch, we walked over to our office. After a tour of the facility, we took the time to sit in my office and talk. All in all, we spent about four hours together. While at lunch, Frank looked at me and said, "When we were in Daryl's (Nancollas) office the other day, I wondered what made you different from the other Senior Missionaries, then I figured it out. The difference is your enthusiasm and excitement. You always are excited and enthusiastic about the work, and you never stop pushing."

"You're right," I said. "I know exactly what the Lord expects of me and what He wants accomplished. So that is what I do."

"Well, Elder, as far as I'm concerned, just keep doing what you've been doing. You've got my support."

"I appreciate that. You will find, Hermano Cevallos, people either love me or hate me. There is no middle ground." With that he laughed.

Allegations of Disobedience

A number of family members have inquired about the status of our office and its future. I will share with each of you an e-mail I received from Brother M., the Director of Temporal Affairs, (DTA) who replaced Daryl Nancollas. He was in a key position and working from Bogotá. After reviewing our progress as an office and evaluating Daryl Nancollas' efforts, as well as my efforts, he wrote a letter to us in which he insinuated that we were dishonest in our administration of the Employment Program; we were in contempt of church authority; and we had placed the church at legal risk. Basically, Daryl and I were liars and thieves who robbed God!

Personally, I was offended, and to be honest, I was angered at what was insinuated. However, I will let you draw your own conclusions. The bottom line was that at no time did Daryl Nancollas nor I do anything dishonest, nor were we in any way disobedient. What we did had previously been approved by the leaders in Salt Lake under the auspices of a pilot program, and with Daryl's approval, the program was developed and administered by Caesar Cacuango, the Area Employment Manager.

Unfortunately, Cesar Cacuango did something—of which I am not aware—to cause the leadership in Salt Lake to offer him, after twenty-three-years of employment, the opportunity to retire from church employment, or he would be terminated. With his options presented, Cesar decided to retire. After only ten weeks in Ecuador, I was advised by Daryl that the Area and church leadership in Salt Lake had approved me to replace Brother Cacuango. We made the transition and I continued to supervise the programs, policies and procedures that were in place under Cacuango. I only made changes when I felt they were needed.

Time passed, and the programs that had been approved were helping to bless the lives of members and non-members alike, and then I received some correspondence from the man who had replaced Daryl. While there were a few in Salt Lake who openly stated that they did not like Elder Whitaker, I was taken back when this letter, with its allegations, was received in my office. I had heard of their dislike, but their feelings were minimal compared to the accolades our office received for doing what the Lord desired in a manner that blessed the lives of the people. This correspondence was drafted based on the opinions of those whom I made uncomfortable, as well as those who tried to bully me, but realized I could not be intimated by their bullying tactics, and by the author of the letter who based his feeling on the allegations of one church employee in particular with whom I previously had a run in. The correspondence covered a period of fourteen months where our programs, policies and procedures were monitored, reported and hailed as highly successful. Here is the letter as received.

"Elder Whitaker:

The problem is not who did what or what was done! Everyone can see that the results are great. The problem has been, is and cannot continue to be the fact that the Quito center has been, is and will continue to be a volunteer operation and we have NOT been playing with the game rules set for us.

We have done things our way and it has worked to a certain extent but we too must consider the fact that, in spite of the great results, we have broken the rules, we are in contempt with church authority and as a result we are out of line and will no longer be supported in our disobedience.

In our effort to be successful, we have exposed the church to additional legal risk, we have spent holy funds that were not authorized for our use, we have set a precedent that will be next to impossible to wipe away and we have given false hope to many people who will now continue to expect the church to continue paying them to do what they should do as service.

I may not be saying this right, so maybe I should summarize it by saying. "In my many years of church service and church work, never have I truly been blessed when I break the rules or am disobedient."

Not all is lost, even though our ideas of using Perpetual Education Funds was not approved, we can still succeed! We can do what we are told, we CAN convince the local leaders to call Service Missionaries, we can use our personal resources, we can give the classes ourselves, we can convince our office staff to give service after hours, we can pray and fast and ask the Lord how he expects us to get the job done "HIS WAY" for he never gives a commandment without preparing the way to comply. I KNOW WE CAN DO IT!! I KNOW WE WILL DO IT! I BELIEVE IN THE PROGRAM AND IT CAN AND WILL WORK!! My only question now is..... CAN I COUNT ON ELDER AND SISTER WHITAKER TO HELP ME?? I can't do it alone, we need your experience, your spiritual strength and your "get up and go."

Let's go do it!!!!!!!"

In all my years in church service, this was the most offensive and degrading correspondence I ever had received. Unfortunately, not only was I accused of wrong doing, but so was Daryl, for it was under his direction, and with not only his permission, but also that of the Area Presidency that we were able to accomplish all that we did. I can't comprehend what it really was that made this man think I came up with this program on my own, did everything under the table and then ran it in an unrighteous manner?

Never at any time did we do anything "under the table." Never was anything done which was illegal, dishonest or immoral. Never did we proceed without the approval of the presiding authorities. Never!

This correspondence was unbelievably offensive. I have been told by a few priesthood leaders that I made them uncomfortable; I have been told they didn't like me; I have had them fly onto the High Council table in anger at something I said, but never has anyone ever questioned my integrity, or insinuated that I have used sacred funds dishonestly, or state that I am disobedient and in contempt of church authority. Never!

After the initial shock and horror of this letter, I did everything in my power to forgive and release it to Heavenly Father who knows the truth. I also did all within my power to put everything in the order required by those above me. My solace rests in knowing that Nancollas and I were completely honest, obedient, and never in contempt of church authority. We were approved by both church authority and the Spirit. What was done at the time was exactly what the Lord wanted done for this office, the people of Ecuador and for the eight returned missionaries, three priesthood leaders and hundreds of people who benefited from the program.

When I shared this with Daryl, he was irate. He called Brother M., the DTA who initiated the correspondence. Daryl told the man that everything we did had the approval of the Brethren. Brother M. apologized to Daryl, but I never received any further communication nor an apology.

Will Cheryle and I serve another mission? Yes. Do we want to serve again Spanish speaking, foreign? Yes. Will I ever again accept another assignment after this assignment concludes to work in the Employment Resource Services area of the Welfare Department? No. You only insult and tarnish my character once. You only question my integrity once.

Will I ever be called to serve in other leadership positions in the church which require greater responsibility? Time will tell. Once you have been labeled a rebel, the tag is usually permanent. And that is my reputation: a rebel, gunfighter and real cowboy, but someone who gets things done where others fail.

Although I have little respect for the individual who disparaged and maligned Daryl and me, his slandering of my reputation has no impact on the fact that I know there is a difference between the Gospel of Jesus Christ and those who sit in paid positions in the organization. *The Gospel of Jesus Christ is true.*

I have been permitted to serve in wonderful callings. I have seen things and been taught by great and magnificent men. I also have been blessed with talents and gifts that appear to be ahead of the understanding of some. With this knowledge, I will continue to push forward.

The Volcanoes of Ecuador

On a special Preparation-day, Cheryle and I went with Quinn and Heidi Johnson and their three children to the Volcanoes Cotopaxi and Pasochoa and its surrounding Refugio de Vida Silvestre Pasochoa. The area was located east of Quito about an hour drive. We were planning on visiting Pinchincha, which was higher, but it was engulfed in clouds, and we felt the experience would not have been worth the drive or the long hike.

They picked us up at 7:00 a.m., and we drove south from Quito excited about the experience, but had no idea how wonderful it would be.

The volcano Pasochoa last erupted in 1976 and blew out the entire west side of the rim creating an enormous valley that resembled the fjords found in Norway and Sweden. The drive to and from the reserve was fun, and we were able to take many pictures.

At the first toll gate prior to entry into the reserve, we had to pay two cents as an entrance fee. The single lane road to the reserve was paved with cobblestones, laboriously laid by hands many years ago, and pock marked with ruts that filled with water every time it rained, which was daily. Within the refuge were homes and ranches—some large, others small.

As we traveled south, I noticed a very large bus heading toward us in the opposite lane of traffic. The bus was the same size as a large Greyhound, however there was one very distinct difference. On the roof were three sheep! They were tethered and standing on top of a bus that was traveling down the highway at over sixty miles an hour, and acting as if this was a daily occurrence and a normal way for sheep in Ecuador to travel. Apparently, it was!

The highway we traveled was probably one of the best in Ecuador, having been improved so that it was flat and smooth which allowed us to cut nearly thirty minutes off the travel time. These improvements were possible because it was a toll road, with dramatically increasing tolls through the years.

Once we entered the park, the adventure really began as the better than average road abruptly ended and we immediately found ourselves back on the typical roads of Ecuador: rough, gravel, pock-marked with deep holes caused by the torrential rains that keep this country beautiful and green, but made travel difficult.

In the park was the volcano Cotopaxi, it loomed majestically on the right as we entered the park. Its snowcapped peak demanded respect from the smaller volcanoes that surrounded it. On we drove until we started to climb up a single lane dirt road cut in the side of the volcano and headed toward the top.

Since we arrived early in the morning, we were virtually alone as we moved up the mountain. On a number of occasions, Quin was required to change the land cruiser vehicle over from the regular drive to its four wheel capabilities. This was a blessing.

Up and up we climbed while the snow grew deeper on either side of the road. Then suddenly it was on the road which made it nearly impossible to continue. I sat in the front passenger seat as Quin threw the gearshift down and we inched our way forward. Suddenly, the wheels started to spin as we hit the snow and ice. Slowly, we inched forward, and then in a heartbeat, we began to slide backwards. In an instant we were sitting on the outside edge of the road with the cliff directly below me. I looked down and over the side as the wheels continued to spin sending us toward the edge looming precariously close. I cinched my seat belt tighter and was a bit concerned, to say the least. Then, suddenly, the tires struck dirt and caught. We came to an immediate stop, and Quin asked, "Well, should we try it again?"

"No," was my immediate reply.

I am not a coward, nor do I back out of a situation which many would consider dangerous, but when the Spirit says no, that is all I need. The answer is no. As I sat on the edge of the side of that mountain, I saw the car in my mind as it rolled uncontrollably down the mountain. We had traveled by car far enough.

Quin backed the car down the steep road until we reached an area that allowed us to back into a space designed for parking. Once parked, the three Johnson children bounded anxiously out of the car. This was their first time in the snow of Ecuador. The four adults followed. We all wrapped up and started to climb toward the snow that covered the side of the volcano. Below the snow level, the mountain was made up of small lava stones and pumice which made climbing as difficult as walking up a steep sand dune at the beach.

At an altitude of about 13,000 feet, breathing was a little more difficult than what was experienced at sea level, and the difficulty wasn't helped by the fact that unless you knew to walk up the side of the steep mountain at angles, you would find yourself taking two steps forward and then sliding three steps back.

Everyone, including Quinn, who was carrying the smallest child on his back, eventually made it to a very large patch of snow that covered a good sized area of the mountainside. For Cheryle, the climb was hard and she remained at the bottom where snow and lava stones met. I climbed higher. It was magnificent!

As the Johnson's and Cheryle stood below, I made my way up the side of the mountain. Below me lay a large plain which had been swept clean of vegetation by past eruptions.

Yet, there were areas that although they had been cleaned of vegetation in the past, now saw the return of life.

After savoring the magnificent view, I turned and walked carefully back down the side of the volcano to an area still well above where the others stood. I then sat down and looked in all directions. The plain before me created a valley which appeared to be about five miles long and three miles wide. In some areas I could see where the force of the volcano had torn its way violently through the valley leaving nothing but devastation. Then in other areas, vegetation had taken hold.

The landscape was beautiful and made up of many shades of green, brown and red. To my left was another volcano, Corazoa. North of it lay Atacazo, and directly in front of me across the plain was Sincholagua. Then farther in the distance lay Pasochoa.

Thick clouds rested on the top of the volcano, Sincholagua, which also had snow capping its pointed peak. Yet, of all the peaks, the most ominous and sinister was the volcano Corazoa. It's craggy, rough and jagged sides testified of the violence that had shaped the landscape many years past.

While I sat on the mountainside, the clouds that had begun to surround the mountain, Cotopaxi, parted. The sight looking up was incredible. There it was, Cotopaxi, majestically sitting like a king upon his throne holding court with the lesser members of his court. It was a court that found some subjects rising majestically toward the heavens, while others had been worn down over the centuries, submissively sitting in evident subjection to he who had proved to be the most powerful: Cotopaxi.

I sat and I marveled. It was the first time, since the fourth grade, that I wished I had a sketch pad. It was in the fourth grade at Monlux Elementary School where my teacher, James R. Klenes, realized that I had artistic talent far and above the other class members. While others remained buried deep in their studies, Mr. Klenes placed a large sheet of brown paper over one of the two blackboards that lined the classroom walls, and I was given the task of drawing a large mural which represented the conquest of Mexico. Every day I drew on the project that took all year. Each day as others were learning math and other critical academic areas, I drew and created a mural that stretched from wall to wall.

So as I sat and marveled at the sight which I beheld in the top of the Andes, I wished I had a drawing pad and pencil with which to sketch some of the marvels I beheld. However, we were able to document this beauty with photographs. All of it will long be remembered.

After sitting alone for a period of time, I made my way back down to where the children were playing in the snow. Once I was where the children were playing, each climbed up a steep snow bank and then repeatedly took turns sliding down the snow and being caught by Elder Whitaker just before the snow came to an end and the lava rocks began. Over and over they slid down the slope and then hiked back up to do it over again. Then Heidi Johnson took her turn. After Heidi, I caught one of the kids when suddenly, bam! A very well placed snow ball hit me in the right side of the head! Looking up the snow bank I saw Quin Johnson with a shocked look on his face. First, he was amazed that the snowball had hit me in the head, but then he was grateful that I hadn't looked up sooner or it would have nailed me right between the eyes. A good laugh was had by all as Elder Whitaker removed small bits of snow from his already near snow white hair.

By this time, we had spent a couple of hours on the mountain, and as it became later in the morning, more people began to arrive. So, we decided it was time leave.

Remember the narrow, one way road heading up? Well, as I looked down into the valley below, I spotted a large tour bus on its way up. Up and up it climbed just like a snail. Up and around it went weaving its way back and forth across the narrow road. My only thought with him coming up was, *How will we get down?* Then the bus stopped on the road below us, and a horde of youth bailed out and started trekking their way up the mountainside through the shifting pumice and rock. Up and up they climbed, all the while the bus sat blocking all cars from coming up, and us from going down. The bus was the width of the only lane, so when the driver saw that he had to do something, he again started to drive up the narrow road. Where he was going to turn around was anyone's guess. No one could pass from below, nor could we pass from above.

Quinn drove to a small bluff just above the bus and using the four wheeled drive gears, pulled back into a small space just off the road. And there we sat. Realizing that he now had a problem, the bus driver decided to climb higher on the mountain. He passed us and the bus tires spun as they laboriously tried to find solid ground under the snow that traced the road.

Fortunately, as soon as he passed us, Quin was off and we were rolling back down the steep mountain grade. How the bus got down off the mountain, I don't know. But it did. The Sunday newspaper did not have an article about a large tour bus driving off a narrow mountain road while trying to turn around on the Volcano Cotopaxi! So I guess all ended well.

Once at the bottom of the volcano, we began exploring the valley. Driving south we passed herds of wild horses, and as we looked toward the south wall of the valley, we spotted something that appeared to be the side of a road. Stopping the car, Quinn and I got out and walked to the area. It wasn't a road but a swiftly flowing stream that seemed not only to wind itself around the base of the mountain, but also cut itself through the middle of the valley.

On we drove and saw more and more wild horses. Then, in the middle of the valley, Quinn pulled off the dirt road—

which was more a path—and drove toward the stream and a waterfall that dropped about five feet as the stream rushed through the valley. It was a breathtaking scene of incredible beauty.

As I stood at the bottom of this beautiful valley which was surrounded by massive volcanoes and traversed by a swift flowing stream, I was in absolute awe, an awe created by the fact that I was standing in the top of the Andes. That, in and of itself, was incredible to me.

I walked over to the stream and looked around. In the far distance was a wall built by the Incas on the top of a hill. Evidently, it was a fortification for the soldiers sent from Peru to protect what was considered to be one of the farthest reaches of the Inca Empire; a fortification which would have been a very lonely, very cold, and very dangerous assignment. I couldn't help wondering who they were. Once again, I was overwhelmed by the fact that we were in the Andes and experiencing this unbelievable beauty.

Gazing across the stream, which was about fifteen feet wide and meandered through the rocks, I saw in the distance what seemed to be sun bleached bones. Making my way across some partially submerged rocks in the stream, I reached the other side and walked to the bones. Next to a rock, I found what appeared to be bones from an animal's ribcage. Not far from there, I found the larger bones, and then the rest of the skeletal remains of a young colt. Although some of the bones had been scattered by predators and large birds, the skeleton was in pretty good shape. With this find, I called the two older Johnson kids to come take a look. They were delighted. Slowly, we put the skeleton back together. Skull, spine, ribs and legs. It appeared that the young colt had broken one of its legs and being unable to keep up with the others, had died.

It is difficult to express the feelings of wonderment and awe I experienced standing on that Andean plain, listening to the rushing of the water, and beholding the beauty that surrounded me. Again, my mind wandered to the past, wondering about the history of the area and what had happened to the Inca soldiers sent to protect an empire that spanned many thousands of miles, but would be destroyed by a few Spanish conquistadors led by Pizarro.

We spent about three hours exploring the Cotopaxi National Park. In all, we left home at 7:00 a.m. and returned at about 3:00 p.m. It was an incredible experience, and although both Cheryle and I returned to the apartment exhausted. It was an experience we will cherish and never forget.

Our Departure from Ecuador

The night of our departure from Quito was cloudy and cool. The sights and sounds of the city we came to love soon would be only a memory as would the nearly eighteen months spent serving the people of Ecuador. When the Elders arrived, they gladly grabbed our suitcases, and hit the button on the elevator that would take us from the eighteenth to the ground floor. We silently left the building. As we entered the back of the mission truck, I looked around one last time.

"Thank you Father for this remarkable experience."

"You are welcome, Richard," was the soft response.

And with that, the mission truck pulled away from the building we had called home for our entire mission.

Although our flight didn't leave Quito until 11:35 p.m., we planned on arriving at the airport by nine. As it turned out, we had made a wise decision.

At the airport, military police blocked all from entering the airport interior, except those who had their passports and ticket confirmation. As we approached the large glass doors that provided entrance, Cheryle and I suddenly looked up and saw that a small group from the office standing beyond the fence waiting to say good-bye. Jorge and Glenda Mena, Pablo and Fatyma Suarez, and President Hernán Herdoiza and Sister Herdoiza. Cheryle and I were rather shocked, but very pleased to see them there. It reaffirmed that we had, even with the difficulty of the experience, touched the lives of many. Of all the good-byes, I think that I always will remember that of Sister Glenda Mena, Jorge's wife. With great tears flowing down her cheeks, she threw her arms around my neck and sobbing, kissed my cheek while expressing her gratitude to me for all I had done for Jorge, for her, and for their family. Her gratitude was genuine, as were the tears of appreciation. These humble people are without guile. They are honest and loving, and they express their feelings in a manner different from norteamericanos. So, as good-byes were said, again I had the reassurance from the Spirit that the Savior was pleased with the sacrifices we laid upon the altar.

Slowly, Cheryle and I walked to the military guard, produced our papers and passports and were admitted into the airport. Those who had come to send us off stood at the glass windows, each with tears in their eyes and waved as they mouthed their final good-byes.

Once inside the airport, we proceeded to the window where we paid our fifty dollars for the privilege of living and safely leaving Ecuador. With receipt in hand, we were directed to the first security station where our papers again were checked and flight confirmation secured. After this was completed, we were directed to another station where more questions were asked and the same documents reviewed. The young man, who was working this security post, saw our missionary tags, smiled, and in Spanish said with a large grin: "I am also a returned missionary." He then directed us to another station where the luggage was tagged.

Following the tagging of the luggage, we proceeded to the next security station where each piece of luggage was opened and thoroughly hand searched. First the large outer suitcase, then the first inner suitcase, then the next, and so on. When the security guard pulled out the two plastic bags I had which contained the tuberculin syringes used to take my migraine medication, his eyes got as big as saucers. "What are these?" he briskly asked.

"They are used to take prescription medication," I responded. "Here is the prescription and here is my Los Angeles Police Department identification that corresponds to the prescription issued by the City of Los Angeles. They are not drugs." I placed these on the bags and watched as he swore softly under his breath and continued the search. He was disappointed he didn't have an arrest! Everything was searched. Absolutely everything.

Then the laptop and Cheryle's carry-on were searched. About thirty minutes later, we proceeded to baggage check-in where we presented our tickets, passports, etc., and placed the luggage on a scale to be weighed and transferred to the conveyor belt that moved it into the rear loading area. Cheryle and I then were directed upstairs to the waiting area.

When we arrived upstairs, we again were stopped, all paperwork reviewed, the laptop taken out, opened and softly shaken back and forth. Then we were asked to remove all metal from our person, and I was asked to unbuckle my belt so the buckle could be inspected. Following this, we walked through the scanning machine. Once through the machine, we were wanded by a security officer using a hand wand, or metal detector. After this, we were approved to go, and were directed to wait in an empty waiting area. We did so and immediately found two seats in the back which provided us a view of what was happening around us. There we sat watching the events not knowing that we soon would be the center of attention. It was now nearly 2:00 a.m., a late departure.

We hadn't been in the waiting area twenty minutes when a uniformed security officer walked directly up to us and stated, "Will you both please accompany me to the luggage area."

"Of course," I responded.

We were led out through a pair of glass doors, down an escalator that had not been turned on, and out into the rear luggage holding area where the luggage for the flight was spread across a concrete floor. All the passenger luggage except ours sat centered in the middle of the floor. Looking to the right, I saw one of our suitcases set off to the side and a drug-sniffing dog wildly circling the suitcase, just like you see on the news when the dogs sniff out a large cache of dope. Around and around he went. His tailed wagged furiously while he jumped around making tight circles, keeping his nose glued to my suitcase. When we entered the area, we were approached by another uniformed military guard who very politely, asked if I would open the suitcase.

"Of course," I replied.

I glanced at Cheryle. She was pale with an expression of dread across her face, for she knew what was in the case.

With the suitcase opened, the soldier proceeded to hand search the contents as the dog continued to sniff and circle. I assumed the position that a catcher would take in baseball behind home plate and calmly watched. Within a short period of time the military policeman removed a bag of migraine medication which contained codeine. The dog went crazy! Calmly, I removed all the required papers and my police identification. As he looked through the papers and my identification, a smile crossed his face. "Policia?"

"Si, policia jubilado (retired) de la ciudad de Los Ángeles, en Los Estados Unidos." Continuing in Spanish, I said, "There are more medications if you would like to see them."

Smiling he said, "That won't be necessary, thank you."

He closed the suitcase, and I zipped it up. We then were escorted back to our seats upstairs in the waiting area. As we sat down, I noted that we had been joined by two other norteamericanos who were seated in front of us. It was apparent that they were oil rig workers. They were still dressed in the clothes they wore in the jungle, and their language was that which was used not only by oil riggers, but also by the cops and bad guys on the streets of South Central Los Angeles. It was rough, vulgar, crude and very offensive. I sat silently for a few minutes listening to the profanity, which was language I hadn't heard for many years, or if I had, I failed to understand it. Cheryle knew what I was thinking.

Calmly and in a very businesslike manner, I walked over and stood directly in front of where they sat. I was dressed in a dark business suit and had a white shirt and red tie. I politely interrupted their conversation and said, "Gentlemen, your language is highly offensive to my wife. We have two options. You can clean it up while in the presence of a lady, or we can move. It is your decision. What would you like to do?"

With that, their heads snapped around, and with each still seated, they just stared at me. I didn't say another word, just looked into each of their faces. Then one said, "We're sorry. We just got out of the jungle. We'll clean it up."

"Thank you," I said.

As I again seated myself, I thought of the scripture in 2 Kings, Chapter 6, verse 16 that reads: "Fear not: for they that *be* with us *are* more than they that *be* with them."

With that, they lowered their voices to barely above a whisper and cleaned up their language. Cheryle breathed a sigh of relief.

Since the terrorist attacks of September 11, 2001 had just occurred, I turned to her and whispered, "I have just identified the other members of my team should we run into problems during this flight." She just smiled.

Our Lives Spared

When I wrote the concluding episode of our experience in Quito, Ecuador, I thought that the final chapter had been written and the book closed. I was wrong. There was more, but before I finish with the final page in this incredible saga, I must regress to Quito and again explain the physical location of the Employment Resource Center office.

The Servicios de Recursos de Empleo, or employment office, was located directly below the Institute of Religion, Colon. We occupied the space in the right front corner of the basement; an office that I designed and then supervised all facets of construction, including electrical outlets and lighting placement, computer stations and interior design and furniture placement. Although I had never done this type of project, between my tenacity and assertive nature, coupled with the Spirit, it all came together nicely.

To reach our office, you entered from the street, walked by a guard station, then walked down a hundred foot declining driveway. At the bottom of the driveway, below street level, sat the lower level of the Institute Building and our office facility.

Our office was surrounded on two sides by the Area Storage facility, or bodega. The other two walls were the exterior walls of the building. The entire basement area sat at a level approximately fifteen feet below the level of the street, with the Institute of Religion sitting elevated about six feet above street level. The drainage for the basin like area in which the building sat consisted of two drainage ducts, one located on each side of the facility. One drainage duct was located around the corner from the front door of our office. Unfortunately, the drainage pipes were rarely cleaned of debris or serviced, leaving them virtually inoperative, an oversight that ended up proving to be disastrous.

Our departure from Ecuador was October 25, 2001. On Wednesday, December 12, I received an e-mail that described the following:

"Throughout Tuesday and Wednesday, December 11-12, the city of Quito endured the worst rain storm it had experienced in the past twenty years. Wednesday might, December 12, at 7:30 p.m. while Carlos Guerrero and another man sat in the employment office working, a wave of water nearly twelve feet high rolled down the long driveway and exploded through the front door of the employment center immediately filling the office to a height of nearly nine feet. With the impact of the water, all desks, chairs, tables, computers and equipment whether secured or not were violently washed to the rear of the office where the two men were seated. Both men struggled out the door of the Director's office and began to struggle and swim through the carnage. Amazingly, they were able to struggle to the small glass front door which had been blown open by the force of the water and they escaped. Both, although losing their shoes and having their clothing torn, survived.

"The pressure of the water caused the office walls to explode out causing a portion of the ceiling tiles to collapse. In minutes the office was totally destroyed. Everything was lost. All the computers, the telephones, the furniture, the copier and all paperwork, computer disks, reports and files. Nothing remained. Additionally, the water caused a wall leading into the Institute to collapse.

"With the implosion of the walls a torrent of water rushed into the storage area where they stored the televisions, VCR's, all manuals, seminary supplies, Books of Mormon and equipment for five South American countries. Everything in the storage area was also destroyed. Water filled the entire basement to a depth of nearly five feet.

"When the water finally drained, nothing was salvageable. And what of the employment office? There is absolutely nothing physically left that would provide any evidence that an office had once occupied the area. Only debris. It was as if Elder and Sister Whitaker had not even been there."

Written by: Danny Mino

I was informed by Danny that the sewers in Quito were so clogged that they literally stopped working. The water that normally would have flowed through the sewers was unable to do so, consequently building up until a wall of water similar to a tidal wave flowed down the Institute driveway gaining momentum as it moved downhill. The worst area impacted was the area of Colon where the Institute was located. Losses to the church would exceed one million dollars.

Not everyone was as fortunate as Carlos and the other church member who were able to escape. In the apartment facility adjacent to the Institute, three people were trapped in a basement elevator and drowned.

I am grateful that the life of Carlos and the other man were spared. I also am grateful that Cheryle and I were not caught sitting in the office where we normally would have been. However, under the direction of the Spirit, we were sent back to the United States six weeks earlier. After I viewed a video tape of the destruction sent to me by Carlos, it was obvious that Cheryle would have been killed, for her area was the first hit as the water surged into the office and where the majority of equipment piled up as the water surged back out through the front door.

I am grateful for the experience we had in Quito. We made a difference, and fortunately, the difference we made will be judged not by what remains of our once beautiful office, but in the lives that were impacted and changed.

Personally, I felt that the office would not immediately be replaced. For now, what the Lord wanted accomplished in Quito had been accomplished.

My reaction to the news probably was different from what many would suppose. I was neither shocked, nor amazed. My reaction was: "We did what we were sent to do, and the Lord was pleased. And when the leaders and members of the church in Quito decide to support the employment program, and when they figure out that the payment of tithing is not financial but based on faith, then, and only then, will the Lord decide that the time is right for another center."

While the employment center as we knew it was never rebuilt, is was announced in the April 2016 General Conference of the Church of Jesus Christ of Latter –day Saints that a temple would be built in the city of Quito.

Ecuador Quito Mission
Perpetual Education Fund
2007-2009

Time to Serve Again and a Change of Assignment

Five years passed before we felt able to serve another foreign mission assignment. Although for a long time I had known that we were to submit our mission papers, each time I mentioned it to Cheryle, I met with so much resistance that I dropped the topic, and although I did not mention it to her, I daily pled with the Lord to touch her heart and reveal to her what I had been told about future service. Time passed and then one Sunday, the miracle came.

If was a fifth Sunday and a combined meeting of the Priesthood and Relief Society had been scheduled. The Priesthood was assigned the lesson. As the Relief Society room filled, I watched a very intense conversation taking place between the High Priest group leader and Relief Society president. Finally it appeared that a decision was made.

With great calm and dignity, the Relief Society president walked to the front of the room and advised all in attendance that unfortunately, a lesson had not been prepared, so in lieu of a formal lesson, we were going to participate in a meeting directed toward worshiping the Savior through singing Hymns of the Restoration.

Cheryle and I took our seats on the second row, left side, directly behind President Ivan Holland and Sister Holland. The room quickly filled to capacity, and a Relief Society sister

TIME TO SERVE AGAIN AND A CHANGE OF ASSIGNMENT

took her place behind the piano. After the opening prayer, the Relief Society president asked that we each select our favorite hymn. From the rear, a Sister's hand shot up. Since the focus of the lesson was scheduled to be on missionary work, she suggested that maybe it would be applicable for us to sing as the first hymn, *Called to Serve*. The room exploded in comments to the affirmative.

As the opening notes of the introduction were played, Sister Lora Dee Christensen, who had served with her husband, Don, as a mission president before his untimely death, recommended that we all stand while that wonderful missionary anthem was sung. All agreed. The standing for this hymn later was not recommended by Elder Boyd K. Packer, so the ritual was abolished throughout the church, including all missions.

Upon our standing to sing, a flood of Spirit filled the Relief Society Room; so strong in fact, that it seemed to suck the air from the room. When we began to sing, I noticed that Cheryle was trembling, and tears were soon accompanied by quiet sobs. Soon, the sobs became noticeable to all in the room, especially Ivan Holland.

When we began to sing the final verse, President Holland turned to us, and with a large smile, said, "It appears that I will see you two in my office very soon."

Later I asked Cheryle what happened when we stood for the hymns. "It was if the ceiling opened and a shaft of light landed one me," Cheryle said. "What did you feel," I asked? "With the light, I began to feel a tremendous warmth and I knew we were to submit our mission papers." So in a miraculous way, my fervent prayers had been answered.

Within a very few weeks, we had begun the mission paper submission process and were seated in his office.

In a short period of time, the papers were electronically transmitted to the Missionary Department, our assignment was made, and a large white envelope arrived in our mailbox.

Excitedly, we opened the envelope. Our assignment was for the Perpetual Education Fund, Tegucigalpa, Honduras. As I stared at the assignment, I knew something was not right. Now don't get me wrong, it is not my method of operation to question the Brethren and those who make the assignments, but every fiber of my being shouted that this was not for us. Now I needed to determine, why.

First, I called my son-in-law, Greg Gardner who not only is a returned Spanish speaking missionary from Venezuela and married to my eldest daughter, Shannyn, but also is a seasoned businessman who has travelled to Mexico, Central and South America on a number of occasions. Once I had him on the phone, I asked his opinion about the level of safety and security we could plan on having in Honduras with my background and if he believed it was safe for us to go. I further explained that my concern was not for myself, for I was able to anticipate danger and react properly, but for

TIME TO SERVE AGAIN AND A
CHANGE OF ASSIGNMENT

Cheryle's safety and my ability to save us both should the need arise.

"Get the assignment changed," was his immediate response. "The crime and murder statistics are higher than anywhere else in Latin America, the gangs are some of the most violent in the world, and with your background, you might as well paint a target on your back. What else can I help you with?"

"I think you answered my question."

"Really, you probably would not live through the assignment."

"Thanks for the candid input," I said as we said goodbye.

My second call was to the American Embassy in Tegucigalpa and I asked if they had an employee who was also a member of the Church of Jesus Christ of Latter-day Saints. They did, and to my delight, the employee was assigned to the Embassy security section. I could not have asked for better!

Once I had him on the phone, I asked about the crime in the city; the support given to senior missionaries by the mission president, and with my background in law enforcement, would my life and that of Cheryle be in greater danger should my past vocational history be known by the gangs.

Like my son-in-law, the security officer was direct and candid. First he explained that he had former law enforcement background in the United States, so he understood my concerns. When I shared with him Greg's answers, he said, "He is right. Additionally, you will have no support from the mission president. Yes, your lives would be in constant danger, and yes, you should call the Perpetual Education Fund leadership and have the assignment changed."

I thanked him for his candor, and after hanging up the phone, I dialed the number for the church office building in Salt Lake City. Once connected, I asked for Elder Richard E. Cook in the Perpetual Education Fund offices.

When I explained to Elder Cook who I was and my background and concerns, he asked only one question: "Where would you like to serve?"

Immediately, I was prompted by the Spirit to answer, "Why don't you send us back to Quito, Ecuador? We know the country, the people and the leaders."

"But we don't have a PEF office in Quito."

"You send me to Quito and you will have the best office in the church. I will organize all aspects of the assignment to meet the vision of the church, and meet the needs of the people."

TIME TO SERVE AGAIN AND A
CHANGE OF ASSIGNMENT

There was a long silence and then he said, "Consider it done."

I always knew that with his business background as an executive for Ford Motor Company and standing as a General Authority, I was blessed not only to secure his backing, but we both knew that my request to have the assignment changed was directed by the Spirit. That one recommendation and change of assignment would pay dividends when future assignments were considered.

The Journey Begins

We left Provo, Utah on July 23, 2007 after spending eight days in the Mission Training Center. It was going to take nearly two days of travel to arrive in Quito, Ecuador. The journey required that we forgo sleep for forty-eight hours and spend twelve hours in San Francisco.

After arriving in San Francisco from Salt Lake City, we were required to store our luggage, travel across the city by either bus, taxi or on foot, find the Ecuadorian Consulate, get our passports stamped, pay a fee for the privilege of entering their country, travel back to the airport and then sit for twelve hours awaiting our flight to Miami.

Before we left Salt Lake, it casually had been mentioned that inasmuch as missionaries in the past had stored their luggage in a small room at the airport, there just might be such a room for us to put our luggage while we travelled to the Consulate's office, however the location of the room was not shared with us.

After securing our luggage, we were not able to find a cart or luggage handler, so we began the arduous process of pulling one hundred pounds of suit cases, carry-on and computer bags behind us as we began the search for the luggage room. We spent over an hour searching and asking every airport employ we could find, if they knew of such a room. Most only looked at us with a blank stare and told us they had never heard of such a holding facility.

Tired, frustrated and feeling overwhelmed, I glanced at my watch. Our time was running out, and I was getting concerned. Salt Lake had given us an appointment time to be at the Consulates office, and advised us that if we were late, they would not sign our passports but require we wait until the next day.

Slowly, and feeling fatigued, we hauled our luggage down to the bottom of an escalator near the rear of the airport and stopped. I looked over at Cheryle and noted that her two suitcases weighed nearly as much as she did. When she added a large carry-on bag and her purse, she was transporting her own weight throughout the airport, and would do so on more than one occasion during our five years in South America.

Standing alone in the concourse, I took Cheryle by the hands and began to plead with the Lord to send someone to our rescue. No sooner had I finished my prayer than a set of large doors opened to our left, and a man walked out. Then I heard a small voice whisper, "Richard, ask him."

"Excuse me, sir," I asked the man as he stepped into the concourse wearing credentials that identified him as an airport employee.

"Would you possibly know where we can store our luggage while we travel to the Ecuadorian Consulate?"

He looked at our missionary tags, smiled and said, "Not only do I know where it is, if you follow me, I'll take you right to it!" Angels come in many forms.

After leaving our luggage, we found a cab driver who knew exactly where the office was located and drove us to the front door.

Walking into the office, we checked in with the receptionist who told us to have a seat and the Consulate would be right with us. We sat in those chairs for two hours, virtually ignored, while the Consulate and a young woman continued their conversation. Patience and dealing with incompetence have never been my strong suits, so it was easy for me to anger; but then I realized this experience was designed to strengthen my weaknesses.

After over two hours of waiting, an employee, not the Consulate, invited us to have a seat in her office. We did so, handed her our passports and other documents which she glanced at, then signed and stamped. It was over in less than three minutes.

Our travel back to the airport was without incident. We retrieved our suitcases, checked ourselves and our luggage in at the airline counter, received our tickets and were told by a smiling employee that we now had a twelve hour wait before our flight departed for Miami. While standing in line to check our luggage, we met a black family who lived in California, but who originally were from Haiti. The family consisted of the mother, father, and three of the best-behaved teenagers I had ever met. We spoke briefly and they saw our missionary tags. We again met up with them while we all waited for the same plane that would take us to Miami. While we sat, we had an opportunity to share with them the fact that we were on our way to Quito, Ecuador to help in a program designed to assist young adults secure education and better their economic standing.

In our conversation, it became apparent that they were devoutly religious. Some time passed when the mother approached and asked if she could buy us something to eat. Thanking them for their kindness, we declined since we had just eaten. About fifteen minutes later, the family again approached and said that they were very grateful that people such as us would give their time to help others. They handed us a $50.00 bill and asked that it be donated toward our mission. Our hearts were touched as hugs were exchanged and eyes became wet.

The flight across country was very uncomfortable, but we finally landed in Miami. We had only one hour to make the International connection, so we knew we had to hurry. The crew told us what gate to go to in order to make our connection. We were advised that our luggage automatically would be transferred to our departing aircraft, so all we needed to do in the short time allotted was find our boarding gate and wait until called to board. *Easy,* I thought. *How hard could that be?* As we deplaned, we noted on a map that our departing flight was at the farthest end of the airport, and we had less than forty-five minutes.

We literally ran through the airport to our next destination. As we approached the boarding area, I became concerned; the area was empty. The counter was closed, and we stood alone in the area. We had not slept in two days, and I don't do well without sleep, so my frame of mind was not real good. I was fortunate to find a telephone and after explaining to the operator our dilemma, we were provided the correct information.

Breaking into a slow jog, we crisscrossed the airport doing our best not to trample anyone while we dodged this person and that. We looked more like two ballroom dancers dressed in formal clothing than missionaries attempting to not miss a critical flight.

Fortunately, prayers were answered, and we were able to locate the correct boarding area. As we sat awaiting the plane, we saw a young lady whom we had met on our first assignment to Ecuador. She was a member of the ward we attended in Quito and had been living out of the country with her husband. Our conversation with her helped pass the time before our flight departed. Three hours later we landed to a wonderful reception in Quito.

The Work Begins

Our first five days in Quito were spent living out of a suitcase in the Hilton, Colon hotel. I learned after our first assignment that it was wise to be in a foreign country and then find a place to live, rather than allow a senior missionary or office Elder to make that decision for you. Our finances, needs and wants have proven to be very different than most, so since I am paying the bills, I will decide on where the money goes. It's that simple.

After five days, I found an apartment in the same building where we lived during our last mission to Ecuador in 2000-2001. While we were on the eighteenth floor our first assignment, this apartment was on the sixteenth floor.

I also was able to get us an office in the church office building. I found it fascinating that my reputation had preceded us. Everyone knew that "Elder Whitaker" was back. I was pleased, if not surprised, by the positive welcome this tough norteamericano received. I guess the black spot on my dossier in Salt Lake had faded somewhat when the "prophecy" failed to come to pass. It was a declaration given by that employee in the Employment Resource Center in Salt Lake who declared that I would ruin the Employment Program in South America

Saturday afternoon, Cheryle and I took a five mile walk around Quito. When we returned from our walk, I sat on the

16th floor in our apartment to write, but it was dreadfully cold, made worse by the fact that the caulking around our large windows disappeared many years ago, thus allowing the wind to whistle through unabated. They said it was summer, but at 10,000 feet in the Andes, summer as we know it, is only a thought.

We had two days of training that basically duplicated the two days in Salt Lake. So after a day, I told the supervisor from Bogota who was lecturing, that he should reevaluate his methodology when training norteamericanos. He asked for some input, and I recommended that he use more hands on computer training and less lecture. He immediately made the change, and off we went. For an assignment, we were given the five stakes in Quito. However, this changed as our Spanish returned.

From the standpoint of exercise, I walked an average of between two to five miles each day as I traversed the city for our assignment. Ninety percent of the time I was alone; Cheryle stayed in the office to complete her assignments. I loved the solitude even though surrounded by people.

For the most part, everything that I requested was granted. The love and adoration for us, as demonstrated by both members and nonmembers, was incredible. One Sunday, as we sat in a church meeting, a man approached and said, "Elder Whitaker, you might not remember me, but you were instrumental in me getting a job six years ago after I took your employment training. I now own a transportation business and am doing very well." With tears in his eyes, he then stepped forward and gave me a big hug. It isn't often we were able to see the fruits of our labors, but since our return to Ecuador, the impact we had during our past mission was apparent. It always pays to follow the promptings of the Spirit, no matter what others might think or say. And so the old adage of, "Dogs bark, but the caravan moves on," continues to be true.

We were surprised at how much the prices in Quito had skyrocketed since our last mission. Most items were between two to three times more expensive. For example: a pair of Levis that once cost $23.00, now cost $76.00-$83.00. I'm glad I brought two pair. Other goods and services also were up. Our supposed furnished apartment was furnished with only the very basics. We ended up purchasing kitchen items, bedding, some furniture, a telephone, and blankets to wrap up in while we sat in the living room with the icy wind whistling through the windows. All bedding was for two single beds.

Food prices also had increased, as did the condo fees, electric and telephone.

It was at this time that a major earthquake hit on a Sunday night. It was about four hundred miles off the coast just above Ecuador and Columbia.

Sitting on the 16th floor, the place rocked, so much so, that I started to become sick to my stomach. First time ever. It's interesting the things that pass through your mind. *Well, here we are. Sixteen floors up, over one hundred and sixty feet above the street, swaying like two stupid birds in a cage in a building built nearly thirty years ago in a third-world developing country. Nowhere to run to, nowhere to hide. So…if the place starts to crumble, I decided I'd just enjoy the ride down and wait until the dust cleared. Really, there were not many options.*

Getting into an elevator would be stupid, and trying to make it down the sixteen floors using the concrete stairwell would be a waste of energy. So, I calmly sat, just staring at Cheryle. After a very quick and fervent prayer, I decided to watch the two chandeliers as they swayed back and forth, their glass bobbles stuck one side of the ceiling, then changed direction and struck the other. On and on it went, one minute, then two, then three, finally ending after nearly four minutes. The old building just swayed back and forth, like a drunken sailor caught on deck in a violent storm. Then it began to subside. As the swaying lessened, I could hear the doors to the neighbors apartments open, and voices began to vibrate up and down the hall. I stepped out into the hallway and watched as our older neighbors from directly across the hall sheepishly opened their door and walked out. They were a formal couple who maintained an elegant apartment, and it was apparent that they and their friends, who always visited on Sunday evenings, were terrified. After asking if they were all right, and receiving their assurance that they would be fine, I began to speak with other neighbors. With the hallway filled, the chatter was animated, and you can understand why. Being reassured that my neighbors were well, I began to find the situation amusing. Here we were, thousands of miles from home, caught in an earthquake, in an old building, with a hallway of older Ecuadorian neighbors who spoke nothing but Spanish, and when excited, it was a Spanish I never before had heard! That began an interesting week.

The work in the office continued to be challenging. To build something, whether an organization or a physical office from nothing, is always a challenge. I was fortunate to have a track record in Ecuador, having planned, organized, built and then supervised the Employment Center during 2000-2001.

A mission is difficult! Since there were no heaters in the apartments, our apartment always was cold. I never found the ideal way to tape all the windows sufficiently; the water from the taps would sputter, cough and then run chocolate brown; there were earthquakes; the sidewalks all were buckled and cracked, which made them hard to traverse; the buses coughed and sputtered thick black smoke that hung heavily in the air until a strong breeze blew it away; sirens cut through the city every ten minutes day and night, and a car alarm sounded every five minutes, whether day or night, which sent the dogs howling; the altitude was more difficult this time; the car was king and the pedestrians were treated like a bull would treat a matador. When I would complain about my shortness of breath, Cheryle would say, "Elder, you are six years older."

Was it worth it, one might ask? Again, the answer was yes.

To have people stop you on the street, remember you from six years past when they sat in the employment course we directed, and with tears flowing down their cheeks, thank you for your time and toughness made it all worthwhile. To have men visit your office, hug you in a tight bear hug and with eyes brimming, thank you for returning to their country to provide service made it worth the sacrifices and discomforts. Just knowing you made a difference was the pay off.

Granted, my reputation of being a tough administrator continued through the assignment, but it was wonderful to know that I had learned to balance the toughness on one hand, with love on the other; the Spirit in one hand, and the sword in the other. And when people saw the results, not only in their lives, but also in the lives of others, they were grateful. Seeing lives change made the difficulties and sacrifice worth the effort.

A Trip to Otavalo

Friday night, our son-in-law, Greg Gardner, the husband of our oldest daughter Shannyn, flew into Quito. He is an executive for a major international company, and when presented the opportunity to conduct some business in Quito, he chose to do so. Friday night, he took us to an excellent restaurant in the Marriott Hotel. Everything was five stars, including the Spanish spoken and service afforded. It was the first time, while in South America, that I chose to eat some beef, and it was excellent.

As with our first assignment to Ecuador, we were blessed on this assignment again to have Patricio Alvarez as a member of our staff. Prior to the weekend, I paid to have Patricio renew his driver's license so he could drive Greg, Cheryle and me to the world famous outdoor, indigenous market in Otavalo. We rented a car and off we went on the hour and a half drive north on winding roads through the Andes. All I can say is that I've driven with taxi drivers in Guayaquil and Tijuana who didn't put as much fear in my heart as Patricio!

The road was a single lane each way with all curves having a thick double yellow line painted down the middle, but one should never worry since in Ecuador, the lines were meaningless, as was a speed limit.

On one occasion, Patricio decided to pass a bus on a hill with a curve at the top. Suddenly, he made his move, pushing the pedal to the metal. The small four cylinder engine failed to respond, yet he began to make his move anyway. When I looked to my right, another car was inches from my window. I literally could have reached out and opened the driver's door. When Cheryle screamed, I looked at the other driver and only saw the whites of a pair of eyes that seemed the size of silver dollars. She swerved to one side and Patricio swerved into oncoming traffic! Then we were alongside the bus with still nowhere to go! Our four cylinder engine coughed, the traffic in the oncoming lanes swerved, and we slipped in front of the bus with inches to spare. The blast of their horn sounded! Ten seconds later, the female driver of the car we nearly broadsided, sped past, and in her own way, flipped us off! And that was only the beginning. On the way home, he missed a couple of turn-offs because of the rain and the slickness of the Andean mountain roads!

When we arrived at Otavalo, we walked and talked to many of the vendors who, when they saw Cheryle's missionary tag, told us they also were members of the church. When Patricio introduced me as the Director of the Perpetual Fund office in Quito, their eyes lit up, and they began to express their gratitude for our service as they shared their success stories related to the program. It was quite an experience.

Walking down one crowded street, it suddenly began to rain. Not the drizzle one might assume, but an Andean mountain downpour, and my jacket was back in the car.

What to do? It was time to buy a serape, or as they are called here, a poncho. I found a nice, gray, alpaca poncho, paid for it and threw it on. Boy, did it work well, but my hair was getting wet. I needed a hat, so I found a black hat the size of an old cowboy hat, and popped it over the hair. Now I was set. Cheryle took one look at me and commented, "You look like a tourist." She knows how I hate to look like a tourist, but I was warm and dry. The serape was a good purchase since later I wore it in the apartment because it was much warmer than any of the blankets we had.

Now, warm and dry, off I went, with Cheryle, Greg and Patricio in the lead. Suddenly, I saw a vendor selling food from a basket. He was selling, small, dark, oblong looking things. I asked Patricio what they were, and not understanding the answer, I took one from his hand and popped it into my mouth, chewing vigorously. It was very crunchy and a bit slimy. Suddenly, Patricio broke into raucous laughter. "Elder," he cried out. "That was a small street snail, and you weren't supposed to eat the shell. You were supposed to suck out the snail, douse it with lime and eat it!" Another first to go with my other experience in Quito when I was served rat.

Well, after a white knuckle drive home, we dropped Greg off at the hotel and Cheryle and I opted to walk back to our apartment while Patricio returned the car. Although it was raining quite hard, we needed the time to try and relax, and walking in the Andean rain always filled that need.

A Special Family

One Monday, we were invited to the home of Wendell Shumway for Family Home Evening. Their home was in Cumbaya, a relatively safe area just west of Quito that had large homes, tall fences with glass and barbed wire adorning the top and security guards.

At 5:15, Brother Shumway pulled up in front of our apartment building and we were off, but instead of taking us the same way Hermano Cacuango had done in the past, today we traveled the back streets over the mountains and through some of the very old and quaint areas of Quito. It was incredible.

The streets were made of brick and cobble stones, each laid by hand. Houses lined the narrow streets that looked like the pictures you see representing old Spain. The road, often only wide enough for a single car, wound in and out of the mountains. Cars coming up had the right of way. Small mom and pop stores, often built right into the front of their small houses, were found everywhere. Houses, or sometimes shacks, were built of every material imaginable; brick, cinder block, wood, and tin. At the bottom of one road, was a magnificent old Catholic church. It was a beautiful structure and still operational.

As we traveled, I was fascinated by the majestic mountains that surrounded us. I looked across a cavernous ravine and saw a mountain that slid during the torrential rains of El Nino. Whole sides of many mountains broke loose and left homes and some apartment buildings hanging dangerously over the edge of steep cliffs. Some homes and their occupants were swept away into the rushing river below. Bridges were weakened, some collapsed, and those that remained were damaged and later destroyed. Yet the beauty of the valleys in which we traveled was magnificent. Large trees sat on the mountainsides and made up forested areas that reminded me that I was truly in the northern most outposts of the Inca.

The road through the town ran at a step angle toward the valley bottom. Where the Catholic church sat, two roads intersected in the shape of an L. At the intersection was a man who, being innovative, decided that he was going to stand at this point and direct traffic. Without him, many accidents would have occurred. Drivers were so grateful for his services, that some handed him coins through an open window.

Once we made the sharp left turn, we continued until we came to the bottom of this stretch of road. Then we had to negotiate another hard ninety degree turn. Hermano Shumway told Cheryle and me that we would get back to this area, and the next time we would have our camera. The road and houses truly represented old Quito, not only in architecture, but also the people.

While the ride at times was hair-raising and always rough and bumpy, Hermano Shumway was an excellent driver and had become quite accustomed to Ecuador and its streets. As I previously wrote, he served his mission in Ecuador where Larry Burns was his Zone Leader. So, all the way home, Hermano Shumway praised Larry for his leadership all those years ago in the mission field of Ecuador.

Wendell Shumway was employed with a major oil company and worked in the accounting department. Their home was a tri-level that sat on a large piece of ground. The house overlooked the valley of Cumbaya and faced the Andes. The entire housing development was walled in and a twenty-four hour armed guard was stationed at the entrance gate. While this façade gave the appearance of being secure, the appearance was deceiving in that burglaries of the expensive homes occurred on a regular basis.

Cheryle and I were very impressed with the Shumway family. Here was a young mother and four children, all boys under ten, the baby just having turned two. Sister Shumway did not speak Spanish, nor did the children. Yet, there wasn't any hesitation to pack up everything they could and go to South America. It took two months for their furniture and personal belongings to catch up with them. During the wait, the family slept on the floor in sleeping bags, and for food, they found what fast food restaurants they could trust. You can imagine the difficulties this good sister had with a young family and a baby.

While dinner was being prepared, the four Shumway boys came into the family room where I was playing the piano. Standing next to the piano, I taught them the background to *Barbara Ann, In the Still of the Night* and *Charlie on the MTA.* They loved it. I renamed them, not the Righteous Brothers, but the Rickety Brothers. We had a good time, and it was obvious they missed their grandparents, so for a few hours, Cheryle and I became temporary replacements.

The dinner was excellent. Following dinner, we had Family Home Evening. The boys led the music, prayed and participated as Hermano Shumway presented a lesson on the temple. We then had desert and Hermano Shumway drove us home. All in all, it was a wonderful evening. A late night, but wonderful.

The Parking Lot Bandit

I previously shared a story about two special people we met during our first assignment to Quito, and upon our return five years later, they were still dutifully working at the same apartment building doing the same jobs. The woman was named Maria, and the older gentleman, Juan. Each went through their daily lives and worked virtually unnoticed by most who passed their way. It was as if they did not exist to those who scurried by in their harried world. Juan was an older gentleman who made a living on the tips he received from parking cars in the apartment parking lot, and Maria was a diminutive woman who diligently swept the floors throughout the street level of our apartment complex.

Juan had to travel by bus nearly two hours each morning before he could take his place in the apartment parking lot to begin the directing of traffic for the early morning grocery store shoppers. Dressed in old gray work pants with stains brought on through years of use and a gray long sleeved shirt with a worn collar, his uniform was topped off with an old tattered gray military hat. In his right hand he carried a bright red handkerchief which he used to catch the attention of the drivers entering the lot. Once he had their attention, he would scurry through the parking lot and while standing in front of an open parking space, direct the incoming car into position. If a car was leaving, he again would scurry to the space, and after walking behind the exiting car, would guarantee them safe passage. Rarely did someone fail to roll down their window and drop a few coins in his weathered and wrinkled hands.

He guarded his lot and his clientele with a passion that was commendable. This was his job and his work. This was his parking lot. One day, as Cheryle and I returned to the apartment building in the late afternoon, I saw that the parking lot was very busy with cars coming and going at a steady pace, but there was something wrong. As we walked closer, I saw that while Juan worked his trade, a usurper had entered the scene. This man was younger than Juan, and it soon became apparent that he was intent on driving this wonderful elderly gentleman into the street and oblivion. Of course, I would not let this happen, so after watching for about twenty minutes, I decided that if this bandit returned the next day, Elder Whitaker would quietly enter the scene.

The following day as we walked back to our apartment during evening rush hour, there he was, the parking lot bandit. In his right hand he too had a red cloth, and because of his age, he was able to out run Juan and guarantee that the tips were his. The clientele paid no attention to the drama that was unfolding, but I did.

I watched the scene for ten minutes, and then watched as Juan walked from the lot toward the bus stop. His red handkerchief was in his right rear pocket, and his hat was at an awkward angle on his bowed head which matched his slumping shoulders. Slowly placing one foot in front of the other, he wearily shuffled on his way. To me, he represented a very discouraged soul whom I am confident believed that he had just lost his livelihood. At the height of his money making day, in these twilight years of his life, he had been driven from the work he loved; but that was not to be, for I had a plan.

I learned long ago that at times, it is justified to use one's title, position and basic clout to rectify a wrong. This was such a case. With dogged determination, and Cheryle at my side, I walked into the apartment building and called a couple of the security guards over. I was fortunate that not only did they know me well from our first mission seven years previously, but also I always had treated them well, remembering them at Christmas with something special and making sure that I spoke to them often. They also knew of my law enforcement background, which literally made me a hero in their eyes. Basically, I held all the right cards.

"I need a favor, my friends," I said.

"Anything, jefe," they both responded.

"There is a man in the parking lot who I don't believe has the permission of the apartment management to park cars. The old man has permission. I would recommend that you advise the new guy that he is trespassing, and if he fails to leave or shows up again, you will call the police."

Both smiled.

"We will take care of it immediately."

With that, Cheryle and I entered the elevator and proceeded to the sixteenth floor.

The next day, when I checked the parking lot upon our arrival home, things were back to normal and Juan, with a smile on his face, approached me and said, "Thank you, jefe, for your help. This is the only way I can earn enough money to live, and when the other man arrived, I didn't know what to do."

"I am happy it all worked out," I said.

Over the years, I have hated to see someone being taken advantage of or bullied. The rights of the little guy matter.

The only two fights I had in high school were because someone bullied my younger brother. Each ended quickly and decisively. The first fight only took a quick left hook and then a brutal right cross to send the bully to the ground. When his eyes opened, he refused to get back up.

The other was a basic street fight. The bully was from New York and decided that my brother was fair game, and I would be a pushover in a fight. With head down and arms flaying like a buzz saw, he charged. I stepped back and with a precision drop kick to the face, sent him flying backwards. When he was able to get up, he ran out of the gym. Neither kid ever bothered my younger brother again.

Serving on a Fractured Ankle

We had about ten months into the Quito Perpetual Education Fund assignment when I rolled my left ankle on a rough cobblestone street and suffered a painful ankle injury. I had been a long distance runner in my younger years and had been injured often playing football, so I thought that the injury was just a high ankle sprain and that with time, the pain would stop. I was wrong. The pain only increased, but knowing that we had an assignment to finish, I walked on the ankle for seven months, limping along and even ran on it when I chased a robbery suspect through the park. But that is another story.

At the end of the seventh month, when the pain became unbearable and my ability to walk was severely hampered, I decided that it was time to visit a doctor. That was quite an experience. His office was located in the complex housing the Hospital Metropolitano which was the largest hospital in Quito. Since most doctors in Quito did not take in-office appointments until after 3:30 p.m., my appointment was scheduled for 4:00.

We arrived at the hospital after a hair-raising taxi ride in a pirated or unregistered taxi cab that wound through the heavy, late afternoon traffic congestion of Central Quito. I guess my look, the sunglasses, our Spanish and my frown intimidated the driver, because he didn't even try to gouge us. Considering the pain I was in, he made a wise decision.

The next challenge was finding the doctor's office in a building complex that reminded me of a newer version of the projects in Watts. Fortunately, I had a small map drawn by Sister Ward, the mission nurse who gave us a general idea where we were going.

Like soldiers picking their way through a minefield, we followed the map and eventually found the doctor's office. Sister Ward said that he understood some English. He did, but we soon realized that our time in his office and at the hospital would be another test of our Spanish language skills. His English was far below our Spanish language skills.

After a brief consultation, we were sent to get x-rays of my left ankle. The tone of the doctor's voice and general demeanor did not elicit a high level of optimism on my part.

He said that in his opinion, I had broken a bone, and since I had walked on the ankle for seven months, there now were problems with the tendons. *Wonderful news,* I thought. Cheryle just looked at me with the look of, "I told you so!"

We left his office, found the x-ray lab, and checked in with the secretary who told us to take a seat because they took all emergencies first, and then walk-in patients. About ten minutes passed when I was called to the counter to register. Again, I was told to have a seat. Being the overly obedient individual that I am, I did as instructed. While I read a book I had brought just for that purpose, Cheryle read a Spanish magazine. About forty-five minutes passed and then my name was called. Since they don't use the letter "W" in Spanish, one listened very carefully if you were a Whitaker.

Time passed. When their names were called, people stood and disappeared through two large white swinging doors. I noted that once beyond the doors, they never reappeared. *Interesting,* I thought. Finally, my name was called. On the other side of those large, white swinging doors, I was met by a technician dressed in a white lab coat. He escorted me, not only to the x-ray lab waiting area, but also back in time.

When I entered the room, my first thought was, *This reminds me of Dr. Frankenstein's laboratory.* The setting literally was like the 1950's where, as a young boy, I had been hospitalized to have my tonsils removed. There was only a single table, stark white walls, the door I entered, and another door on a side wall. Patiently, I sat on the examination table and waited for about thirty minutes until a technician finally arrived and escorted me to an inner chamber where he x-rayed my ankle. The equipment was old, and the surroundings were bleak. As I sat on the examination table waiting for someone to appear, all was quiet; no talking, no elevator music, nothing just the thump, thump, thump of my heart, and the longer I sat, the louder it became. I had now left Mary Shelley's *Frankenstein* scenario and entered Poe's *Pit and the Pendulum.*

After three x-rays of the ankle, the technician walked out. I replaced my sock and shoe, and then stood in the empty room awaiting further light and knowledge. Nothing. *Maybe I am to return to the lobby.* The thought sent me walking back out of the x-ray room doors to the door we had entered. The doors were secured and only could be opened by using a card key. *What the heck?* I pulled out my wallet and ran a couple of plastic cards through the reader. The door didn't budge. *This can't be that sophisticated!* I thought. Next I ran my plastic entry card from our office through the reader. Still nothing.

While I was shaking the doors and trying to get the reader to accept one of my cards, a patient stepped forward from the waiting room on the other side of the door and began tugging in an effort to help. He pulled one way and I the other, but the lock was smarter than the two of us combined.

There I was, trapped. My day wasn't going well, and at this rate, I was becoming impatient for the doctor to look at the x-rays and give me his final opinion. Slowly, I walked back to the x-ray room, slid onto the table, looking like an idiot in a rubber room at a mental institution. There I sat with a foolish grin on my face. About ten minutes passed before the doors opened to the hallway. There stood the technician. "Sorry," he said, "I forgot you were in here, and I didn't open the doors to the waiting room. I cannot let you out this door, but if you will go to the door on the other side of the room, I will open that."

Suddenly, a side door opened. Startled back into the present, another technician asked me to follow him. *Gladly,* I thought.

Silently and just happy to be released from my detention cell, I walked to the other door and made my way directly into the main concourse of the hospital. Cheryle was there to my left, sitting and reading. With the experience behind me, we left the hospital, walked a distance, found a Taxi and returned home.

My follow-up appointment with the orthopedic surgeon was scheduled for the following week. We travelled to the same hospital, and after about fifteen minutes, we were able to find the correct pedestrian bridge to cross from one side of the complex to another. This time we easily found the doctor's office. When I handed the doctor the x-rays, he threw them up on the lighted screen, stood for a few minutes, mumbled a few words, shook his head and then took a seat behind his large wooden desk.

"Mr. Whitaker, the fibula is broken. You broke it straight across, leaving the upper bone to rub on the lower portion each time you took a step. Because of the friction, new bone could not grow. The bone is like mush. You need surgery."

"No wonder it hurt so bad for the past seven months," I mumbled.

While I thought that this was just part of my tough guy persona, Cheryle made it clear that in her opinion it was plain stupidity. She was right.

With that information and the knowledge that I had walked on the break for seven months, Cheryle and I decided that our assignment was finished, and we would return to the United States for surgery. One week after our return, through the efforts of Don McClelland, I was in the operating room where our bishop, Rob Tait, a wonderful orthopedic surgeon performed the surgery. He had to break what the bone had attempted to mend, and he then placed a plate and attached it with five screws to the bone.

Since then, I seriously have rethought the tough guy image, and for the most part, I've put him to rest.

Are You A Whitaker?

About four blocks from the church office building at the corner of Amazonas and Patria is the Hilton Colon Quito Hotel. It is a nice facility in an area that is somewhat dangerous at night. This meant ignoring the prostitutes on the corners, and making it to the safe zone of the hotel.

Approaching the front, visitors were met by a doorman dressed in a dark suit, tails and a large black top hat. With the appropriate beard, he would resemble Abraham Lincoln.

Large revolving glass doors provided an entrance into a very modern lobby with an upscale restaurant and buffet located to the right. The restaurant provided five star service and food, and was such a treat that we made it a point of dining there at least once a week.

The rooms were clean and reasonably priced, especially when one was afforded the church rate. It was here that Cheryle and I stayed for ten days at the beginning of our assignment while we searched for a permanent apartment.

It was a beautiful March afternoon when we, accompanied by another couple, decided to walk to the hotel and have lunch.

Amazonas was crowded with locals and an influx of tourists, mostly from Europe, since the US government had published warnings about government unrest in Ecuador. As far as I was concerned, the warnings were unwarranted.

Entering the restaurant, we were met by a cordial host and seated in a quiet section that would allow for conversation.

Cheryle and I took seats that faced the interior of the facility which allowed us to watch while the restaurant filled. Before sitting down, I removed my suit jacket that had my missionary tag attached to the left pocket.

We had just begun our meal when I noticed that a man across the dining area was staring at us. He would stare, turn and comment to a member of his party, and turn back and stare some more. While it did not bother me, it was so apparent that Cheryle commented that he was making her nervous. After twenty minutes, the gentleman left his seat and approached our table.

"Excuse me," he said in English, "I hate to bother you sir, but can I ask you a question?"

"Of course," I answered.

"Are you a Whitaker?"

Here we were thirty-five hundred miles from home, in a foreign country and in a different hemisphere, and someone wanted to know if I was a Whitaker. I could not believe it!

"Yes, I am."

"I knew it," he said, "I knew you had to be. It was the silver hair!"

"You've got to be kidding," Cheryle said laughing.

"No, I knew it right away."

"Where are you from? I asked.

"Heber, Utah. If you are related to Tom and Doug Whitaker, I was their high school football coach."

"They are my cousins," I said. "What a small world!

A Belligerent Cop
Fails the Attitude Test

While I served as the Director of Perpetual Education in Quito, Ecuador, I became aware of the fact that a Roberto Gomez, (not his actual name) was a member of the church who had returned dishonorably from his mission and was behind in this PEF monthly payments. Additionally, he was employed as a police officer for the Policia Metropolitiano and was considered by his stake president to be an apostate. After being loaned money from the Perpetual Education Fund program and after making only one payment, Gomez decided to stop paying on his loan. Since the funds used for the Perpetual Education Fund were considered to be sacred, his refusal to abide by the contract he made with the church and the Lord was of grave concern.

A review of his situation and discussion with priesthood leaders indicated that Roberto had avoided all church contact for about four years until the previous Wednesday when Patricio Alvarez and I tracked him down on the streets of Quito.

The method of us locating Roberto was interesting. First, I sent Patricio Alvarez to interview Roberto's last known stake president. He did so and was supplied some pertinent information. The stake president advised us that Gomez was in fact a police officer for the city and was last known to be working the area around our office. Armed with that information, Patricio and I set out to walk the streets in hope of either finding Roberto or locating some police officers who knew him.

We had not been searching long when we noticed a group of four cops standing on a street corner talking. As we approached the group, I removed one of my Los Angeles Police Department business cards. The card had my badge, identified me by name and showed that I was a retired detective. Turning to Patricio I said, "Let's see if this works! I want you to introduce us and then tell them that I am a retired detective from Los Angeles and an administrator for The Church of Jesus Christ of Latter-day Saints and we are looking for Roberto Gomez." Patricio complied, and when the four police officers turned to me, I presented them my card, shook all their hands, thanked them for their service to the community and told them I would appreciate it if they told Roberto that I would like to speak to him in my office, which was only three blocks away. It was apparent that I had made four friends, and they not only agreed to find Roberto, but also guaranteed that he would came see me.

About two hours passed when my telephone rang, and the receptionist downstairs advised me that I had a visitor named Roberto Gomez waiting in the lobby.

"Please send him up."

Roberto entered my office dressed in his uniform, armed to the teeth and displaying a surly attitude.

"Please have a seat," I said.

He hesitated.

"I have something I would like to discuss with you."

Still no movement.

Then Patricio spoke to him and Roberto grudgingly sat down in the chair on the other side of my desk.

As I looked into his eyes and studied his countenance, I realized that it had been some time since I sat in front of anyone who had a countenance as dark as his. When I began to speak, he interrupted and assumed the role of the bad cop in the bad cop, good cop interrogation process. He was angry, belligerent and threatening. Unknowingly, he challenged the wrong person.

I began in a nice, quiet, Christ-like manner. I spoke softly and only asked pertinent questions. When he shared that a year ago he had lost both his parents, I truly felt his anguish and expressed my sorrow at his loss. He did not respond, but continued to sit, arms folded, leaned back and glared at me with deep animosity.

It was apparent that his only thought was to intimidate the silver haired old guy. That was his undoing.

Leaning forward in my chair, I looked him directly in the eyes and spoke. My voice was still soft, my demeanor

A BELLIGERENT COP
FAILS THE ATTITUDE TEST

controlled. While this situation might have been new to Roberto, it was not my first, nor would it be my last.

I told him that he owed the Lord over $540 dollars in PEF payments. I explained to him that he could make minimal payments, for the money was not as important as his keeping the covenant he had made with the Lord. I explained to him that we would do all we could to be of assistance.

He continued to glare, and his expression became more hateful.

Then in an aggressive voice, continuing his attempt to intimidate me, he shouted, "I don't need your help, and I don't plan on paying you or anybody else any money!"

Patricio, who had acted as translator throughout the conversation jumped back, a look of fear crossing his face. It was obvious that he was very afraid of the police in Quito.

It was now my turn.

I leaned closer to him, and in a tone of voice that cut him to the core, I explained that he had the choice either to work with us and begin making the minimal payments, or I would write a very detailed letter to his commandant explaining the nature of the problem, his attitude and the fact that it was my opinion, as a retired detective administrator from the Los Angeles Police Department, and administrator for the Church of Jesus Christ of Latter-day Saints, that the Quito

Metropolitano Police Department had hired a liar, a thief and one who robbed God.

He went nuts. He jumped from his chair and with his hand resting near his weapon, screamed, "Nobody threatens me," and threw twenty dollars on my desk.

I stood, walked around the desk and stepped directly in front of him. If someone understood the role and demeanor of a US Marine Drill sergeant, they would know how close to this man I stepped.

My voice had changed. No longer was it the soft, smooth voice of one who had been misjudged as being weak, but the voice of one who, when he walked into a room filled with strangers, bad guys and the wicked, commanded attention.

Leaning closer to him, I said, "It's not a threat my friend, it's a promise. I don't like your attitude, your demeanor, and throwing hateful looks in my direction will serve no purpose."

I then threw my police identification on the table. He was startled.

My directness and hardness shocked him. It was obvious that he had never sat before an LDS administrator this direct and forthright who also carried a badge.

A BELLIGERENT COP FAILS THE ATTITUDE TEST

He walked toward the door, but hesitated when Patricio told him he needed his banking coupons to pay the debt.

"I'll pay the entire $540 dollars," he screamed. His words spewed forth through clenched teeth. I stepped forward; my voice now had a very street cop like tone.

"You'll pay the debt by the end of this week, or I'll have your job! Again, no threat, just a promise!"

He backed off, turned and stormed out the door.

He made the mistake when entering my office of telling me he had been on the force only six months. With that, I knew I had a great deal of leverage.

The next day, Patricio delivered the payment coupons to his commandant and I received a telephone call from one of his police partners. Both Patricio and I explained that we first offered the man the option of paying the loan off at $8.00 a month, but when he failed the attitude test, I demanded full payment. I told his partner that he acted as though he thought he was going to intimidate or scare me.

The partner knew that this man had chosen the wrong person to confront. The entire experience was not any different than the many interviews I had in the mission presidency. For some reason, there are those people who think that because you are in a mission presidency, or the director of a church program, you don't have a spine and won't brace them and push them to the wall. Never do they have any idea that they are dealing with an experienced, ghetto street cop who has seen it all.

The next day, Roberto Gomez paid off the loan.

Confronted by a Deranged Woman

The distance between our apartment building and the church office building was about three miles. When it wasn't raining, and often when it was, we walked the distance and took in all the sights and sounds of the remarkable city of Quito.

On this particular day, as Cheryle and I walked from our apartment building and up a side street, we were met by a distraught and disheveled old woman who was walking up and down the street screaming like a banshee. As we approached, she blocked our path and continued to rant and rave. Upon closer examination, I noted that her hair had not seen a comb or brush in months; her clothing was dirty and mismatched, and when I looked into her eyes, my first thought was, *the lights were on but nobody was home.*

Realizing that the situation could turn ugly at any time, I gently pushed Cheryle toward the street and told her to cross over to the other sidewalk. When I did this, the woman stepped directly in front of Cheryle and in a high pitched voice that had a German accent, demanded to know if Cheryle spoke English.

"Yes I do."

"I vant your cell phone," the woman screamed.

"I don't have a cell phone," Cheryle replied.

"You're lying," the old lady screamed. "I know you do! I can tell by the way you are dressed! Now give me your cell phone! I need to call 911!"

By now the old woman was trembling, and her demands were punctuated by violent arm motions and odd hand gestures.

"Looks like a street robbery in progress," I mumbled under my breath.

Cheryle did not think I was funny.

"I'm scared," she whispered.

Quickly, I stepped between the crazed woman and Cheryle, and forcefully told her to go away.

Rather than leaving, she became more enraged and took a couple of steps toward me. When she did this, my collar turned, as we would say on the street. Removing my missionary tag, I placed it in my pocket and I became the street cop of years long past. The transition only took seconds.

"You're crazy, now turn around and go away," I commanded.

"I'm going to hit you in the face," she screamed. Then she picked up a brick.

"That would be a mistake," I growled as I stepped forward and braced for the attack.

She stopped.

While my confrontation with the woman was ensuing, Cheryle tried to push me up the street. However, I didn't move and was now in a combat mentality. No one, not man, woman or a child gets a shot at either Cheryle or me, especially not on the streets of Quito. Seeing that I did not retreat at her threats, she continued to scream.

"I'll get you, I'll get you!"

"I've heard that before," I mumbled as I turned and escorted Cheryle across the street.

After we crossed to the other side of the street, I kept a vigilant eye on the old lady, watching as she shook her fist at us while running toward us and then back, all the time screaming threats on how she was going to do us great bodily harm.

Welcome to South America, I thought as a large smile crossed my face.

Later that afternoon when we returned by the same route, we were stopped by one of the men on the street who directed the parking of cars. He told us that the woman was so angry, that she threw a brick through the window of a business.

The next day, I again was told by the same man that she returned looking for us. Had she found us, she probably would have tried to attack Cheryle first, and that act would have been detrimental to her health and well-being.

Evil Walks the Streets

I have mentioned before that Cheryle and I loved to walk the streets of Quito, which included an area midway between our apartment building and the church office building. This area was called *Gringolandia*, because it was a hotbed of tourist activity. It was also a high crime rate area inhabited by prostitutes, bandits, pick-pockets and generally some real bad guys. But that never stopped us from walking through there.

One day, about five in the afternoon, we were walking back to our apartment and were about half-way into the adversary's territory when I had a new experience, at least new for down here.

We were approaching an intersection when five men turned the corner to our right side and brusquely walked in our direction. Each was dressed in black clothing with black jackets, long black unkempt hair, chiseled features of the Mayan Indian, dark and sinister countenances and each appeared determined to take up the entire sidewalk. They were so evil in appearance that I instantly discerned no light in their countenances. It is not uncommon for me to encounter one such individual in my travels, but five was a first.

Upon their approach, they separated slightly and began to surround us. As the circle formed, one turned, stopped and with a contorted and dark, satanic expression—the kind carried by those in the army of darkness—began a deep unnatural throaty growl and shook his head rapidly from side to side. While his long hair flew helter-skelter, he snapped his teeth as a wild animal would when trying to paralyze its prey for the kill. He never bothered to look at Cheryle, just stood directly in front of me snarling and shaking his head, snapping and grinding his teeth. There we stood, face to face, neither of us moving; a confrontation of light versus darkness, good standing before evil. As I faced this enemy of righteousness, I was aware that they were only seen by me.

In my mind, I calmly thought, *"By the authority of the Holy Melchizedek Priesthood which I hold, and in the name of Jesus Christ my Master, I command you to leave!"* My lips never moved, nor was any sound uttered.

When the final word was thought, this personage of darkness suddenly bowed his head, turned and hurried away. Then, as quickly as it began, it ended and in the twinkling of an eye, they were gone.

I had on many occasions seen that darkness and those vile expressions, and unless one has beheld that depth of evil, it is difficult to put it into words, for there is no light, absolutely none emitted from their person. They are not from this side and their spirits belong to those who serve the Master of Darkness. This was the first time that I had been confronted on the street by such a large group of these demonic entities, but not the first time I had seen them in a large group.

An Attempt to Murder Two Senior Missionaries

Our apartment building in Quito was a wonderful eighteen story structure that provided not only a safe environment, but also had a super market on the first floor and small shops on the mezzanine and second floors. Since it was considered one of the finest apartment buildings in the city, it also was home to other missionary couples.

One such couple was Elder and Hermana Ward. The Wards were in their early seventies, and their backgrounds were far different than ours.

Hermana Ward served as the mission nurse, while Elder Ward was the mission financial officer. They were soft spoken, quiet, spiritual, and as non-confrontational a couple as you could find. They were the salt of the earth and true peacemakers.

It was a Thursday morning about 7:30 when the Ward's stepped from our apartment building parking lot and began their walk up La Nina to the church office building. Elder Ward carried an umbrella against the threat of morning rain.

As they walked and talked about the coming day, they suddenly heard rapid footsteps approach from the rear. Before they could turn around, a man jumped in front of them holding a glass bottle with a screw on cap. In an instant, the cap was off, and both Elder and Sister Ward were heavily splashed with gasoline. The assailant then whipped out a pack of matches and attempted to ignite the gasoline that soaked their clothing.

Reacting to the danger, Elder Ward pushed Hermana Ward behind him and using his umbrella as a weapon, beat the man back, striking him on the head, shoulders and arms. Confused by the matches not igniting and Elder Ward's aggressive defense, the assailant threw the empty bottle to the ground and fled leaving the Ward's in a state of shock.

When I came into the office, Cheryle told me about their experience. My first response was anger, then, after two or three deep breaths, I realized that Elder Ward was not alone in this confrontation. Under the direction of the Spirit, and with the companionship of the angels of heaven, the manner in which he handled and diffused the danger was perfect.

My concern was now for Elder Ward who believed that he should have done more to protect his companion. Being a private person, he was reticent to talk about the situation, but quietly processed it in his office.

For those who have been confronted by a violent aggressor intent on doing you great bodily harm, and who were able to neutralize the situation using whatever means available, silence was not an option for future success should a similar situation occur. Prior preparation, mentally, physically and emotionally was required to guarantee that in the future, one would not seriously be injured or killed if again menaced by an insane attacker.

To guarantee future success if again confronted, one must review all aspects of the initial confrontation, and if necessary, seek guidance that would allow for the implementation of additional precautions.

Basically, you must strategize and map out what actions you would take under every situation imaginable.

Knowing that Elder Ward was shaken and needed to talk, I sought him out in his office where I found him seated, leaning forward in his chair, head in hands, and body trembling.

Lovingly, I place my hand on his shoulder.

"Elder Ward, let's talk about what happened."

He lifted his head, and an expression of gratitude crossed his face.

"I would appreciate that," he said. He then recounted what had happened and his reaction, sharing that afterward he felt that the attack never should have happened, and when it did, he reacted incorrectly.

I explained that he did fine in protecting his companion, and that he must know that those matches failed to ignite because angels of God were in attendance.

AN ATTEMPT TO MURDER TWO SENIOR MISSIONARIES

When he had calmed down, I showed him how he could use his long umbrella, with the finely pointed tip, for additional protection if again confronted by this type of attacker. I was loving and direct, and he was appreciative.

As we talked, he soon realized that he was a hero who performed admirably in a life and death situation.

When the severity of the attack was confirmed, and I applauded his actions, a thin smile crossed his lips.

As I shook his hand and turned to leave, I looked him in the eyes and said, "Elder Ward, you did just fine."

"Thank you, Elder Whitaker. Coming from you that means a lot."

Tears filled his eyes and we parted.

A Difficult Assignment Comes to an End

The journey was coming to a close. I had walked on a broken ankle for seven months, and it was time to get it repaired. The Spirit testified that we accomplished what it was we were asked to do, so we began to wrap up our assignment. Because of my broken ankle, and Cheryle experiencing severe pain in one of her knees, Mission Medical recommended that we return to the states and get our orthopedic problems resolved. We were in full agreement.

As I sat in our apartment and penned my final thoughts, heavy sheets of hail were cascading across the building while thunder ripped through the heavens. We were going to miss this climate, the beauty of the land of Ecuador, and the love of the people.

During this assignment, we made wonderful friends. Daily, we were greeted by security guards, shopkeepers, handicapped beggars and street vendors that we had now known for eight years. What a special feeling it was to have a nonmember ask us to pray for their family, and when they were told we were leaving, tears filled their eyes as we shared our final hug.

We did our best, and in doing so, we had a positive impact on the Perpetual Education Fund Program within the country of Ecuador.

On our final day, we received an e-mail from Salt Lake asking us to travel to Salt Lake to report on our success, and to make recommendations as to how the program could be strengthened throughout the world. That would be a special meeting and one we would look forward to. The request came from Elder John Carmack, the Executive Director and Elder Richard E. Cook the Managing Director of the Perpetual Education Fund. Both are Emeritus members of the Seventy and had the responsibility for the PEF program throughout the world.

On Sunday night, Cheryle and I attended a PEF meeting in the Colon chapel that was held for two stakes. In attendance were Elder Cook, two stake presidents, a number of bishops and other priesthood leaders as well as many PEF participants. Prior to the meeting, Elder Cook, Cheryle and I met with the two stakes. They were very complimentary and gracious about the work accomplished by our office. During Elder Cook's remarks in the main meeting, he said:

"The PEF program as it is organized and running in Ecuador, is closer to what President Hinckley envisioned than anywhere else in the world."

When I met personally with Elder Cook regarding his visit, he told me that both he and others in Salt Lake were so impressed with what was occurring in Ecuador, that it was decided he would travel to Quito and see for himself if it honestly was happening. After his arrival, he met with a number of stake presidents who were very complimentary about the work and what Elder and Hermana Whitaker had accomplished. In those meetings he received his answer.

When we reported to Salt Lake for our after action report, I was wearing an orthopedic boot and hobbling.

A member of the PEF staff picked us up at the airport and drove us to the Marriott Hotel. We checked in and then drove to the church office building for our meeting. The meeting was attended by the entire PEF staff, including Elder Carmack and Elder Cook. However, before the meeting started, an interesting conversation took place in the hallway.

As I stood awaiting the meeting, both Elder Carmack and Elder Cook approached me and asked if I would be available to fill a special assignment. My response was immediate; "Yes, but let me take care of some of our medical issues first."

"Oh, it will be down the road," replied Elder Cook, "We'll be in touch."

South America Northwest Area Perpetual Education Fund Special Project 2009-2011

Evil Tries to Thwart a Special Assignment

It was mid-April, 2009 when I received a telephone call from Elder Richard E. Cook asking if Cheryle and I would fill a special Perpetual Education Fund assignment to Lima, Peru. He told me that nothing of its type had ever been done before, and that I would have the responsibility to write and supervise a special program directed at focusing on the priesthood and applicable priesthood correlation. I further was advised that I would be working with the Area Presidency, five countries that included Venezuela, Ecuador, Colombia, Peru and Bolivia, and a number of Area Seventy and numerous stake presidents. In addition I was told that my traveling companion would be an Area Seventy. Upon consultation with Cheryle, we accepted the assignment and scheduled an arrival date in Lima.

During the month of June, I received two telephone calls from Elder Marcus B. Nash, the Area President over the South America Northwest Area. On both occasions, he explained his focus and that of the Area which was based on Doctrine and Covenants 84:106. He stressed this during both calls and asked if I felt that I could support the presidency. My answer was a resounding, "Of course."

With those two calls, an eternal friendship began.

On Tuesday, September 2, we were in Salt Lake for our one day of training. The day began with a meeting which included Cheryle, myself, Elder John Carmack and Elder Richard E. Cook. We spent an hour with the Brethren and I was advised by Elder Cook on three different occasions that "The church cannot afford to have you fail in this assignment, Elder Whitaker." The weight of the assignment began to sink in as did the reference Elder Cook made to the 121st section of the Doctrine and Covenants.

We then spent the remainder of the day with other Perpetual Education Fund staff members and were given a preview of the direction the Perpetual Education Fund would take. At five o'clock, we again met with Elder Cook, and again the serious nature of our assignment was stressed along with the impact it would have throughout the church.

Sleep came hard that night, and at about 3:00 a.m., my entire body was seized upon by an unseen force while a thick darkness enveloped me and pressed down upon my body with a force not unfamiliar, but one greater than I had ever before experienced.

A struggle then ensued between my spirit and the powers of darkness that lasted until 7:00 a.m., when Cheryle awakened. During those four hours, I contended with an onslaught of evil spirits in a combat that seemed never to end. Unlike times past when similar confrontations occurred, on this occasion the heavens literally were sealed as I fought to dispel the thick blanket that held me powerless to move or call out. Even my thoughts, designed to dispel the evil one through the name of Jesus Christ, failed. In my life, this was the first time I felt so powerless against a force that drove me deeper and deeper into a despair that began to overwhelm my spirit.

If one never has had this type of experience and the accompanying feelings of solitude, they will not understand my inability to provide an adequate written explanation.

I must emphasize that this was not only a physical, but also a spiritual confrontation accompanied by feelings of despair and discouragement that were some of the gravest and most profound I had ever known.

At the end of the four hours when I finally was able to dispel the forces of evil by commanding them to leave through the use of the name of Jesus Christ, I thoroughly was exhausted.

When able to do so, I sat up, looked at Cheryle and with words reeking of discouragement whispered, "I don't know if I can do this."

With a tone laced by an exasperation that dripped from each word, she bolted into a seated position, looked at me and blurted out, "Then why are we here?"

Immediately, I asked, "Father, art thou there?"

When the quiet reassurance settled upon me testifying to the depths of my soul that I was not alone, I knew that I had been called of God to accomplish a task that would prove to be one of the most difficult assignments of my life.

"Turning to Cheryle, I said, "Let's go home and prepare for the assignment."

The Adventure Begins

We left Las Vegas the morning of September 8, 2009 and flew to Los Angeles without incident. Don McClelland took us to the airport and after ten minutes, we had our luggage checked, boarding passes in hand and we were on our way. We easily cleared security and were pleased when it went so smoothly.

In Los Angeles, as we approached the security area, a TSA officer looked at us and stated, "VIP's go through this line. Please follow me." So Cheryle and I fell in right behind the man and circumvented one very long line while others were trying to figure out who the silver haired guy was with the blond.

I continue to be a strong advocate of the importance of a professional business-like appearance, missionary name tags and dark, aviator sunglasses. This coupled with what I call my "street persona," has carried us successfully through two assignments to South America and will do so during our third.

When we arrived at security scanning, another TSA representative looked at us and then our name tags. "You have a very important and distinguished name." With a huge smile crossing his face, he escorted us directly to the security screeners and we were processed ahead of others. Time elapsed; not more than five minutes. I was so impressed with the professionalism we experienced that I sought out a TSA supervisor. I introduced myself and told him that I was retired from the Los Angeles Police Department. "Oh, our Chief Executive Officer for TSA in Los Angeles is a former member of your department. His name is Larry Fetters."

"Larry was one of my training officers when I was sent to Wilshire Division as a young police officer," I said. "It's a small world."

He agreed; we exchanged business cards and he told me that he would give Fetters my warmest regards.

We then proceeded to our gate. With this, our luck began to go south.

Arriving at our departure gate, we found seats in the waiting area and hunkered down for what we believed would be a normal wait. We were wrong.

We had been seated no more than two hours when we were told that they found mechanical problems with our aircraft. We were advised that we would be notified within the next three hours what the game plan would be. This was at two o'clock. At five, they told us that we had a gate change and would be leaving for Lima at eight thirty, so we continued to wait.

The new waiting area was full, which indicated a full flight. When the time approached to board, I pulled a Bob McKee and Don McClelland maneuver.

For those not privy to this creative maneuver, it is that when you have handicapped status and the proper credentials, you use them whenever you can. Since Cheryle has two bad knees, and my ankle is still a problem along with my old football injuries to both feet and neck, we both had the proper handicapped credentials that allowed pre-boarding.

Quietly, I approached the attendants, advised them of our plight and asked to pre-board with either the handicapped or First Class passengers. They were thrilled to be of assistance, so when the time came, we pre-boarded and found our seats without being part of the cattle-call that was to come.

I found it interesting to note that we were two of the few non-Asians on the flight. Even the Latinos were sparsely represented. There were three large Asian tour groups traveling on the plane, so I nicknamed the flight the Orient Express.

The flight went smoothly. LAN Airlines is far superior to any US carrier. They not only had comfortable seats, but also excellent food and there were more than enough flight attendants to accommodate a full flight.

On Wednesday, September 9, after nearly twelve hours in the air, we arrived in Lima. Exiting the plane brought with it another intense experience, albeit it one more intense for Cheryle than me.

When the plane came to a stop and the unfasten seat belt sign was turned off, I stepped out of my seat, reached up to the luggage bin and was just about to pop it open when a male Asian behind me tried to push me out of the way so he could elbow his way to the front of the plane. As he put his elbow in my back, I stepped firmly into the aisle, blocked his passage, and glared at him through my sunglasses. Again he began to push me out of the way. I turned and in my best police voice commanded, "Back off, pal!" Shocked, he immediately stepped back.

I opened the luggage bin, pulled out Cheryle's carry-on. I retrieved my computer bag, slipped on my jacket and again turned toward the guy, said nothing, just looked him in the face. With this, he decided discretion was better than increased stupidity and that his trying to push me to the side and back into my seat was not the best idea. When this slight confrontation ended, we followed the forward passengers to the front and exited the plane.

We now had been up, and going for twenty-seven hours.

Finding an Apartment

As previously mentioned, we arrived in Lima on September 9, 2009. After exiting the plane and finding our luggage, we headed to Customs. Since they were comfortable admitting Mormon Missionaries to their country, especially senior missionaries, we passed through Customs without incident and stepped outside to find our contact. We had been told that we would be met by a senior missionary assigned to the Perpetual Education Fund office. As we stepped into the common area, we were not met by the senior missionary, but by a younger man named Henry Utrilla who was the PEF Call Center Manager for the South America Northwest Area. Henry was a young man with a great personality. He spoke English, and it wasn't ten minutes in the car before we knew we were on the same page of the hymnbook. We also felt strongly that we knew each other from somewhere but could not pin it down. My relationship with Henry would turn out to be a wonderful blessing.

Leaving the airport, we experienced our first glimpse of what to expect for the next eighteen months. Picture, if you will, a narrow three lane road. Put into it some lane stripes. Now picture making five lanes from the three and add Destruction Derby combined with bumper cars. You now have the traffic in Lima. Until experienced, it is inconceivable. They have the European circular round-a-bouts and it is first come, first served. Most intersections are not controlled by signals. You just inch forward and tap the gas until you have cut off everyone else and are into your desired traffic lane. What is amazing is that although you might find yourself only inches from the car next to you, they usually don't collide; that is, most of the time. On occasion, you have a small bus slightly larger than one of our twelve passenger vans with traffic helpers hanging out the passenger window.

The traffic helpers were called "monkey's" in Ecuador. It was their job to signal the traffic on the right when the bus driver wanted to move over. Unfortunately, at times, if they made an error in judgment and told the driver to change lanes when the lane was occupied by another car or especially a bus, the mistake was fatal. The death rate amongst those who worked in this profession was high since the "monkey's" in Lima leaned out the window to their waist.

After a lengthy drive in heavy traffic, our driver entered the Area facility. In the Area offices we were introduced to many people. It was interesting that we already knew a number of the staff from our two assignments to Quito, Ecuador. We were taken to meet Elder Cesar Hooker, an Area Seventy and the man who was over the Area Welfare Services which included PEF. After the introductions, we went to see the apartment that we had rented, sight-un-seen. This proved to be a financial and emotional disaster. Another lesson learned…the hard way.

When we received our assignment, I sent a senior missionary and an employee of the Area my apartment requirements. When they told me they found a nice place, I told them to proceed. That was a tactical error. I had been prompted before we left Las Vegas to stay in a hotel our first week to ten days while we looked for a place and to hold onto any deposit. I did not follow the prompting. Going against the prompting, I placed my confidence in this senior missionary. That decision later became a financial debacle.

With our luggage piled high in the Area van and accompanied by two area employees, including Henry Utrilla, we drove to the apartment. I was hoping that the apartment would be suitable since I was required to pay $1800 dollars upfront. That was for the first and last month's rent plus a $600 security deposit.

When the van turned off the main street and into the neighborhood, I knew we were in trouble. The area was a ghetto; much like what one would find in North Las Vegas or near the crime ridden area referred to as the "Naked City" located around the Stratosphere Casino. Groups of bandits hung out on each corner and when we pulled up to the building, I noted that the "Security Guard" stationed out front was drunk, used a bicycle for transportation and sat in a plastic chair.

We stepped from the van and unloaded our luggage. This was done to eliminate any temptation for the bandits who now faced our direction and were watching our every move. Dragging four suitcases and some other incidentals, we walked through the first security door leading into the patio area and then up the steps to the glass doors leading upstairs. On one of the glass doors was posted a large note warning people of the criminals in the area and the number of robberies that had occurred and were continuing. I was now in full combat mode lacking but one critical item…my gun.

Wonderful, I thought, as we hauled our suitcases up to the second floor. The apartment door had four deadbolt locks. Edwing, our Area contact, put the keys into the locks. Nothing happened. The locks were so old that the tumblers were not working properly. He struggled for about twenty minutes and finally got them open. As he opened the door, we stepped across a thick deposit of dirt and dust. We had been told by the senior missionary that the apartment had been readied for us and cleaned. Someone lied. Standing just inside the front door, I knew this was not going to work. Then, it only got worse.

After shutting the front door, I noted a large iron bar which slid into a clamp, securing the door. For a former street cop, this was just another indication that someone made an error in judgment when they told us that the place was acceptable. While it might have been acceptable for a missionary couple who hadn't done this before, it was not acceptable for a couple who had served in Latin America three times during the past nine years. Bottom-line, unless I was living alone and had my choice of hand guns and semiautomatic weapons, this dive, which I nicknamed Fort Lima, was not an option.

Exiting the living room, we walked into the kitchen. The stove didn't work and there were screeching parrots just outside the window. The strong aroma of cooking food filtered from below, and when we stepped into the laundry area, we saw that one entire window was missing and the space was open to the outside. We were told that this was done to allow the air from the outside to blow into the apartment and dry the clothes. As we walked from room to room, we noted that the place was filthy. All that was missing were the cockroaches which were regular inhabitants of the apartments in Ecuador.

"Disappointment and a high level of frustration laced my words as I said, "This is not acceptable."

Both Henry Utrilla and Edwing Ramirez stood in front of me in abject fear not knowing what this commanding norteamericano with the silver hair and aviator sunglasses was going to do and say next.

Edwing's face went white. He felt that it was his fault and knew that we would lose all or part of our $1800 dollar deposit. I was not real happy, and this seemed to impact poor Edwing.

FINDING AN APARTMENT

"We need a place to stay," I said. "Take us to the Marriott."

We were driven to the Marriott, Lima, which was located about one hundred yards from the ocean. Some might think that the ocean view would be beautiful. Guess again. Lima sits in the fog most of the year and has a climate not much different than San Francisco and a number of cities in the US Northwest.

On Thursday, a driver picked us up early to go to the Area office. Once in the building, I began the process of looking for an apartment. While organizing the search team, Elder Hooker recommended that we change hotels and check into a five star hotel closer to the Area offices. So, we drove back to the Marriott, checked out, schlepped our luggage to the van and began the one hour drive across town. Now, no commentary would be complete without a few comments on the drivers and traffic in Lima.

As we began looking for another apartment, and after talking to the brethren who worked in Quito and were reassigned to Lima, it was obvious that the cost of this assignment would be more than double anything we had previously experienced. The debacle of the first apartment cost us $900.00. A tough lesson learned, but one that reminded us that we were in South America.

So, there we sat with not enough money left for a deposit once we found another place. I didn't know how I was going to handle that situation. On a bright note: We had lunch with Henry and Arturo Fernandez and found out that Arturo worked not only for the church in the area of travel and visas, but was also an attorney. At lunch, he gladly took on our security deposit problem and told me he would do all in his power to get something back. But as hard as he tried, no money was ever refunded.

We also needed to hire a driver just to get around safely since many of the taxi drivers were thieves and drug dealers and the buses were, as in Quito, havens for pickpockets and thieves. They were also known to be the main means of transportation for the traveling flea circuses.

In talking to the brethren in the Area offices, it was contemplated that our rent alone would be in the area of $1200-$1500 dollars a month…..or more!

On Friday, with the help of Henry and Arturo, we found a nice apartment near where the members of the Area Presidency lived. To enter the area, you first were required to pass through a security gate manned twenty-four hours a day by a guard. And unlike the first apartment, he was in a security shack, had a telephone and was sober. After passing through this checkpoint, we drove onto a street that housed five large apartment complexes. Our building was not the largest on the block, but it was well maintained. After parking, we were met by the realtor. As a group, we walked to an iron electronically operated security gate which also could be opened with a key. Entering, we walked down a short flight of stairs and to the elevator. *So far, so good,* I thought. Security appeared to be tight. The elevator was small, but accommodated the group. The realtor pushed the button for the second floor, and up we went. When the elevator stopped, a key was required to open the door. Once open, you stepped directly into the apartment.

The apartment was large with two bedrooms, two bathrooms and a well equipped kitchen. It also had a television sitting area down one hall and a spacious living room. Oh, and I forgot, the place was fully furnished, with picture windows that looked out toward the front. The only drawback was that the master bedroom was only fifteen feet away from a high wall that separated the building from the spacious homes to the rear. And in South America, when you have spacious homes situated on large parcels of land, you have loud parties that go on for days.

We told the realtor that we liked the apartment and if the owner approved, we would meet with him in a few days and sign the papers. The cost to rent? $1350 per month. When you included utilities, etc., it would run about $1750. As Cheryle and I reviewed the rental cost, we had to laugh. Our first apartment in Quito cost us $450 a month. When we returned to Quito for our second assignment, we were in the same apartment building as the first assignment, but the monthly rent was $550. Now we were at $1750. However, since security was a critical factor, we decided to make it work.

On Saturday, we did what every new resident to a city does: We found a large, modern mall and walked, and walked and walked. We also found the food court which was extensive. So all in all, the day was a success!

The mall was about a ten minute drive from our current hotel and from the apartment we hoped to rent. It was twice the size of the Galleria Mall in Henderson and had every store found in Las Vegas. The parking lot must have accommodated at least five thousand cars, and what struck me as interesting was the number of sales personnel employed. If you had a question or needed something, you never had to look for help. The name of the place was Jockey Plaza and it had a huge movie theatre that showed some G-Rated films in English with Spanish subtitles. The place appeared to be the same as our Cine Max theatres.

Sunday was spent in our meetings. Our hotel had taxis in front, so the only challenge was to get the driver to understand where it was we wanted to go. This took some doing, but eventually we arrived at the chapel which also was the La Molina Stake Center located adjacent to the Area office facility and Lima Mission Training Center. Travelling a new city and doing so using only Spanish is always a challenge since most taxi drivers do not know where they are going. As I found in Quito, and it was reaffirmed in Lima, if I didn't tell the driver what street to use and what turns to make, we never would have arrived at our destination.

Monday we were advised that the owner of the apartment we wanted to rent desired to meet us. The meeting with the owner went well. He attended Syracuse University in the US, spoke great English and we hit it off quite well. A monthly rental price was agreed on, payment method was arranged and we were able to move in within the next two days.

On to Interpol!

Our second week in Peru found us reporting to the Interpol International Police Agency. No, we had not violated any laws, nor were we on the International Terrorist watch list. Our appointment was a registration process required of all foreigners who would be residing in Peru for any significant period of time, and that included Mormon missionaries.

It was an overcast morning when we were told that we had an appointment that morning. When I asked about our paperwork, I was told, "Not to worry!"

Trust me; I have heard that line before!

We left the Area offices with President Arturo Hernandez driving. I failed to realize the size of a city like Lima until I was immersed in its traffic. Then the fact that it had a population of nearly nine million became a reality, and it appeared that seven million were all driving at the same time.

We were accompanied by a wonderful young lady named Mya. She was bilingual and worked for Arturo Fernandez in the Travel and Visa Department. The route to the office was new to us, but rather than drive downtown as we had done for a previous appointment when we were required officially to check into Peru, we found ourselves driving through some very beautiful and well-manicured neighborhoods. After about forty minutes, President Fernandez pulled onto a wide, long tree-lined street and parked in front of a group of small, nondescript, white buildings.

Stepping from the car, we were ushered into the front lobby of the largest of the three buildings. Walking through the solid doorway, we stepped into a dimly lit and cluttered office. To our right, seated behind a small metal desk, was the receptionist. She sat in a weathered old secretary's chair and had in front of her an antiquated computer. Nothing in the office looked new, or well cared for, nothing that is, but the young receptionist. She was attractive, had a beautiful smile and appeared just to be happy to have a good job.

Old metal index card boxes lined the shelves. It appeared that most files were still maintained on index cards and sheaves of paper, and carelessly stored in the many metal file cabinets that lined the walls. Papers were piled everywhere: on top of her desk, on the top of a number of other old desks not being used, and on top of the many bland gray metal cabinets.

"Please take a seat," the receptionist said. "I also will need your paperwork and credentials."

Mya stepped forth and produced the required documents. We found two uncomfortable purple plastic chairs from a group of ten that lined the center of the office and began our wait. I hoped that it would not be long. I was wrong.

After about forty minutes, our names were called to be fingerprinted. I was first.

The fingerprint counter was very similar to those used in the decade of the sixties in all the jails in Los Angeles. A small wooden board was attached to the top of a table and a metal frame was used to keep the fingerprint card in place.

Now the fun began.

"Please relax and give me one finger at a time, beginning with your index finger." The technician's monotone voice held absolutely no emotion.

As directed, I produced my index finger. The technician was dressed in a soiled white lab coat and was wearing white latex gloves smeared with old black ink. With each daub of ink and twist of a finger, my prints were affixed to the fingerprint card, as his gloves were quickly becoming a greasy black. *No need to worry Richard,* I thought, *it is all part of the process.* As soon as both hands had been printed, he removed the cards, shook them a few times and then placed them on an adjacent table.

"Señora Whitaker, you are next!"

"Now this will be something to watch," I whispered to no one in particular.

Both Cheryle and I glanced at the black gloves and then at each other. I could tell from her expression that she was praying that he would change to a new pair of white latex gloves.

"Please step to the podium, extend your right arm and give me the index finger of your right hand."

Cheryle threw me a look that said, "I can't believe this!" but without a word, she complied.

The technician stepped forward, filthy gloves and all. The process then began.

The ink on the gloves was now darker than that on the fingerprint cards. Smudges and slight smears appeared not to be a problem. *Extend finger, roll on ink pad, and roll on card....next!*

When all ten fingers had been printed, both palms then were inked with a rubber roller and with that, the process was completed.

Cheryle stood silent, her face having lost some color and her lips pale from being pinched together.

The attendant then stripped off the old gloves and using his ink stained hands, drew on a new pair of blue latex gloves. Once on, he picked up the black greasy fingerprint kit, and while transferring ink from the kit to his fresh gloves, placed the kit in a drawer. The new gloves no longer were clean. *Why even change gloves,* I thought, but discretion was the better part of valor, so I kept my opinion to myself.

Smiling, he pointed with an open hand to an adjoining room and said, "Please follow me." We shot each other a look and proceeded in a strained silence.

We stepped through the doorway and our senses were met by what appeared to be a B-movie replication of a torture room from a Bela Lugosi horror movie.

Planted firmly in the center of the concrete floor was an old dental chair with a dented silver tray bolted to the left arm. Next to the tray sat a large green metal circular light that sat atop a six foot tarnished pole that had to have been used in the old horror classic, *The Bride of Frankenstein.* When the technician turned on the light, the entire unit bobbled back and forth like the broken neck of a dead chicken since it was only being held in place by a loose fitting bent gooseneck extension.

Expressionless, the technician turned to me and in a low mumble, said, "Please have a seat in the chair."

"Why?" I asked.

My questioning his procedure appeared to take him back.

"Because, we need to check all your teeth, and we need to identify any abnormalities or dental changes. We do this so that if you die and the body is damaged, you can be identified from your dental records and the body shipped home." Then he smiled, his expression never reaching his eyes.

"Comforting," I said as I sat down on the long vinyl chair, extended my feet and threw my head back onto the headrest. Closing my eyes, I attempted to travel to a different place, but that did not happen.

Where was the elevator music, I thought, *or the pretty dental assistant?*

Once seated, the interrogation lamp was thrown on and the room became awash with a brilliant white light. I squinted my eyes and then squeezed them tightly shut. B*etter not do that,* I thought, *my life might hinge on my ability to flee should the need arise!*

The technician snatched a soiled rag from the tray, wiped some of the black ink from the latex gloves and grabbed a clipboard and a pen.

"Please relax and become comfortable."

All we need now is a rubber hose and some electrodes.

"Please, open your mouth!" he commanded.

With my mouth open wide, he began to check each tooth and make the appropriate notes to the dental chart attached to the clipboard. Over and around each tooth the latex gloves slid, guaranteeing that each became a victim of this procedure.

The gloves left a strange taste in my mouth. And since he wore no surgical mask to cover his mouth, I was soon overpowered by the odor of onions and garlic he had consumed at breakfast.

Out of the corner of my eye I caught a glimpse of Cheryle. Her face had lost all color.

By now, I was numb and barely felt anything as one ink stained glove pulled my cheek from one side to the other while the other pried open lips that inadvertently tried their best to close.

When the technician was done and all of my teeth had been checked and documented, he turned to Cheryle and asked her to have a seat in the chair. I was told to step back into the waiting area and take a seat. As Cheryle slowly slid into the dental chair, I could see a feeling of discomfort cross her now colorless face. I watched as she glanced at the same ink stained latex gloves and then into the face of the technician. When she looked at me, calmness had been replaced by fear.

I forced a smile, shrugged my shoulders and found an empty plastic chair.

Her procedure was identical to mine, and although her body language radiated discomfort and fear, she never complained or said a word. Within twenty minutes the ordeal ended. As she sat down next to me, all she could say was, "That was horrible!"

Again, it was another first.

"Onward Christian Soldiers!"

Elder René Loli and
Our Trip up the Amazon River

As we sat in the offices of the Perpetual Education Fund in Salt Lake City preparatory to our flight to Lima Peru to fill a special assignment from the brethren, I was approached by a staff member.

"You're on your way to Lima?" he asked.

I respond in my usual longwinded, jubilant manner, "Yes."

"Great city, but it is too bad you will be working with a man who is known to dislike norteamericanos and is hard to deal with."

"And who might that be?"

"His name is René Loli. He is the manager of the MTC, an Area Seventy and a hard case. I don't envy you."

"Thank you for your concern," I said and ended the conversation by turning and walking away.

How interesting, I thought. This was nearly the exact dialogue and warning I received from a number of sources when we were called on our first assignment to Quito. The first individual I was warned about was Cesar Cacuango, and as I have outlined in earlier writings, he and I forged a strong friendship and became eternal friends.

The second warning about Elder Loli came when I received a telephone call from Lima. An individual working in the Perpetual Education Fund felt it important that I knew of, "Loli's dislike for norteamericanos and how difficult he was to work with."

I found the telephone call strange and the caller out of his lane in that he was a seasoned church administrator, former missionary to Lima as a youth, and a former mission president in Peru. He told me that he and his wife now were serving a senior mission to Peru working in the Perpetual Education Fund office and were required to work with Elder Loli, an arrangement that he openly said they did not like.

During the conversation it became apparent that because Elder Loli did not have a great deal of formal education, this leader treated him in a very condescending manner. They butted heads daily and little was accomplished. I was told at the end of my conversation with this senior missionary that the bottom-line was he did things his way and refused to work with Loli.

I had three thoughts when the conversation ended. The first was that the telephone call was unwarranted, and because of the tone of the conversation, pride was more a factor than Elder Loli's weaknesses. Second, I was determined to decide for myself whether or not Loli was capable. Third, I would make my own determinations as to how my relationship with Loli would go. I vowed long ago to do my best to work with anyone, and Loli would be no different, especially in light of the fact that he currently was serving as an Area Seventy.

I stored this conversation and the previous warning away knowing that under the direction of the Spirit, my evaluation and assessment of Elder Loli would be correct. If he refused to work, I would roll over him. I knew when the rubber hit the road, I had the full support of the General Authorities in Salt Lake which included the First Presidency and also that of Elder Marcus Nash, the South America Northwest Area President. So, my first challenge would be to develop a good working relationship with Elder Loli. If he was a hard charger, we would make a great team.

Elders Carmack and Cook, both General Authorities had given me my assignment. They explained that I was to organize a priesthood directed pilot program and assist a number of Perpetual Education Fund participants to recognize that the Perpetual Education Fund was based upon the making and keeping of sacred covenants, therefore it was first and foremost spiritual, and then temporal. It was to be designed so as to lead participants back to the temple. Secondly, it was to assist them in their educational and vocational pursuits. The program would be monitored both by Salt Lake and by Elder Nash, the Area President. One final stipulation was that the program needed to be designed so that it could be reviewed by Salt Lake and then replicated throughout the world. It was that simple. I also would be responsible for coordinating the effort in five different countries while training twenty-three other Area Seventy about the program and processes developed. The assignment was the South America Northwest Area, with the involved countries being: Venezuela, Colombia, Ecuador, Bolivia and Peru.

After we arrived in Lima, it took nearly three weeks to find an apartment and settle in. Once that was done, I began the process of having my office enclosed, a front door added and the office divided which allowed Cheryle to occupy the front while I worked in the back. It was apparent from the start that never before had the presiding area authorities worked with a senior missionary as hard charging as Elder Whitaker. Fortunately, my background, past assignments and reputation for getting the job done eventually found my unusual requests granted. Once we were settled into our office, I knew that it was time to meet this Elder Loli and evaluate how the work would move forward.

I called his office and he picked up the phone. Boy was he difficult to understand! Yet, through it all, I was able to set an appointment for us to meet that afternoon in his office. Fortunately, the Mission Training Center in Peru was located adjacent to the South America Northwest Area office building so travel time was about five minutes. Accompanied by Henry Utrilla, we walked to Loli's office.

After pleasantries were exchanged, we took seats around a small round table located in a corner of the office. Loli was not a large man, and after we entered and were seated, he leaned back in his chair, looked at me and said, "Elder Whitaker, when are we going to start?"

For a moment, I felt a pang of fear shoot through my body, and in my mind I began to make excuses. *My Spanish isn't good enough; I don't even know what I'm doing.* And then, from somewhere deep within came the words, "Immediately, Elder Loli." With those words, he broke into a large smile.

"Good," he said as he slammed his palm down on the table.

And so the journey began.

We took the entire month of October to organize our travel, and the work. As we spoke, it became apparent that the senior missionary who had called me at home and expressed his dislike for Elder Loli, did nothing to train Loli as to the Perpetual Education Fund Program, nor did this senior missionary try in any way to outline Loli's responsibilities or make any effort to include him in a program for which he had priesthood responsibility and was the presiding authority. Basically, I was starting from scratch. Not only was I responsible for writing the new program and organizing the efforts in five countries, I also would be responsible for training Elder Loli, and as time passed, I also would have the responsibility to include training for the other Area Seventy in the South America Northwest Area.

During the last three weeks of November, Elder Loli, Cheryle and I travelled to special meetings with eleven stakes in Lima, and then into the Amazon Jungle to visit the Amazon basin city of Iquitos where we provided priesthood training to stake and ward leaders.

The first meeting was in Lima and was conducted by Elder Loli. It was a remarkable experience. I have attended many priesthood leadership meetings in my over forty years of church service, but none have had the impact of this meeting. All eleven stake presidents attended, as did their counselors, high priest group leaders, high council members, elders quorum presidents, branch presidents and secretaries. The total attendance was nearly two hundred priesthood leaders. I had never seen that percentage of attendance in the United States.

As we travelled to the meeting, Elder Loli, who was driving, turned to me and asked, "How much time should I take, and what should I speak on?"

"Since you preside, I will take thirty minutes and you take the remaining ninety," I said. He laughed and responded, "You take the ninety and I will take the thirty."

What was funny was that he was serious. We later laughed about that conversation when he admitted that he needed to hear me first so he, under the direction of the Spirit, would know the path to follow. And so it went.

I took my thirty minutes and he, under the direction of the Spirit, taught the brethren the doctrine of the new Perpetual Education Fund Program that I had drafted.

About that program, allow me to digress for a moment.

When I was given the initial assignment by Elders Carmack and Cook, I was not given any idea on what to do or how to proceed. All they said was that I should follow the Spirit, write the program, and be obedient to the members of the South America Northwest Area Presidency.

After Elder Loli and I first met, I went back to my office and began to ponder what direction the Lord wanted me to take. I sat in my office for two weeks with an empty piece of paper before me, not knowing what to write. Then, after two weeks of pondering, praying and pleading, the answer came. *"Richard, remember, all roads lead to the temple. Members need to be reminded of their covenants and commitments. Stress this rather than money. The money will come as the Saints become more worthy to enter the temple. First rescue those who hold temple recommends and are not paying."*

So there it was, and it was around that counsel that the new program was developed.

Later he would refer to this meeting, and our other meetings in which we spoke, by saying that he was Alma, and I was his Amulek.

In our first Priesthood Leadership meeting, the pilot project was discussed and it centered on the Doctrine and Covenants, Section 84:106:

"And if any man among you be strong in Spirit, let him take with him that is weak, that he may be edified in all meekness, that he may become strong also."

My responsibility was to outline the program, explain how it should be implemented, address the concepts, stress the need to use that doctrine as the *How,* while the W*hat would be to rescue, minister and retain all participating in the program;* and it was emphasized that it would all begin with the priesthood.

Together, we taught the spiritual and temporal sides to our project, concluding with the fact that when all was said and done, all roads led to the temple and it was the responsibility of the priesthood leaders to identify, involve and instruct participants on the importance of keeping their sacred covenants.

In a second meeting in another stake, the format was similar to the first, except we had additional Area priesthood leaders in attendance. Cristobal Garcia made a wonderful presentation representing Public Affairs, and then I provided about forty-five minutes of priesthood training, a feat that President Bob McKee would have loved, since I never spoke much while serving in his mission presidency. Then Elder Loli and Henry Utrilla powerfully honed in on how our pilot project would change the mind set and culture of the Peruvian people. Those present took notes and asked questions, and I could see in their faces that they understood and were catching the vision.

We experienced a true unity of the faith as we were inspired by each speaker, knowing that we all were on the same page with the teachings and counsel which the Area Presidency taught.

The next day we visited another stake near Lima, and the following Friday found us in the Lima Airport boarding a flight for the city of Iquitos which was located in northern Peru on the Amazon River.

This trip placed us in the Amazon Jungle, or *silva,* visiting the three stakes in Iquitos. We arrived at about 8:10 Friday night, and immediately felt that we had stepped back in time. The weather was hot and humid; the airport was small and reminded us of the first time we flew into Quito in 2000. After landing, we walked down the boarding steps and straight onto the concourse. From there we could see the remnants of old airplanes that apparently had not been as fortunate as we were to make a safe landing. Fuselage bodies were pushed to the side and rusted out shells occupied an area of a deserted portion of the landing field.

Once we exited the plane, we walked through the small airport and soon found ourselves on the street surrounded by the many mototaxi drivers and a few cab drivers hustling fares. A mototaxi basically was a three wheeled motorcycle with a bench seat for passengers and a motorcycle seat for the driver. This unique contraption was covered by a canvas or cloth headliner that protected the passengers from the elements. Normally, the rain fell at an angle, so whether you stayed dry or not was a fifty-fifty proposition. I'll explain a little more about the mototaxi later.

"Elder…Hermana," the voices shouted as we walked through to a mototaxi procured by Elder Loli. Stepping up to the car, it was obvious that the taxi had seen its better days, and what I learned when traveling with Elder Loli was his propensity to find the most beat-up taxi, then barter the driver as far down in price as he could. *There was a method to his madness,* I mused.

Climbing into the rear, we sat on springs covered by a thin cloth. The headliner and side panels long since had disappeared, and it took the driver two or three turns of the ignition to get the sputtering engine finally to kick over. Once the engine began to rumble, we were off.

As we travelled toward the heart of the city, all we saw coming at us were long lines of the mototaxis. They were the primary transportation used in the jungle. Some were fancy, others more humble, but all were built in Iquitos where the primary factory was located. To get a better idea of this unique contraption, imagine a rickshaw, set it over the frame of a motorcycle, add a driver and some canvas side flaps, add a top and you have the primary land vehicle of the jungle. It is the primary three wheeled vehicle in many parts of not only South America, but also the world. Cheryle immediately fell in love with this mode of transportation and tried her best to figure out how to get one back to Las Vegas!

In Iquitos, we noticed that there were a few main roads that were paved, but once we got off the beaten path, we were on dirt and mud filled side streets lined by shacks whose roofs either were rusted corrugated steel or thatch. Water was delivered by water truck, and many of the neighborhoods near the Amazon were some of the most dangerous in the world. The area within the city was some of the most impoverished I had seen. And yet, life continued.

Since Elder Loli wanted to make sure we were safe and well cared for, he chose the nicest hotel in Iquitos, The El Dorado. Inasmuch as we paid for all our trips from our own funds, I was grateful for nice accommodations. The hotel was beautiful and very secure and it did not take long to find out that the bellboy was LDS, a Perpetual Education Fund participant and very delinquent in his payments.

ELDER RENÉ LOLI AND
OUR TRIP UP THE AMAZON RIVER

Saturday, from 9:00 a.m. to 3:30 p.m. we toured Iquitos in a mototaxi with a young man named Jimmy who was handpicked by Elder Loli to be our guide. I recall hearing Elder Loli's last words to Jimmy: "I expect you to take good care of Elder and Hermana." And he did.

As we toured the city, he was very adept at maintaining a constant speed, which usually was greater than the flow of traffic, and while horns honked, he effortlessly darted in and out of traffic. If he heard the horns and comments about his driving, he acted unfazed, and we continued our circuitous route. Before our boat trip up the Amazon River, we toured the entire city of Iquitos.

We travelled up and down dirt roads and around deep pot holes filled with muddy rain water deposited by the storm the day before. We saw what little modern conveniences were at hand for the occupants of the city and were constantly reminded that the only transportation into and out of this jungle city was either by boat or plane. No outside roads entered the city because of its depth in the jungle. We visited a zoo occupied by half-starved animals, and after walking the beach, we headed for the boat dock.

Finally, we reached our destination, the docks along the Amazon River. Invigorated by an hour of adrenaline rush, we disembarked the mototaxi and immediately were met with the combined odors of rotting fish, engine motor oil and garbage. Loud music blasted from the many small open bars, and as usual, none of the radios were tuned to the same station, which resulted in a cacophony of noise! Lining the walkway were small tiendas or shops where the fishermen, their families and the few tourists that visited the area could buy bottled water, soft drinks and homemade pastries.

We walked into the main area, stepped up onto a narrow wooden plank walkway made of weathered wood and proceeded to what was identified as the boat we would take up the Amazon River.

Slips had been constructed and were lined with boats which all basically looked the same; only their sizes differed. Each craft was long and narrow, with the entire vessel covered by a long v shaped canopy that was supported by a number of poles. The more expensive crafts were partially enclosed with a fiberglass shell containing windows which offered greater protection. Each boat was equipped with a large outboard motor and life vests to accommodate the passengers.

Our boat came right out of the movie, *The African Queen,* lacking only Bogart and Hepburn. It was about fifteen feet in length, had four chairs bolted to the floor, a canvas canopy overhead, a seat in the front for the "Captain of the Craft" and a smaller seat near the large outboard Evenrude engine for his crew member and spotter, who in our case, was the skipper's twelve year old son. It was his responsibility to make sure the engine had gas, or petro as it was called in South America, and then go to the front of the boat and watch for any debris that might be in the water. All tasks the young man did quite well.

The name of our Captain was Luis. His son was Miguel. The only things colorful in the boat were the bright orange life jackets which appeared to have been in use since white men first began to travel the Amazon. The craft also was outfitted with blue and white fiberglass seats. When Luis seated himself next to the engine, Miguel scurried to the bow of the boat.

Standing, the captain pulled the rope starter. Nothing happened. He tried two more times and still nothing. Calmly, Captain Luis walked over to a bench, lifted the top and took out a glass bottle of gasoline. Unscrewing the top, he poured some gas into the carburetor and primed the engine. Again, he pulled the rope. Success! The engine sputtered and coughed, began its throaty growl and we were on our way.

While constantly fighting the current, Luis slowly and with great effort turned the boat up river. The engine strained as it pushed the small craft through the rough silt-filled water. Although the water was choppy and threw the small craft from side-to-side, we could not contain the large grins that crossed our faces as the spray from the river soaked us, and we realized that we actually were traveling up the Amazon River, both of us dressed, not as tourists, but missionaries outfitted with bright orange life vests. What a sight we made with me in my white shirt, missionary tag and black dress shoes, and

Cheryle in her orange blouse, missionary tag, long ankle length skirt and platform shoes. As you can guess, our dress was not appropriate for our jungle exploits and would instill into this adventure some wonderful humor and memories!

As the old engine struggled against the current, our attention was drawn to the old buildings and partially sunk vessels that lined the river bank, remnants of silent sentinels to times past and tragedies real, each testifying to the extreme elements found on the Great Amazon River. When we approached the middle of the river, we saw where the Amazon converged with the Marañón River.

Entering the point of convergence, our small boat was more turbulently tossed up and down. Hanging onto the sides, we marveled at the fact that although the two rivers met, the waters never mixed, each keeping to itself forming a straight line with the waters of the Amazon being a light brown, and the waters of the Marañón a dark muddy brown.

Our first stop was one of the two native villages we were to visit. Rounding a bend, we saw a rickety wooden dock that extended about twenty feet out and three feet above the river. With finesse, Luis headed in that direction and within minutes after arriving at the ancient structure, Luis firmly secured our craft.

Both native villages were very different. In the first, we were invited into a large circular thatched hut which served as the tribe's main meeting place. The hut was constructed of two large tree trunks placed about fifteen feet apart in the middle of the structure. On these trunks, the roof was built by placing poles in a circle like an umbrella, and then tying all these poles together with smaller poles that held the roof up and were placed in the ground. The roof was covered with thatching. The sides were made of the same poles as the roof but set in a vertical position and made to encircle the hut. An opening was left for the door. The floor was dirt. To the left of the door and on the left side of the structure were two large hollowed out tree trunks that were supported by an A-frame apparatus that pulled the drums off the ground. It was these large jungle drums that were used to keep the solid beat as the people danced. Hanging from the walls were many of the items the tribe had made that were for sale.

We were greeted by about twenty members of the tribe. While the men beat out a driving rhythm on the drums, half-naked women and younger members of the tribe performed their native dances. They wore their conventional costumes which included bare breasts and a loin cloth bottom. First, Cheryle was invited to participate in the dance. Laughing, she stood and soon was circling the hut with the other members of the group.

I am in trouble if they ask me, was my only thought, for I remembered that Cheryle had the camera and I boldly was wearing my missionary tag! Suddenly, a bare-breasted woman stepped in front of me, smiled, stretched out her hand and grabbed mine. Before I knew it, she had painted the area around my mouth with black paint that made me look as though I were tattooed. She then placed a hat of green feathers on my head, and before I could say a word, she pulled me into the swirling, dancing throng. All I could do was laugh and enjoy the ride. As I slid by with my bare-breasted Indian escort, Cheryle jumped up, yelled, "Smile," and snapped a photo! The experience now was documented for the ages.

When only the men were asked to perform in a line, I participated. My only thought...*I certainly hope that the Brethren never see the photos taken by Cheryle of this experience.*

We spent about an hour with these wonderful people before Luis advised us it was time to leave and continue our trek up river. Since it had rained the day before our arrival, the murky Amazon River was even darker than usual. The river in this area was low, nearly fifteen feet below the usual height, even with the torrential rain the day before.

Upon our arrival at the second village, we saw that there again was a small dock protruding into the river. Attached to the dock were about thirty steep stairs that climbed the muddy embankment and provided access to the flat area above. The steps were made from logs and other miscellaneous bits and pieces of wood that rolled terribly with each step taken. There was also a rickety hand rail made from two inch wooden poles that rocked back and forth as we climbed. I watched as Cheryle took a step, grabbed the handrail, steadied herself, and then took another step. Remember, she was wearing a long skirt and her wedge sandals. Not the ideal clothes for roaming around the Amazon Jungle or climbing muddy river banks, but through it all, she never complained.

At the top of the steps, we were met by a tribal elder who was barefoot, wore a loin cloth, had beads and feathers strung around his neck and a headband with a feather at the back. He stood about five feet in height and his countenance was warm. We were invited to follow him, so we stepped onto a muddy path that led to the village and back in time. Our walk to the village took care of my spit shined black shoes. I learned that day always to have an additional set of casual clothes, for we never knew when or where the next adventure might take us.

With the tribal elder in the lead, we followed the path deeper into the jungle, walking below large trees and into dense under growth. Suddenly, the path opened into a clearing where the village was located. The primary structure was identical to the one we visited in the last village: a large circular hut with a thatched roof and doorway that measured about six feet across. I ducked as I entered the hut that was not designed for a tall norteamericano. The inside was dimly lit by the rays of sun that peeked through the thatched roof and sides. Wooden benches cut from large trees lined the periphery of the hut whose circumference was about forty feet.

It was a ceremonial hut, and we were invited to take a seat. We were alone in the village with the natives, and it was apparent that they all knew we represented the Savior, since our missionary tags were read immediately upon our arrival. Then something very interesting happened. The tribal elder, who was an old man about seventy years old, and who in stature came up to just below my shoulders, began to tell us the history of his people. He spoke rapid Spanish and directly to us. When he had finished, he looked deep into our eyes, then using his tribal tongue and not Spanish, gave each of us a blessing. Both of us immediately knew what was happening. We felt honored that this religious leader, who represented the Lamanites from generations past, would honor us in this way.

When he finished the blessing, we stepped outside where another native was holding one of the tribe's long blow guns that shot six inch darts that were usually tipped with deadly poison. Since Cheryle was the first to exit the ceremonial hut, she was handed the fifteen foot long blow dart gun. The young man to her side handed her a dart and pointed to a small metal target about twenty-five feet away. The target was the size of a small monkey and Cheryle was invited to take aim and let loose. Without hesitation, she slipped the dart into the hollow end of the gun, put the long hollow tube to her mouth, took a deep breath, and blew; A miss, but not by much. I refrained saying anything about hot air.

ELDER RENÉ LOLI AND
OUR TRIP UP THE AMAZON RIVER

Then she was handed a second dart. She again slipped the dart into the blow gun and again let it rip. Another miss, but the villagers were delighted that the blond white woman came so close to the target. They whooped and hollered, and then handed me the gun.

I took the weapon, slipped a dart into the end, pulled a Davy Crocket and tested the windage, then elevated the end of the blow gun slightly, and after taking a long, deep breath, let it rip. A perfect shot. The monkey was hit dead center! You should have seen and heard the reaction from the tribe. They were astonished that a white man could successfully use the weapon.

I then was handed a second dart. It was apparent that they wanted to see if the first shot was luck, or if the white man was as good as it had appeared. I slid the dart into the end of the gun, placed it to my mouth, slid my left hand down the hollowed out piece of bamboo to balance it, lifted it up and took aim. Again, the same procedure was followed.... a deep breath and sudden blow. The dart flew out the end of the gun and landed next to the first. Both ten ring kills. Now the tribal elders went wild.

They danced in circles, patted me on the back and shouted and laughed. I instantly became a folk hero to those sweet people, but I never mentioned that I could do the same with the white man's gun! Then we bid them goodbye and turned to walk back to the skiff. I was told that I was the first white man ever to have accomplished the feat of two kills.

As we approached the edge of the cliff and the steps that led back down to the boat, I was stopped by another native who explained that he was another of the religious leaders, a priest in the village. He thanked me for coming to his village since they had very few white religious leaders make the trip. I thanked him for the earlier blessing and for his kindness, and after placing a hand on his shoulder and looking deep into his eyes, in Spanish I told him, "God bless you for your work." He smiled; we shook hands and then Cheryle and I began our journey back down the mud inlaid wooden steps with the rickety hand rail.

We travelled back down the river some distance, and I was intrigued and impressed by the density of the jungle. Were it not for a few hand cut paths leading from the bank into the deep foliage, travel would have been nearly impossible.

Returning via the same route we had taken to the villages, we pulled up to the original dock, thanked Luis and Miguel for their time, disembarked and trudged back up the muddy slope to the small sidewalk where Jimmy, our mototaxi driver was patiently waiting for us.

We climbed back into the mototaxi, toured more of the city and in the late afternoon, Jimmy returned us safe and sound to our hotel. It was a wonderful afternoon, but the day was not over. Later we met with three stake presidencies and priesthood leaders from each stake. My responsibility was to provide priesthood leadership training as it pertained to the Perpetual Education Fund Program that I had authored. The brethren from these stakes absorbed the training given by both Elder Loli and me, and it was apparent that they were very grateful for our taking the time to travel from Lima to their stakes. When the training ended, we were taken back to our hotel to rest before another full day that was planned for Sunday.

Sunday morning, it was raining sheets of water. Unfortunately, we had no umbrella and only the clothes on our back, which were our church clothes. I wondered if Elder Loli would change his plans to attend two Sacrament meetings that morning, visit two different stake Family History Centers, and all of this before a five hour priesthood leadership training meeting. I learned that day that not unlike President Bob McKee, Elder Loli never cancelled a meeting or appointment. So, we attended two Sacrament meetings where the Primary children made their presentation.

I have noted that at times in the United States, informal dress has replaced what I was trained to wear. I was taught by priesthood leaders many years ago that informality in dress equates to informality in worship, while formal dress, as depicted by the attire of the General Authorities, reflects a commitment to worship the Savior in a manner different than when dressed in Levis and tennis shoes; now to my point.

In South America, the members of the church *always* dress in their best clothes not only for Sunday worship, but also for any meeting during the week or special occasions, which include church parties and other social events. Both Cheryle and I were impressed that not only did the parents always look sharp, but also the children.

As we sat and listened to the Primary children in each ward, both Cheryle and I again were astonished on how intelligent these young children were. We watched as five year olds stepped up to the podium and read their parts without any promptings or help from parents or primary teachers. Not once did any child stop and ask for help. Then we watched as many others had their parts memorized, and that included all the words to the songs!

Finally, during the meetings, we listened as both the children and the youth of Zion bore strong testimonies. They did so without any help, and the amazing thing was that they bore a true testimony as taught by the Prophets and Apostles. There were no stories about vacations or personal feelings, just a simple pure and sweet testimony. It was quite refreshing.

During the second Sacrament meeting, as in the first, after the children had their program, Elder Loli took a few minutes to teach from the pulpit. He, who had served as a former bishop, stake president and mission president was a great teacher who always taught from the scriptures. He also spoke so fast that when we were alone or traveling, I had to ask him to slow the conversation down. He would laugh, slow down for a sentence or two and then shift back into the machine gun mode.

Well, just as he stepped up to the pulpit, a guy walked into the building right off the street and sat down directly in front of Cheryle and me. He appeared to have slept on the street for the past year. He had a scruffy, unshaven face, his clothes were filthy, his long black hair was matted, and his eyes were darting and dancing around. It appeared that he was casing the room, looking at the purses and drooling at the young women, but what sent me over the top was when he began scratching every part of his body because of the fleas that infested his clothing. Then his hands moved to his hair and scalp that were infested by head lice. He shook his head, scratched and then ran his fingers through the matted locks, all the time waving the contents of his hair backward and onto my lap. I wanted to hit the clown upside the head, but remembered where I was and who I represented, so discretion won out, however, that didn't save me from the fleas that seemed to gravitate to me. I've been told they are attracted to O blood type, so I become a living feast for every flea and flesh consuming bug in the country.

Besides decking the guy, my only other option was to begin dusting off my clothes as rapidly as possible. But, it seemed the more I dusted my pant legs and coat, the faster he shook his lice filled hair sending the matted mass in my direction.

Because of the high esteem that the members of the church hold for their priesthood leaders such as Elder Loli, and because of the great respect I received, I simply could not get up and leave. To do so while an Area Seventy was speaking, would have been considered disruptive and rude, therefore it wasn't an option.

I just sat there squirming and dusting myself off as rapidly as possible. When I glanced over at Cheryle, she was doing everything in her power not to break into raucous laughter. That lasted until the closing prayer ended, and then she burst out laughing as I jumped up and headed to the rear of the chapel, never taking my eyes off this guy who continued to case the place.

Suddenly, I found myself in police mode. I slipped on my sunglass and when he turned in my direction, he knew that someone whom he didn't want to confront was watching him. I continued this until he finally slipped out the front gate and disappeared down the street.

After Sacrament meeting, we had a five hour training meeting, and then we raced to the airport to catch our flight back to Lima. It was around midnight when we finally pulled into our apartment building. Although we were exhausted, I had the satisfaction of knowing that we had accomplished what the Lord desired. I was really proud of Cheryle. In each and every meeting held, she was invited to share her testimony, which she did without notes and in beautiful Spanish. Her love of the people and their love for her was remarkable and evident no matter where we traveled.

I continued to be amazed at her ability to speak and understand Spanish. As I have mentioned before, she was highly respected and greatly loved by the Saints in Peru, as she was in Ecuador. The Area Presidency, as well as the Director of Temporal Affairs and many of the other leaders in the Area offices, as well as Elder Loli, thought that she was the greatest, and all of them mentioned how blessed the Area was to have her serving there, and how fortunate I was to have her as my eternal companion. I agreed one-hundred percent on both counts. She was one of the few North American Sisters who could communicate in Spanish, and for this reason, the people respected and loved her.

Our flight back to Lima was uneventful. On the next Sunday we were up early and traveling by car up the Pacific Coast toward the towns of Barranca and Huacho. Elder Loli drove the trip of nearly three hours each way. Considering the descriptions I've given of how the majority of drivers operate behind the wheel, one might ask about Elder Loli's driving ability? Cheryle claimed that during the drive up and back, she lost all circulation in her hands because her knuckles were white from gripping the armrest so hard. Each time I looked over at the speedometer, it wasn't below 130 kilometers per mile, or 80 mph, except when he saw a police car in which case he slowed slightly! So, I have named this our "White Knuckle Journey" up the Peruvian coast.

Our first meeting was in Barranca. The day was similar to that of the past Sunday, with attendance at Sacrament meeting, then a full day of training. Again, the reception we received was remarkable. After Barranca, we drove south to Huacho for more meetings and priesthood training. What continued to amaze me was when an Area Seventy requested a meeting, and the priesthood leaders were told of the meeting and advised that special training would be provided, all invited priesthood attended, and not only were gracious, but highly receptive and grateful for the time and teachings.

Our Return to the Cities of the Amazon

A few weeks passed and it was necessary for Elder Loli and me to return to the Amazon Jungle basin. We started in Iquitos, the city made famous in my own mind, by me picking up stomach parasites.

We returned to Iquitos Friday night after working a full day in the office. Saturday afternoon we met with the three stake president's and provided six hours of training. In the mission field and in South America in general, when a presiding authority travels any distance to train the priesthood, the meetings are long and intense. Lunches are provided by the Relief Society, and after a thirty minute break, it is back to work.

Both Elder Loli and I trained the brethren and it was well received.

The temperature was 92 degrees, with 70% humidity. I was the only person in the entire city wearing a suit. The looks I received were almost laughable. There I stood, dark aviator sunglasses, silver hair and a dark suit, coat jacket and all. That is a tough habit to break, for it has been my priesthood uniform for so many years that I believe that habit never will be broken.

Following the lengthy meetings, we returned to our separate hotels anticipating Sunday and more meetings and travel. I went to bed and suddenly felt something crawling up my arm.

I am at war! I thought.

Gently, I leaned over and switched on the light as the enemy continued his aggressive march toward my upper arm. With the stealth of a Navy Seal, I sat up. There he was, moving slowly through the forest created by the hair on my arm. A sinister grin crossed my face. My mind shot back to the thirty flea bites I currently was suffering from that were just beginning to heal. With the precision of a surgeon, my right hand moved toward my vigilant adversary. Suddenly I struck.

"Gottch ya!" I exclaimed with glee.

Between my fingers I now had the first flea I've ever captured in our three assignments to South America; assignments that have seen me suffer through hundreds of bites. With great determination, and a feeling of revenge surging through my body, I squeezed my thumb and forefinger together. I waited. When I opened my fingers, I dropped the flea into the palm of my left hand. There he was.....dead. Then suddenly, the little bugger began to crawl up my hand. I couldn't believe it. It couldn't be! He had to be dead. He was moving as if nothing had happened!

As I honed in for the real kill, his movement increased slightly, and in the blink of an eye, he was gone, having jumped to the floor! My disappointment was evident as my eyes scanned the busy hotel carpet. It was apparent that I had won a small battle, but lost the war. He was gone!

Slowly, I leaned over and turned out the light, hoping that somehow even fleas feel lucky when they have escaped their own demise. I hoped he would not again climb skyward.

Sunday morning, I was up at six. First, we attended a Fast and Testimony meeting, and then prepared for our flight to Pucallpa, another city that sits on the edge of the jungle on the west side of Peru. After our Sacrament meeting, we had about an hour to kill, so we walked up the street for the weekly military parade and band concert. Every branch of the Peruvian military was represented with hundreds of active and retired personnel all dressed in uniform and marching to the cadence of the drums and the squealing of the brass horns.

The members of the military carried rifles with bayonets, but no ammunition clips or live ammunition. The rifles looked wooden; however, the array of uniforms was quite impressive. Flags fluttered in the hot morning breeze, and everyone tried their best to stay in step. Some were better than others which made it fun to watch. When a member of the parade saw one of their friends or family standing on the parade route, they would smile and try to sneak a quick wave.

After the federal forces came the municipal. The police were represented by both men and women who marched in segregated units. I chuckled when I watched the women march by and saw that while they all had a black holster on their hip, no one had been issued a gun. The holsters were empty. They were followed by a very small group of fire fighters, woman's service organizations, youth groups, and then the retired folks.

The final group consisted of women in blue skirts and pale blue jackets. Their average age was at least seventy-five, but there was no way they were going to be left behind. In high heels they shuffled along paying no attention to the drum cadence. From the smiles on their faces and the animated chatter of conversation, it was obvious to see that they were grateful to be alive and able to represent their part of the Iquitos community.

As the five hundred or so parade participants marched through the streets, they eventually came to the parade stand where the band had mounted and the city officials and dignitaries stood and presented salutes. The band played on as column after column marched past. After about thirty minutes, we returned to Elder Loli's hotel and caught a taxi to head to the airport.

Airports in South America were an experience in and of themselves.

As I mentioned the last time I wrote about Iquitos, we only could get to this city via air or water. There were no roads cut through the jungle that entered the city, so the number of cars were limited, taxis being fewer, thus the reason for the mototaxi.

The physical airport structure in Iquitos was a rectangular building about half the size of a football field. There was no air conditioning and no fans in the main concourse area, so when a couple of hundred people were packed in, it was really hot.

We were told that they had not yet determined if we would have a flight, so we waited, and we waited. After ninety minutes, our flight was verified. At this airport, as in many in the jungle, only one plane flies in at a time. This time, we were on Star Peru which is a smaller airline than LAN with flight attendants a notch below those working the major carrier. It isn't that those working for Star didn't do a good job, they did, but it was apparent that physically they did not meet the standards of beauty required by LAN. In Latin America, employers go for beauty and intelligence. There was no Affirmative Action south of the border. If you were a single female interviewing for a job, the employer had the right to ask about your social and sexual life, and they were even able to ask when you last had any sexual relations.

I personally heard this question asked, so I know it happened. The employers also were able to require and request a specific type of look; light skin color, height, weight, figure, bust size, and even a specific length of hair. They controlled every aspect of the hiring process. If they didn't like a woman's looks, she didn't get the job.

Finally, after standing for more than ninety minutes, we were checked through security and into the waiting area. I thought that the general public area was hot. Boy, was I wrong! The pre-boarding area was a smaller room equipped with three floor fans that worked feverously to circulate some of the hot, humid air. I laughed as I watched some maneuver to get as close to the fans as possible, turning the bases to ensure that they were the primary recipients of the blowing air. Others just sat and waited.

After another forty-five minutes, our flight landed, the passengers disembarked and we walked across the tarmac to climb a ladder to get on board. If anyone couldn't climb the ladder, they didn't fly.

The flight was uneventful, and we arrived in Pucallpa in time to grab a sandwich in the small airport restaurant before hailing a taxi and driving to our first meeting.

In Pucallpa, our meetings began at 2:30 p. m. and ended at 9:00 p.m. The meetings held with the stake presidents were what are referred to as Coordinating Council meetings. Being able to have an Area Seventy as my companion, and be invited to these meetings, was quite an honor since this happened nowhere else in the church. This was the only such companionship of its type: Loli and Whitaker; Alma and Amulek.

Medications Held for Ransom

One of the challenges to serving any assignment in a foreign country is to identify the process required to receive your prescription medications. Serving in Lima, we found it more difficult than Ecuador. Let me explain. Here is the Peruvian process I went through to be able to get my necessary medications:

First, I had to have my U. S. doctor supply me with a copy of the prescriptions, the dosage, and the quantity etc. This had to be accompanied by his signature. Next, I had to find a company that delivered to Peru; in my case it was FED EX. I was only allowed to ship three prescriptions at one time, and they had to be accompanied with the required paperwork and necessary documentation. At the FED EX office, I had to pause and take a deep breath because the cost to send two pounds or less to Lima was in the area of $115.00. It was a bit steep, but I had no choice.

Now the fun started. It only took a few days for our box to arrive in Lima, but in order to get it out of Customs, not only did we have to have in our hand our personal copy of the prescriptions signed by our doctor, but also my passport, my Peruvian Identification and some additional cash, as well as a letter from a doctor in Peru stating that I was who I said I was, and the medications were needed. Then all of this had to be approved by the *National Ministry of Health.* My small, inconsequential box of three migraine medications needed to be given the papal blessing by someone representing the federal government! So there it is! It's always best to take all of your medications with you when you go foreign.

It became somewhat of a game to see how long they could hold my medications hostage. I was fortunate in that during our last assignment to Ecuador, our daughter, Jamie, got us what we needed, and this time Don McClelland, in his infinite patience and kind heart, worked through the process with me to see if we could make the system work.

Unfortunately, my medications languished in country for over a week and sat in what I envisioned as a small dark room, on a small out of the way shelf in the catacombs of the Customs office while the paperwork rested at the bottom of a stack of papers in the Ministry of Health.

As I wrote this explanation, a man arrived at the Area offices who, I was told, had been assigned to resolve my problem. In hand, he had a note detailing my prescriptions and began to ask questions about usage, availability, for how long had I taken the medications and how much longer I would be taking them. Additionally, while I did my part, the staff upstairs in the South America Northwest Area offices were trying hard to solve the problem, but it looked like approval to receive the medications monthly, would not be granted.

So the options were either to locate and buy the medications in Peru at an exorbitant price, which would be catastrophic since I received the prescriptions free from the City of Los Angeles due to my stroke in 1981, or stop the medications and hope for the best, or punt. I placed it in the Lord's hands. I had done all I could do. Now, only time would tell.

I walked upstairs, and after stepping into the office of Andres Ramos, who was the Director of Temporal Affairs for the Area, I explained to him the problem. An hour later, much of the problem was resolved which meant I might see the box Don McClelland sent. Finally, on October 15, the ransom was paid and the medications were delivered.

Our Efforts Acknowledged by the First Presidency

On April 1, 2010, Elders John Carmack and Richard E. Cook, presented our work of the past eight months to the First Presidency of the Church of Jesus Christ of Latter-day Saints. What began as a concept in the minds of Elder Carmack and Elder Cook, became a pilot program and then, with the presentation to the First Presidency, it became an Area program designed to involve the priesthood and rescue the Lost Sheep involved in the Perpetual Education Fund program.

To accomplish this, the effort was placed under the direction of the Area Seventy. They in turn worked closely with their stake presidents. My role was to train the Area Seventy in the new program and accompany them while they visited the stakes. This, coupled with the changed and increased involvement of the Call Center PEF specialists, whom I label as specialists because I do not believe this to be a volunteer church, but one of assignment and accountability, the development of this program with its implementation that realized a success not before seen in this type of a program in the church.

It was humbling to see a photograph of Cheryle and me on one of the slides presented to the First Presidency. It also was amusing when I was told that Cheryle's quote, "I love my job!" was shared with the Presidency and brought a smile to

OUR EFFORTS ACKNOWLEDGED
BY THE FIRST PRESIDENCY

President Monson's face as he enjoyed her positive attitude and exuberance for the work.

In May, Elder Loli was released, and I was given the charge to outline and implement a program that would see twelve Area Seventies trained in this effort. It was designed to stress the spiritual and not the financial side of the Perpetual Education Fund, an emphasis that had been ignored for the past ten years, even though we all know that all things are first spiritual, then temporal. Unfortunately, the cart was put before the horse, and for several years, many had been negatively impacted and had fallen away. It was the goal of this program, and the desire of the First Presidency and our South America Northwest Area Presidency, to reverse this trend and return the Lost Sheep through priesthood correlation. The ultimate goal was to see the Perpetual Education Fund Participants hold current temple recommends, and those who didn't have a recommend, to secure one and see them return to the Temple with a better understanding of the making and keeping of sacred covenants. It was that simple.

What began as an assignment for a missionary couple became a unique team effort that involved three General Authorities, twelve Area Seventies, five countries, and an entire PEF Area team that also included nine Call Center specialists. Although I was but a soldier in the operation, I was given the responsibility to plan, organize, direct, coordinate and control the effort while training the Seventy. I cannot express what type of experience that was. I also was given a new nickname by the brethren: "The General!"

I still believe that "El Soldado" would be more appropriate, but having the respect of great men has been, and continues to be, a blessing.

Machu Picchu

Christmas this year was different than any we have celebrated either at home or in South America. On Thursday, December 17, 2009, Shannyn, our eldest daughter, her husband Greg and their three boys, Jake, Nick and Nate arrived in Lima for a two week stay.

Before knowing about our assignment to Peru, Greg and Shannyn booked a trip to Lima during Christmas that would allow Greg to attend a wedding for one of his coworkers. When they heard we would be assigned to Peru, they offered us a once in a lifetime Christmas present; a trip to Machu Picchu and Lake Titicaca. The week spent traveling to those locations was remarkable.

They arrived at our apartment after being picked up at the airport by a driver we had secured. That night we spent getting settled, and then Friday, using the same van and driver, we headed into Central Lima to visit many of the historic locations that included several cathedrals, and watching the guard change in front of the Governor's Palace. It was a great day!

Saturday, at four-thirty in the morning, we were on our way to the airport for our flight to Cusco.

The flight was short and uneventful. Shortly after we arrived in Cusco, which was at a higher elevation than Lima, I began to feel the effects of the altitude change. After checking into our Four Star hotel which had been secured by Greg, we walked the streets and visited a number of old cathedrals and museums. We then had lunch at a pizza restaurant. That was my first mistake. I have mentioned before that this assignment was brutal on the head because of migraine headaches and also my gastrointestinal system. In Cuzco, the health issues were intensified.

The pizza made me violently ill, and I immediately was struck with a migraine. I returned to our hotel and was sequestered in a dark room for the remainder of the afternoon. That migraine continued for the next seven days, but fortunately was controlled by medication. Nevertheless, the pain and discomfort never abated. An additional reason for the headache was that we were now at 13,000 feet. Saturday in Cusco was a bust. *Whitaker,* I cynically thought, *this is a great way to see one of the wonders of the world!*

In Cusco, we stayed at the Libertador which was a marvelous hotel. Sunday, found us in another van traveling the eight hour drive to Ollantaytambo which sat in the Andes. It was from here that we took a ninety minute train ride on PERURAIL up the mountains and through the passes on our way to Machu Picchu. It is difficult to put into words the thrill it was traveling on this restored train as it slowly plowed its way through the Andean canyons and up the mountain. From the windows, we watched as ancient Inca terraces that were carved into the mountains crisscrossed the landscape and connected the Inca Trail with the ancient city of Machu Picchu.

The railway paralleled a sacred river, so on one side we had the fast moving water, and on the other were the steep cliffs of the mountains. Dispersed in the mountains were remnants of Inca walls, homes and other buildings.

When the train ride ended, we found ourselves in the small town of Agua Caliente where we climbed on special tour busses that transported us to the entrance of Machu Picchu. But I'm ahead of myself. Agua Caliente offered us two very different experiences.

First, the hotel that Greg had made reservations at was a place called Gringo Bill's. Seriously, that was the name of the hotel. After getting off the train, we grabbed our rolling luggage (Greg and Shannyn bought us new travel suitcases since we didn't have any in Peru) and schlepped our suitcases through the markets and in and out of the side streets. Finally, after asking directions more than once, we saw a small sign nailed to a wall that had an arrow pointing up another incline. "Gringo Bill's" was painted below the arrow. The size of the sign and its location should have warned us of the adventure that would come.

The hotel was located on the side of a steep hill. After a healthy climb up a number of steps, we came to the entrance. While we all waited in the dark lobby, Greg walked up to the front desk and gave the receptionist our information. "I am sorry, but we don't have any reservations for you, Senior Gardner." Like a cat on a hot tin roof, Greg changed gears and became a little more forceful. After another short conversation, the receptionist told Greg that his reservations had been cancelled and they had "no room at the inn."

With that, Greg's voice raised two octaves, and I turned and walked toward the door. Greg told the receptionist that we had reserved three rooms, and would take those three on any of the four floors of the hotel, and I'm using the term hotel loosely. Hostel might be more appropriate, but we will leave it with a loose translation of hotel. Better yet, I would refer to it as the "Old Bates Motel." If you never have seen the Alfred Hitchcock movie, *Psycho,* you will not understand the reference, and may have to look it up. For those who have seen the film, the structural edifice of this place could be the twin to the Bates Motel! To add to the incredulity of the situation was the fact that other than our group, only two of the rooms in the entire place were occupied. *Full?* I thought.

"Oh, but one of the three rooms is not ready," Greg was told. "But it will be soon."

It appeared that December was their off season. Weren't we lucky!

So, now you have a very unhappy Greg, Shannyn, Cheryle and the three boys who are tired and hungry, and Elder Whitaker trying to remember that he, for the first time while traveling, actually was wearing his missionary tag.

That's right; I usually don't wear the tag when I am on the street. Cheryle wears hers, and that is sufficient.

After about an hour, we were told that the rooms were ready, so with suitcases in hand, Greg, Shannyn, three tired boys and Cheryle with two bum knees, and I began our climb to the fourth floor of the hotel.

I forgot to mention another important fact. When we walked into the hotel lobby, we noted that it was quite dark. Then we saw the candles and were told that all the electricity in the town had gone off about three hours earlier, and they thought it would be restored sometime the next day! Fortunately, we still had sunlight to guide us up the treacherous rock stairs, but at night, that would be a different story.

Slowly, we trudged up the steps. Cheryle firmly placed one foot in front of the other and never complained about the pain. If you haven't guessed it by now, Hermana Whitaker is quite a trooper, especially since she had done the South America mission assignment three times.

Once we made it to the fourth floor, we all stopped to catch our breath. We found the three rooms, but discovered ours was still not ready, so Cheryle and I found a couple of seats on a veranda and spent the time scanning the city below. After about thirty minutes, our room was ready. Entering the room, I flipped the light switch; still nothing. About ten minutes passed and a hotel employee brought a candle and matches to each room. While Greg, Shannyn the boys and Cheryle opted to take a walk in the remaining sunlight, I chose to wait in the room, sit on the porch and read.

About an hour passed before they returned. Greg had a flashlight in hand for each room. Slowly, darkness closed in on the Andes, but before it fell, Cheryle and I decided to take one last tour of the small town nestled in the mountains. We walked down the stone steps and into the lobby, and then stepped out onto a narrow cobblestone street. Making a hard left, we took a short walk and found ourselves in the plaza.

On one side of the plaza were small cafes, and on the other stood a small church. We headed toward the cafes where we were confronted by an old drunk whistling and screaming at the top of his lungs, "MACHU PICCHU! MACHU PICCHU!" Suddenly he stepped in front of Cheryle and grabbed her arms! Immediately, I stepped between him and Cheryle causing him to loosen his grip. Then he grabbed me, and continued to whistle and scream, "MACHU PICCHU….MACHU PICCHU!" My first reaction was to slug the guy in the mouth, but I didn't, because the thought raced through my mind, *Remember who you represent, Richard.*

As I broke his grip on my arms, two waiters grabbed him and pulled him out of my reach. If was after that incident that I again had confirmed to me that although they have uniformed police walking the streets in Peru, they are of no value what-so-ever. None! Basically, you are on your own.

After that excitement, we walked away, but my adrenaline was still pumping and I was angry that some drunken clown would touch my wife. So I told Cheryle I was going back to "Have a talk with the guy," but she became adamant that we just move on down the street and leave it alone. As badly as I wanted to return to the scene of the crime, I didn't. The old saying, "You can take the cop off the street, but you cannot take the street out of the cop," is so true.

Exhausted, we trekked back to the hotel and up to the fourth floor. After about another hour in the candle light haze, the lights went on. A roar erupted from all four corners of the small village, the music started again and the cracking of firecrackers and bottle rockets again filled the air. Agua Caliente was a nice place to visit, but I wouldn't want to spend another night there.

The next morning we were up early for the bus ride to Machu Picchu. Travel books fail to capture the magnificence and grandeur of the ancient city. Leaving the bus, we were surrounded by clouds and pelted by rain and a heavy mist.

We climbed the ruins for over three hours, and Cheryle never said a word about her knees, although I was certain that she was in pain. What I found interesting was that when we arrived at the entrance to the ruins, the mountain was shrouded in clouds and it was raining heavily, but as time passed, the rain stopped, leaving us in a cloud shrouded place of enchantment. We also were blessed to have a wonderful guide named Franklin Cuba. He was knowledgeable and spoke English which helped the three boys enjoy the site far more than if we had a guide who spoke only Spanish. Machu Picchu truly is one of the wonders of the world.

Walking through the heavy mist and climbing the solid rock edifices allowed my mind to reflect upon the majesty of this people and the cruel, lustful intent of the Spaniards to destroy them. It's a sad commentary to the greed of man.

Leaving the site, we boarded our bus and travelled back to the "Bates Motel" where we got our luggage and headed for Puno and Lake Titicaca; but before we left, Cheryle was involved in another incident. This time it was very positive.

While Greg was checking us out, Cheryle walked to the post office located down the narrow street just in front of the hotel. When I looked out the lobby window, she was surrounded by about twenty young women and was carrying on an animated conversation. It turned out that they were in Peru doing service for their church and wanted to know why Cheryle was here. The group was from Australia and was captivated by the blond norteamericana. Another teaching moment presented itself as she quickly slipped into the nature of our assignment to Lima.

From Agua Caliente, we climbed back into our van and headed for Puno. Upon our arrival, we were more than grateful again to be staying at another Libertador Hotel. We slept well that night and were up early the next morning for our trip on Lake Titicaca, which is the largest navigable fresh water lake in the world. Our guide for the day picked us up and we walked from the hotel to the boat landing.

Setting out in the boat, we traveled to the famous floating reed islands inhabited by the Uros Indians. They were remarkable, as were the very humble and highly religious people that inhabited the islands. We quickly made friends, and felt an instantaneous bond with the two families we visited. We were able to buy some wonderful hand woven tapestries. From there we travelled across the lake for two hours to a larger island where we had lunch. While Greg, Shannyn and the boys hiked the island, Cheryle and I went back to the boat and travelled around the island to meet the kids. Then we had another two hour boat trip back to the hotel. After a wonderful dinner, we headed for our rooms. The next day we traveled by van to the airport and then back to Lima. All in all, it was a remarkable week. We were back in our apartment on Christmas Eve. Both Cheryle and I will forever be grateful for an opportunity we would not have had were it not for Shannyn and Greg.

Terror in a Taxi

It was March 8, 2010 and Elder Loli and I were back in the Amazon Jungle. We had travelled to Pucallpa to meet with the stake president and other leaders in a Coordinating Council meeting. After the meeting, we held a Perpetual Education Fund meeting for leaders, the youth and their parents. From this one stake, we had approximately two hundred in attendance while in the three stakes in Iquitos, about seventy-five attended. Leadership makes such a difference.

We left the location of the meeting and walked down a dark side street onto the main street where we hailed a mototaxi, who, for one dollar, took us to the airport. With Elder Loli and me in the back seat, and our luggage and his computer stacked on his lap, that little motorcycle engine struggled, coughed and chugged all the way.

We checked in at a near empty airport and waited until we were advised that we could begin the process to clear security. After passing through security and entering the waiting area, my boarding pass with the tariff stamp was scanned.

"Oh, Señor Whitaker, you are on the preferred customer list," said an attractive airline employee. "You will board first." How that happened, I did not know, but as I was moved to another line, Elder Loli only smiled and gave me a wink. That worked for me. Women, children, the sick, lame and the lazy, and the gringo in a suit, all pre-boarded. Unfortunately, Elder Loli was in the longer line and his seat was about ten rows behind mine.

The flight from Pucallpa to Lima was uneventful, but once we landed, the excitement began. We touched down at 11:30 p.m. I was tired, but not so tired that I had lost my edge.

Elder Loli found us a taxi that cost twenty-five dollars to my apartment and then back to his car which was parked at the Mission Training Center.

We got in, and left a very crowded airport. At first, the ride was uneventful with the driver adroitly maneuvering through the freeway traffic and then onto the main streets. About ten minutes into the ride, I noticed that his driving had become erratic. It didn't dawn on me that we had a problem until another taxi driver pulled alongside and started yelling out the window at our driver. Our driver said nothing, just slowly pulled forward when the light changed green. Then, down the street we roared, and suddenly, he slowed down, crossed into two other lanes, then back into our lane and crept to a stop at the signal.

The dude is loaded, I thought.

I looked over at Elder Loli and he had his eyes closed, oblivious to what was going on.

When the signal changed to green, the driver hesitated, then slammed the gas pedal to the floor and roared down the street. When we hit a straight-away, the car slowed, then sped up to about fifty and slowed again as we veered to the left and toward a curb and center divider. Straining, I looked into the driver's rearview mirror…..his eyes were closed. Unbelievably, the guy was asleep! I glanced over at Elder Loli. He also was resting his eyes, while this clown roared up and down the street with Whitaker in the backseat of an out of control two thousand pound projectile. Dying in a traffic accident in Lima, Peru was not on my to-do list, so the cop that's still part of me, took over.

Angered, my right arm reared back and leaning forward, I slammed my right fist into the driver's right shoulder and screamed in his ear…"Wake up! Open your eyes!"

My blow slammed his shoulder against the driver's door and his hands that had dropped to his lap suddenly flew to the steering wheel as he pulled his head out of the headliner. His eyes shot open, and as he straightened out the car, I could see that the sleep from his eyes had given way to abject terror not knowing what the crazy gringo in the back seat would do next. Looking in the rearview mirror, I could tell from his eyes that in his mind, he was terrified that my next blow would probably send him flying out the door and down the street!

TERROR IN A TAXI

Quickly, I glanced over at Elder Loli. He was sitting in quiet desperation to my right, his eyes wide open, staring straight forward! It appeared that he thought I was yelling at him!

My eyes shot again to the rear view mirror. The driver appeared to be awake, but then suddenly, I watched as his eyes began to close. Leaning forward to where my mouth was close to his ear, I screamed like a drill sergeant in the Marine Corp…… "Open your eyes!"

Again, his eyes flew open as his body shook and tensed in anticipation of a second blow that never came. Now he was awake and trembling.

My next counsel might shock some, but without a second thought, I shouted into his ear, "If you need to get a cup of coffee, do it, because I am not dying in your cab!"

Throughout the experience, Elder Loli didn't say a word, just continued to sit, his face pale, his eyes open and a small quiver showing on his bottom lip. I was so sorry that he thought my threats were at first directed towards him, but when we arrived at my apartment and I explained the situation, he roared with hearty laughter, first at me, then the driver, and finally at himself.

Cheryle Blows a Fuse!

It was a Monday morning. Down the hall in the South America Northwest Area conference room, there was a large special meeting of the ten new mission presidents assigned to the Area. The meeting included the presidents, their wives, the Area Presidency, Andres Ramos the Director of Temporal Affairs and Javier Gonzalez, the Area Systems Manager.

Winter had set in, and as it became increasingly cold in our office, Cheryle decided to plug in our small heater. Climbing under her desk, she pushed the plug in and returned to her chair. About ten seconds passed, and then suddenly, all the computers in half the building shut down, including ours. That encompassed the computers and audio-visual machines being used for the mission president's presentation. I was told that everyone in the room looked at Javier Gonzalez thinking it was a computer systems failure. Little did anyone know that it was Cheryle's small heater that caused the problem. When she plugged the heater into the wrong socket, it blew fifteen circuits and shut down half the building!

She knew immediately that she had caused the problem. Shooting me a look of distress, she sheepishly whispered, "I think I just blew the circuits!"

I didn't say a word, but walked out of the office and found Rudy, our building maintenance supervisor. When he came to our office, he verified that the plug Cheryle used was not configured to handle the heater, so he plugged it into another outlet and all was fine. Cheryle later told Andres Ramos she was sorry for shutting down his presentation.

"You are a very honest person, Hermana Whitaker," he said.

The entire office building had a good laugh over that one incident and Cheryle learned that before she plugged anything in, she first needed to verify that the outlet could handle the increased workload.

Cheryle earned herself a new name—"The UL Lady," with UL standing for the Underwriters Laboratory, but that was not where the story ended.

Later, she was moved across the hall into an area previously used by Henry Utrilla, the Call Center Manager, and Henry was moved into Cheryle's area in my office. This was done for a number of reasons, with me being asked for my approval before it happened.

It was another cold morning and by lunchtime, the offices had not heated up. So after lunch, Cheryle did the logical thing; she plugged in her small space heater located on the floor adjacent to her desk. As she slid the plug into the electronic strip, there was a loud "POP," and just as suddenly as the last time when she shut down all the computers in half the building, it happened again! But this time it was different.

Instead of everyone milling around trying to figure out what had occurred, half the first floor of the building rushed into the long corridor and in unison, began to laugh and point at Cheryle as she stepped out of her office. It was quite funny, since it was a repeat performance of a month earlier. Soon, the entire corridor was filled with people laughing and chanting, "Hermana Whitaker, Hermana Whitaker!"

When it was verified that Cheryle once again had blown the main circuits by plugging in the small heater, Javier Gonzalez again referred to Cheryle by her nickname of the "UL Lady." He explained that had it not been for her second test of the system, they would not have known that the problem persisted. Within minutes, all computers were back up and running and a new procedure for plugging in the space heater was developed!

Peru's Answer to the French Guillotine

On a crisp winter afternoon in the city of Lima, we nearly lost Sister Whitaker when she almost became the victim to the Peruvian answer of the French guillotine. I called ours the Guillotine de Grifo since the beast stood at the entrance to our office complex on a street named Grifo.

One notable difference however was that in France, the blade was made of sharpened steel; in Lima, it was crafted from two large, thick pieces of lumber that were the two motorized cross-bars allowing ingress and egress to the Area office parking lot. Okay, I know I have piqued your curiosity, so I will elaborate.

One day when we were returning to the office after lunch, we decided to enter the facility via the vehicular driveway rather than use the pedestrian door which was adjacent to the driveway and controlled by security personnel. Walking briskly, Cheryle stepped into the driveway where the two heavy wooden cross-bars were both in an upright and open position. And even though there was a sign posted warning pedestrians to use the pedestrian door, we saw the path clear and decided to shoot the curl and enter through the vehicle zone, blatantly ignoring the warning sign.

As Cheryle stepped forward, someone in a car called her name, and then drove off. With a smile on her face, she stepped forward just as the cross-bars were lowered. Now one might think that these two messengers of severe blunt force trauma would be lowered slowly. Wrong! Nothing could be further from the truth. This was South America, and when the wheels of security were in motion, they traveled faster and with more force than Superman fleeing from a piece of rogue kryptonite.

As the bars fell toward the center of Cheryle's head, I screamed at her while the security guard flew out of his office shouting a panicked warning in his loudest and most incoherent Spanish. Fortunately, Cheryle froze just as the left cross-bar slammed down, missing her nose by mere inches while brushing against the front of her coat and sliding down her leather jacket. Had she been more womanly endowed, she immediately would have lost a few pounds.

Startled, she stood frozen yelling to the guard about how sorry she was to have caused him any discomfort. Never did she express any fear or concern about herself, but was more concerned at causing the guard to fly out of his security booth in an action that probably took ten years off his life. As I stood behind her and assessed the situation, I could see that had the cross-bar struck her on the top of the head, it would have broken her neck. While some might think that she was just lucky to have eluded what would have been a fatal accident, I knew that she was protected by unseen hands.

Do Not Defile the House of the Lord

On Saturday, June 19, we had a meeting of the Lima Norte Coordinating Council. The meeting was attended by Elder Carlos Solis, a new Area Seventy, sixteen stake presidents, a district president, and President Perez, the Lima Norte Mission President, President Bowman, President of the Lima Temple, and one soldier, Elder Whitaker. To sit in that room and have the responsibility to teach these priesthood leaders was a humbling experience.

President Perez, President Bowman and I each were given twenty minutes. I went first. My training was directed toward errant members of the church; those who had made a covenant with the Lord to pay back their Perpetual Education Fund loan, and were not keeping their commitment. I explained that these individuals, leaders and members alike, had received loans from the sacred funds of the Lord, and in not keeping that commitment, were robbing God. It was that simple. I pointed no fingers; however, as I looked around that room, I was aware that more than one priesthood leader fell into the delinquent category. After I concluded my remarks, I sat down. You could have heard a pin drop.

President Bowman then addressed the topic of Temple work, and after some housekeeping items, he asked the stake presidents to turn to Doctrine and Covenants 97: 15-17. He proceeded to read the verses and explained that the doctrine taught that when one entered the temple unworthily, the

Spirit did not enter. And if the Sprit failed to enter with one person, it would not be in attendance in the temple nor in the particular session attended by that unworthy member. When he finished, the room was stone cold silent and a look of astonishment could be read on the faces of those in attendance. He then went on to further explain that those with current recommends had three financial responsibilities:

1. Tithing

2. Offerings

3. The Perpetual Education Fund

Since President Bowman had been a mission president in Lima, the Lima MTC president and also the Lima Temple president, he was well qualified to teach the priesthood leaders. I could not suppress my delight when he finished and I told him so. He smiled, and from that moment on, he would be a great support to me.

This was critical in that in the beginning of this assignment, I did have some in Salt Lake arch their backs and bow their necks at the fact that I first was stressing the spiritual aspect of the program while also addressing the fact that many who possessed a current temple recommend were late in their payments, and some priesthood leaders, including stake presidents, had not made a payment in six years. Those few in Salt Lake balked at my asking if someone 150 or more days late held a temple recommend. That was all that was asked. They needed only to respond, yes or no. Nothing more. Nothing about worthiness was addressed; that was the responsibility of the stake presidents and bishops. So while the few in Salt Lake balked, the priesthood leaders in the Area were thrilled with the information, and through their efforts, change ensued.

I was delighted that one, who held the keys, spoke, taught doctrine and addressed a critical worthiness issue.

At the conclusion of President Bowman's remarks, there was no doubt in anyone's mind about what was taught. When he sat down next to me after one such session, I leaned over and thanked him. He smiled and we agreed that what we were doing was helping to change a cultural mindset. I later was told that he addressed this issue again in other Coordinating Council's where the problems also were severe.

When one was given the responsibility to do something which never had been done before, it was wonderful to have the total support of those presiding. I literally can say that I stood amazed at what the Lord allowed us to accomplish when we listened to the promptings of the Spirit and followed the Brethren.

When the meeting ended, my driver was there and we began the long, difficult trip home. Traffic in Lima normally was horrible, but on Saturday night, the streets resembled the Los Angeles freeway system at rush hour. Gridlock would be an appropriate description.

My driver, seeing that the main streets were jammed, decided to try some side streets, so off we went weaving through the ghettos of Lima. Unfortunately, other drivers had the same idea, and within a short period of time we ended up on a one-way-street with traffic stopped. Nothing was moving. I looked around at the area, and had I not been with a driver secured through the church, I would have sworn that I was being driven into areas where robbery would have been the motive; it was that dangerous.

So, there we were not able to move forward, but we had some space behind. Slowly, we began to back up, then with great skill, he got us turned around and in minutes we were back on one of the main streets. Inch by inch we were trudging forward, when suddenly, I heard a band playing. The music sounded like a funeral dirge. Looking to my right, I watched as a large band and about one hundred dancers moved slowly up a dark side-street. The rippling of their bodies looked like a wave moving across a darkened sea. As they came closer, I saw that in the middle of the group was a large platform being carried on the shoulders of a group of men. On top of the platform was a large replica of a specific Saint worshipped by the members of the community. Yes, some communities have their own patron saints. The entire event was made more interesting in that the street was poorly lit, and as the procession passed under a dim light, it more resembled a funeral procession than a festive religious activity.

After nearly an hour, we arrived safely at my apartment. It was the end of a long day and very interesting night.

Required to Return to United States

In August I received notification from the City of Los Angeles that I was required to travel from Lima back to Henderson, Nevada and meet with my Worker's Compensation Physician, Dr. Lisa Haworth for an examination. Failure to keep the appointment would see my Worker's Compensation life-time medical benefits placed in jeopardy and my prescriptions, which were approved and paid for by the City of Los Angeles, cancelled.

It didn't take a brain surgeon to figure out what I would be doing in the future. I contacted Elder Nash and advised him of the situation. He then contacted Elder Clayton, our Area contact and one of the Seven Presidents of the Seventy. At first, Elder Clayton suggested that we end our mission and return to Henderson. However, after Elder Nash explained the criticality of our assignment, Elder Clayton agreed that it would be best if we made a quick trip back, have the appointment and return to Lima.

When I notified President Ivan Holland, our stake president of the requirement to return home for a week, he, knowing the criticality of our assignment and the fact that we had been hand chosen for the work, offered to assist in offsetting some of the cost for the airline tickets. This was greatly appreciated and with his help, we made the plans.

The week of October 4th through the 12th was blocked out for this trip. I contacted Dr. Haworth and we scheduled an appointment. Then I advised our Area Travel representative that I would need tickets. An interesting side note: when I spoke to Elder Nash on the telephone, I was positive that he said I would be returning to Henderson…alone. While that did not ring true, when I talked to travel, I advised them I would need only one round trip flight ticket. When I was given the flight packet, there were tickets for both Cheryle and me. When I told Cheryle that she was now going, she was happy, but wanted me to promise to let Elder Nash know of the ticket mix-up. I was able to speak to him at church, and when I explained the situation, he told us to go, take care of the appointment, and then return.

I wanted the trip to be kept under wraps, so other than Dr. Haworth and Dr. Tait knowing we were coming, only Don McClelland was notified. I notified Dr. Tait, first because he was our bishop, and secondly I needed an appointment with him because of the severe pain I was experiencing in the top of my right foot. I also wanted his opinion as to the feasibility of removing the steel plate and screws he had placed in my left ankle after our last assignment to Quito.

At 8:30 p.m. on the night of October 4, we were picked up by our personal driver, Eric Noel and driven to the Lima Airport. We checked our luggage with LAN Airlines and after paying our tariff of $31.00 each, we headed for the security screening. Because I won't carry luggage onto an International flight, it was relatively easy passing through security. Then we headed for the boarding gate. This is when it became interesting. During this flight experience, we underwent new screening procedures both in Lima and Los Angeles; but first, Lima.

While we were seated in the boarding area, there was a sudden flurry of activity in front of the ticket counter. We watched as seven LAN employees, all very young, began to bring small square plastic tables and some chairs into the area. Then, for the next two hours, we watched what only can be described as a three-ring circus minus the Ringmaster.

First, the tables were lined up in one place, and the entrance to three boarding lines established. Then, not satisfied with the first arrangement, everything was changed to a different configuration. This was repeated five times; each time allowing a different employee to make what they believed to be the best configuration. Then it happened…right before pre-boarding, the arrangement was approved.

All passengers were told to secure a spot in one of the three lines according to their seat assignment. Those in wheelchairs or needing special assistance were advised to come to the front. When I saw employees behind the tables putting on surgical gloves, I understood what was going to happen.

Our flight had been chosen to be involved in a security training exercise for the new LAN employees!

First, two very elderly women about eighty years old were wheeled up in their wheelchairs to the first plastic table. They were gently lifted from the chair, and patted down. Then as they stood trembling, their purses were dumped on the table and all carry-on items were searched thoroughly. Both Cheryle and I were also patted down, and when we passed the search, having no carry-on items, we were allowed to board the plane. All two hundred plus passengers went through the same experience as had the elderly women. EVERYONE! They were patted down, purses dumped and all luggage hand searched.

The flight to Los Angeles was uneventful, except for the five hour layover at LAX until our American Airlines flight to Las Vegas became available. Since we knew the procedure, we headed directly out of the International Terminal and into the rain to get to the Domestic Terminal. Arriving at the long line for the security check, we were told it would be at least an hour and a half because the terror level had been elevated. About this time, another little miracle occurred. An airline employee took nearly thirty of us from the rear of the line and walked us back to the same area we just had left. We were told we would go through security at this point and then be bussed back to our gate.

The beginning of the security routine was the same as before at LAX, that is until we both were asked to step out of line and proceed to the x-ray machine. That's right, the silver haired guy in a suit and wearing the sun glasses, along with the blond, again were patted down and x-rayed! Fortunately, we passed and were escorted to a bus to be driven to our American Airlines boarding gate. The flight to Las Vegas was short, and we were met at the airport by Don McClelland, the greatest friend one could ask for!

The itinerary for the week then was discussed with Don. Oh, I forgot something. A week before we left Lima, I received an e-mail from Lisa Haworth advising me that she had been diagnosed with breast cancer and her chemotherapy would begin the week we were scheduled for my city medical. She told me not to worry since one of her friends, a neurologist, would handle my appointment. Other medical appointments had been scheduled for me with Drs. Tait and Torgesen. Cheryle also had an appointment with her doctor.

The days were busy as were the nights, and we felt like ducks out of water being somewhere that felt foreign. Prior to our arrival, Warren Gray, our son-in-law, spent weeks cleaning the house and doing yard work. As we entered our home, it still held the same sweet spirit as it did when we left over a year ago. However, we both felt awkward being in Henderson at this time and could not wait to get back to work in Lima.

After the medical appointments, I was advised by Dr. Tait that the plate and five pins in my left ankle could come out since it was causing some discomfort. I also had two bones in the top of the right foot rubbing against each other which had caused arthritis and a bone spur. However, no bones were broken. It was recommended that a staple be placed in the bones of the right foot allowing the bones to fuse, thus eliminating the pain. After further discussion, it was recommended that I receive a shot in the foot every four months rather than the surgery.

Our return to Lima was uneventful and our release date from the assignment was scheduled for the 27th of February; that was unless our assignment had been finished and my medical issues became unbearable. Then, we would leave early, which is what happened.

Fiestas in Lima

It started as a low rumble; a slow moving wave of sound that eventually reached our fourth floor apartment. Instantly, the windows began to shake and the ground trembled. At first, I thought that it was an earthquake. However, when I opened the front glass window, my ears were met by a loud, high pitched scream that overshadowed the rumble and shattered the quiet Friday evening. I looked at my watch. It was ten o'clock. The Friday night rock concert at Jockey Plaza had started. Then, from my right came another scream and a different rock band came to life in what appeared to be a quest to scream louder and more often while playing harder than the group at Jockey. As the intensity mounted, a third paper shredding scream that sounded like fingernails clawing at a blackboard entered the mix! It was indescribable. Within six blocks, we had three bands vying for the attention of their audiences. This battle of the bands would continue unabated until nearly three in the morning.

To add to the problem, directly behind our bedroom, was a vast fenced-in-area and a private residence that was rented out for concerts and parties lasting twenty-four hours a day for up to three days at a time. The residential property line was fifteen feet from our back bedroom window, with the residence about a hundred yards from that. The fence dividing the properties was about twenty feet in height with an additional twenty feet of canvas attached to the top of the wall. Since we were above the fence and behind only canvas, the noise flowed unabated into our bedroom.

You have all heard of the Bermuda Triangle? We now were living in the Devil's Triangle of Rock and Roll, and since the police and the Mayor were paid very well to look the other way, they refused to enforce noise restrictions. It appeared that this would be our lot while we served in Lima or until we moved.

The noise became so intolerable that we finally moved two twin beds together in the spare bedroom and hoped that the next battle of the bands would find us in a quieter room with less window space and thicker concrete walls. Unfortunately, it didn't work. Not only did we find that we had to contend with the bands on a regular basis, but now added to the mix were the private parties which surrounded our apartment. The last party came the night before a national holiday. It began at two one afternoon and ended at five the next morning. While we thought that the holiday was the cause for the celebration, we later learned that it was a wedding celebration. We have grown accustomed to the fact that the noise, parties, and lost sleep were the price to be paid for living in Lima.

There was one party that began at 2:30 in the afternoon and lasted until 4:30 in the morning; a tortuous fourteen hours with the bass volume set at full capacity. It was the loudest rock and roll I had ever heard.

What was interesting was that no one in the area complained. In another effort to get some sleep, we decided to take the sofa cushions from the chairs and couches and put them on the front room floor in the corner room that was farthest from the bedroom noise. We closed all the doors hoping that we could sleep, even if it required sleeping on the floor.

That too, didn't work.

After the marathon rock concert on July 3, I enlisted Olger Lopez, one of the tenacious young men who worked in the Perpetual Education Call Center, to set his sights on helping me eradicate the problem. When I first gave him the assignment, he immediately ran with it.

First, he went to the office of the Acalde (Mayor) and secured a petition which they told him would need to be signed by all the complaining neighbors and accompanied by a letter from me and my personal documents and identification. Also requested were supporting documents such as photographs, etc. Olger had me complete the top part of the petition, and then he placed it at the front security post for our area and asked the vigilantes, or security guards to secure the signatures. Within a week, we had the names, addresses and identification numbers of twenty-seven neighbors who were signing the complaint. We were on a roll.

I then wrote a letter to the office of the Acalde and submitted it with the two page petition. Yet, with all that work and effort, the problem continued. The massive parties and music continued to blast through enormous speakers. The activities occurred on Wednesdays, Thursdays, and each Friday and Saturday night. At times, it involved two massive homes to our rear and a large home in front, all three rocking at the same time.

Wanting to see the exact locations where each party was held, I walked up to the fifth floor of our building. There, I found a metal ladder that protruded through a small square hole granting access to the roof. In my suit, I climbed onto the roof and walked over to the ledge, where I was able to view the largest homes, both of which were rented out for the parties. They were incredible residences, each with a swimming pool, massive green laws, and one even had a large enclosed patio that seated at least seventy-five guests. With that, I knew what I was up against. Armed with information and confident that the local police were receiving additional funds for turning the other way, Cheryle and I decided it was time to find a new apartment and make a move. We had stayed at this location for a year, and that was more than enough. After our assignment ended and we were back in the States, I learned that although thirty neighbors had signed the petition, nothing was done since the owners were personal friends of the Mayor. When Olger called us, we were advised that the old Mayor had been removed and a new one installed which eliminated the noise.

Throughout this difficult time of dealing with unbearable noise, we were very busy. During a mission conference we met with Elder D. Todd Christofferson of the Quorum of the Twelve; we travelled up the Amazon River; visited native villages, and humble wards then flew back to another area of jungle and a city named Pucallpa; and we conducted a number of meetings with church leaders in Peru. This was accompanied by the continued organization and coordination of our assignment.

Should We Rob the Silver Haired Gringo?

How I did it, I did not know, but I developed my third urinary tract infection within a sixteen month period of time. Dr. Slingerland, the mission doctor for the South America Northwest Area advised me to walk down to a pharmacy and pick up the required antibiotic; so, with paper in hand, off I went.

The day was one of the first we had where the sun was actually shining. Yet, even with the sunshine and increased heat, I still wore my suit coat, something many senior missionaries never did unless they were at a Sunday or special meeting. Yet, old habits were hard to break…for me, impossible. No matter where I was, except while in the office, I wore my coat. I did this always to remind me of who I was and who I represented. If I was in a suit and tie, I was also wearing the coat. I was never without mine because I just didn't feel adequately dressed without it, and since the jacket hid my weapon for many years, it was just natural to wear it.

I left the Area office building and decided to take the long way to the pharmacy. So there I was walking down the street; suit and tie, silver hair, dark aviator sunglasses, my shoulders thrown back and a stride that reeked confidence and indicated I had somewhere to go.

The walk to the pharmacy was uneventful. I made my purchase and started back along Avenida Tristain. The street was wide with two traffic lanes traveling in each direction. It was separated by a well maintained center section dividing the east and west bound traffic. Both the vehicle and foot traffic were light, and it was a beautiful day for a walk.

For the past forty-five years, it had been my habit always to know who or what was to my front, rear, left and right. Basically, my head was on a swivel, and often I would stop and just turn around to take a look. Today was no different.

Thirsty, I decided to find a small tienda, or store that sold Gatorade. Just before I found a store, two street bandits, who appeared to be in their early twenties, stepped onto the sidewalk from the street, and while talking and walking in my direction, stepped in front of me and tried to block my path. There was no doubt in my mind that their intent was robbery. Shooting each a hard, cold, glance and not breaking stride, I looked at each and said, "Not today boys." As I spoke, I tensed my shoulders, and as they moved closer one to another with shoulders touching, I slammed through them, knocking each back and creating an avenue that allowed me to pass.

One chided and laced me with profanity.

Nice guys, I thought.

When I glanced back, I found that their intensity to complete their appointed task had increased and they had doubled their effort to follow me down the sidewalk.

Quickly, I asked for that divine protection I have had throughout my life. It immediately was present.

Two to one odds, I thought. *Add the angels of heaven, and the odds are in my favor. I can handle that.*

As the suspects approached closing the distance to about ten feet, I glanced back over my shoulder and quickly stepped toward the street, which, because of their nearness, caused them to become confused and forced them to walk past me.

Before they could turn around, I darted into the small store. Once inside and seeing that they had not followed, I bought a glass bottle of Gatorade. My right hand fit smoothly around its neck, and the balance was perfect. Today, I did not plan on being a victim.

Perfect, I thought.

I opened the bottle, took a few swallows, screwed the cap in place and stepped back out onto the sidewalk. The two bandits had crossed the street and from the far side were looking up and down trying to find me. When they saw me, one spoke to the other, and nodded in my direction. While they were doing this, I stood facing them, drinking my Gatorade and smiled. It was evident that the old gringo was not intimidated. I should mention that I was not wearing my missionary tag, and in South America, one is often not identified as an American because of the suit and sun glasses, but thought to be a European businessman working in the city.

There was more conversation between the two, furtive looks into some businesses, and then their attention focused back to me. It was obvious that they wanted me to get ahead of them which would give them some room to cross, and then once again behind me, they could close the distance.

I turned and started to walk slowly down the sidewalk in the direction of the office, never taking my eyes off them, and each time I stopped, I stared directly at them and smiled. Not a friendly smile, but more of a taunt. Then, I would turn and continue on. They followed, drawing closer.

Again I stopped, and took another drink. The distance between us closed. When I stopped, they stopped.

I waited.

Slowly, my right hand slipped under my left armpit to an invisible shoulder holster. I shrugged my shoulders, adjusted the nonexistent holster and made it look like I was adjusting what appeared to be a weapon. They never took their eyes off me, nor I them—another swallow, another look, another taunt. They didn't move. The bottle now was empty. In my right hand I firmly gripped the cool glass. My attitude and cool demeanor had them confused.

With the bottle in hand, I rolled my wrist, and then meticulously tapped the bottom of the bottle into the palm of my left hand. Again, I smiled. Again, they conversed, tossed looks in my direction and debated. The hunters had now become the hunted, and they knew it. With my missionary tag hidden, they had no idea who I was. In South America, a silver haired man wearing a suit and aviator sunglasses was not a tourist.

I never had been a victim and wasn't going to start now.

Apparently their confusion about me generated some argument between them.

I turned my back and continued to walk leisurely down the sidewalk with them in deep discussion walking parallel to me, from across the street.

When I looked over my shoulder, I was met with more hateful looks and profanity.

Rapidly their side of the street began to veer toward my side. They needed to make a decision.

Do we rob the silver haired gringo, or do we pass?

Slowly, they angled toward me. I stopped, stared, smiled and tapped the bottle in the palm of my left hand.

They hesitated.

They realized that I was showing no fear, quite the opposite of what street thugs expect.

The one who had sworn at me when I pushed them to the side in our earlier confrontation, spit in my direction. Another thirty feet, another hard look, a final spit directed toward me, some profanity shouted at me, and then they turned and began their walk back in the direction they had just come.

As they turned, I stepped onto a small pathway leading off the sidewalk and watched. They never looked back.

For two street bandits in their early twenties, they actually acted very wisely that day when they decided that the silver haired gringo in the dark suit was probably not the right mark.

Much like animals, criminals can smell fear, and the greater the fear, the greater their bravado. They also sense indecision and just as a good street cop can, they are able to look at someone and size them up fairly quickly. People, especially senior missionaries, make themselves victims by not always being aware of their surroundings, by showing weakness through their physical actions, and giving off a portrait of fear rather than confidence; weakness rather than strength. Gratefully, I never had that problem.

Travel Home and Divine Intervention

With the completion of one assignment came the need to prepare for the next. For us, the door to our Perpetual Education Fund assignment in Lima was closing, but before it could be shut, some departure preparations were required. They were preparations that would see us safely home where we could take care of some minor medical needs, that, when completed, would allow us again to fill another assignment for the Lord, one which already had been discussed with the Brethren.

Our airline arrangements were coordinated by Sister Day who worked in Church Travel and with whom I had worked during our second assignment to Quito, Ecuador. However, this time it was far more complicated. Originally, I had given my travel requests to the Area Travel Coordinator, but he soon sent me an e-mail stating that Church Travel could not make my arrangements as requested.

I had requested to fly by LAN to Los Angeles, then Los Angeles to Las Vegas. Sister Day's e-mail to our travel coordinator was forwarded to me. It said that the plans I requested would cost me $4,000 out of pocket, whereas if I travelled by Delta, it would cost me nothing since the church had a contract with that airline, and our return home was covered in our missionary transportation. So what did I do? I called Sister Day.

At first, the reception was chilly, but considering all the hassles and complaints she dealt with from around the world, I couldn't blame her. She explained the cost of LAN, and then told me my travel dates on Delta were all booked. She tried flight after flight and nothing. Then suddenly, she said, "Whitaker? Are any of your relatives from Beaver Utah?"

"My grandfather, Orson Adelbert is from Beaver," I said.

Suddenly, she laughed.

"Your grandfather and my grandmother were brother and sister. It appears that we are related!"

With that, the tone of the conversation changed dramatically. We were family!

"Give me a minute," she said, "and let me try this again."

Not more than three minutes passed and she was back on the phone. "I have made your arrangements; however, you and Sister Whitaker will be sitting one behind the other on the flight from Lima to Atlanta, Georgia. You then will have a two hour layover and leave Atlanta for Las Vegas at 10:45 a.m. Both flights will be on Delta and will not require any out-of-pocket funding by you. Will that work for you?"

"My dearest cousin, you are wonderful!"

She laughed. "I try to be."

So with a little divine intervention and the help of a distant cousin, the travel arrangements were set in stone. As it turned out, both flights were booked full and we were happy just to have seats.

Since we were only allowed two suitcases and 100 pounds each while traveling, we were required to leave some clothing and kitchen items in Lima. It was not a problem dividing up the items, and once this had been accomplished, each of the four suitcases was under the fifty pound limit.

Now we faced the problem of the weather in Atlanta, Georgia. We were scheduled to depart Lima on Friday morning, January 7, at 1:25 a.m. and arrive in Atlanta at 8:45 a.m. This was in the middle of a huge and violent snow storm that blanketed the East Coast, and the last thing I wanted to see was Cheryle having to sit in a cold airport for a day or so waiting for the weather to clear until cancelled flights would be resumed.

In past assignments, we had a twelve hour layover in San Francisco, and because of mechanical problems with the aircraft, we spent eight hours in Los Angeles. In these situations, the only thing I could do was pray and exercise the priesthood.

For the two weeks prior to our scheduled departure, I requested that angels be assigned to the Atlanta Airport on Thursday, January 6 and Friday January 7. I further prayed that the weather and snow storms cease for those two days so that we would have no complications travelling home.

On Wednesday, the weather was clear and continued to be clear until Saturday morning. Then another heavy storm rolled in with so much snow that it caused the airport to cancel most flights.

I never have enjoyed the chaos of airports, so that part also was included in my prayers. "Please assign angels to assist and lessen the chaos, and let us find everything easily and not experience some of the severe complications as we have in the past." I made this plea on many occasions. When I received that calming assurance that all would go well, I moved on to other items.

We left Lima at 1:25 a.m. and arrived in Atlanta at 8:45 a.m. The storm had stopped and the weather was clear.

My prayers and supplications had been heard and answered.

Inasmuch as we were the first plane in that morning, the airport was empty. After following the directions as to where to claim our luggage, we found ourselves in a medium sized room with baggage carrousels. Walking past the row of luggage carts, both Cheryle and I grabbed a cart. As we did, a smiling Skycap stepped forward and offered his services. His cherry attitude, and the fact that I did not enjoy schlepping fifty pound suitcases around, closed the deal. I handed him our tickets and off he went.

We were in his hands, and he treated us like royalty, as did the Custom's Officer, the two women who opened the VIP line for us to go through screening, and also the TSA employees! It was wonderful. They smiled and we smiled. They looked at our missionary tags and the way we were dressed, and coupled with a positive attitude, which is often foreign when traveling, they could not do enough to make our experience the most pleasant possible. *Angels come in many forms!* I have learned that a word of appreciation, a smile and a wonderful tip…in advance can do wonders. In South America, many North Americans and especially senior missionaries fail to realize the fact that those working in the various service positions rely heavily on tips to make ends meet, and to feed their families. Unfortunately, this is not always understood by the Americans living in country. Therefore, I made it a habit of tipping generously and it paid dividends.

The long, uncomfortable plane flight was just that….a long, uncomfortable plane flight. We arrived in Las Vegas at 12:45 p.m. and were met by our faithful and wonderful friend Don McClelland who has become so dear to us. After the short ride from the airport to the house, we were home. Within a few days, it was as though we had never left!

Reporting to the Brethren

On February 11, 2011, we received a wonderful letter from Elder Richard E. Cook thanking us on behalf of the Perpetual Education Fund and the First Presidency for our service. He summed up all aspects of the assignment and with love, expressed his personal gratitude and that of the Brethren for what we had accomplished.

As we prepared to travel to meet with and report to the Brethren, the weather became cold and it started to snow in Salt Lake. We were scheduled to fly from Las Vegas on Monday, February 28, stay at the Marriott Hotel that night and then give our report on Tuesday, March 1.

Tuesday morning, March 1, we reported to the Church Office building. Mishael Sedas, as in the past, picked us up at the hotel and drove us to the building. At 9:30 a.m., Elder Carmack, Elder Cook, Tom Rueckert, Cheryle and I, along with a number of PEF staff met in the conference room for our report.

The first question asked by Elder Carmack was, "How is your health?"

After we answered, both he and Elder Cook said some very kind words about what had been accomplished in the South America Northwest Area and then requested our report.

We were given an hour to report on all that was accomplished during the Lima assignment. The report went well, and I was very open about explaining the process combined with the great challenges and ultimate successes. When we had completed the report, Elder Cook asked that I take five minutes and share the story about the two bandits who thought that the silver haired gringo in the business suit would be an easy mark for a robbery. As explained in an earlier chapter, when the experience ended, two street thugs made a wise decision in not aggravating the silver haired gringo.

While I recounted the story, I thought it humorous to look into the eyes of those in attendance and watch as they became larger and larger. At the end, when I explained that in our two assignments to Quito, I had been shot at each time. It soon became apparent that no one in the room had ever come across another senior missionary like Elder Whitaker!

When I finished, Elder Richard Cook asked Cheryle and I to come into his office. Once seated, he shut the door. He began by saying; "We are family, so let's talk."

After discussing some very personal items related to himself and to us, he looked at and me and said, "I want to ask you a question."

"Go ahead, "I responded.

"Elder and Sister Whitaker, would you consider serving in Santiago Chile and replicating the program you so successfully developed in the South America Northwest Area?"

Silence filled the room. After a brief pause, I explained that we had some medical needs to take care of and needed a little rest and time to visit our family. The brethren knew that this was the most difficult assignment either of us had ever had, and some rest was much needed before journeying out again.

"You can go according to your time schedule, and I can guarantee you that I will set the foundation with the Area President, Elder Amado, who is a dear friend, so that you will have his full support, like the support you had from Elder Nash. I also will bring the Area Welfare Manager and Area PEF Coordinator to Salt Lake so we all can meet, and they will understand exactly what you would be doing and that you have the total support of the First Presidency, Elder Carmack, me, and also Elder Amado."

"Let me pray about this, "I answered.

"I know that Elder Gavarret and Elder Nash would like you in Salt Lake, but I don't see you here. You need the challenge of being in country, with the Saints and working with the priesthood and the brethren."

"You are right," I agreed.

"Well, keep me informed about your health, and let me know when you and Cheryle are ready to go."

By the time Cheryle and I called Elder Cook to advise him of our availability, we were told that the spot in Santiago had been filled. Concluding that conversation, I said, "Before we leave, let us tell you a quick story about our youngest grandson and our mission callings."

"I would love to hear it," he said smiling.

Then, Cheryle continued with the story. "Upon our arrival home, we had the opportunity to visit two of our daughters who live in Southern Utah. While we sat with the families and eight of our twenty-one grandchildren, one of the granddaughters asked, 'Grandma, are you going to serve another mission?'

"Yes, I think we will."

"Why?" asked another granddaughter.

Without hesitation, Tucker, our four year old grandson answered with as much authority as he could muster in his voice, "Because that is what Grandma's do!"

So there it was, out of the mouth of babes. "That is what Grandma's and Grandpa's do."

And so we concluded four and a-half years out of ten, serving the people of Ecuador, Venezuela, Colombia, Peru and Bolivia.

Uruguay Montevideo Mission Leadership Support
2012-2013

Amid Chaos and Catastrophes

After nearly eighteen months at home, both Cheryle and I felt that we could serve again and began to consider submitting our papers.

While pondering this, we received news that a friend from our Lima assignment had been called to serve as the mission president in the Uruguay, Montevideo mission. After discussing the matter, we felt that we could be of assistance to this new mission president and offered him our services.

A week into this process we received a telephone call from the South America Northwest Area asking if we were available to return to Lima and serve as one of the secretaries to the Area Presidency. Humbled to be considered for the position, I felt that a commitment had been made to the mission president and advised Lima we were not available. In hindsight, that probably wasn't the best decision, and will be explained in the Uruguayan experience as documented in the coming chapters.

Reflecting on our four assignments to South America, I believe that one of the most difficult things to achieve was some normalcy and consistency to everyday life. In Montevideo, I struggled with that aspect of the assignment, mostly because the mission president was changing what was done in the past and focusing on what he believed should be done in the future. As is the norm, change came hard.

Our Arrival

Our air travel to Uruguay, when compared to other flights, was very uneventful. We arrived in Montevideo on September 20th 2012, one day after a devastating storm slashed its way through Argentina and across Uruguay. The storm cancelled all flights from Buenos Aires to Montevideo and was so vicious that it uprooted nearly seven hundred very large old trees in and across Uruguay. It was quite a sight to see trees with a circumference of four and five feet literally ripped from the ground and thrown onto houses and across roads. The clean-up took months.

The Mission Home

When we arrived in Montevideo, we did not have a place to live, and we soon would discover that we also didn't even have an office where we could sit at a desk. This was nothing new, for in the past three assignments, the creation of a work station, whether it was in an office or just a place to sit, was always left to my own ingenuity. And so it would be on this assignment. However, that task never was accomplished.

On our first assignment to Quito, Ecuador, the Employment Office was so small and crowded that I sat outside on a concrete wall the first three months while I developed the plan on how to build an office and run the center. I wanted to do the same on this assignment, but I was unable to do so. Unfortunately, the support we had in our prior three assignments to South America never materialized in Uruguay.

Since my first assignment to serve in a mission presidency in 1995, I was of the opinion that a mission president had the most difficult calling in the church. This feeling was reinforced in the six months spent in Montevideo.

Let me share with you my reason for this opinion. I will start with the mission president's home where we lived in a small bedroom for our first three weeks in country.

The mission home originally was built in the early 1960's. It was the same mission home that the mission president reported to when he was assigned to serve his mission in Uruguay and Paraguay from 1976-1978. Unfortunately, the mission home was basically the same as when he served.

Without prior living accommodations being made for us, we stayed in the mission home guest room located on the first floor. The room was small and cramped, but that was not the problem. The difficulty lay in the fact that throughout the house, they had problems with the water and electrical systems. There was often no running hot water to the second floor where the president and his family lived, and the electrical that operated the garage door and many appliances was so old, it was unreliable. In our shower, as with upstairs, you had either scalding hot or freezing cold water. There was no happy medium.

When we needed to shower, the process was simple. We cupped our hands under the cold water faucet, got as much water as our hands would hold and then quickly dumped the water onto whatever body part we wanted to wash. We did this over and over until we had taken a brief thirty second shower, or were shivering sufficiently to call it quits. We did this daily for three weeks. When it was reported to the physical facilities department, a man came out, said it was repaired and left. Unfortunately, the maintenance man either misunderstood the problem or was incompetent, for nothing was ever resolved. I later would learn that the latter was true.

That problem, combined with many others that should have been repaired by the physical facilities department, would "be fixed" one day, and break the next. When the managers were confronted about the shoddy work and why they just didn't replace the antiquated parts, they would reply, "When we can no longer fix it, we will replace it." It became apparent that because of a lack of mechanical skill, and what they perceived to be a shortage of funds, which was not the case, and fear that if they asked for something they would be placing their jobs in jeopardy, nothing was adequately repaired. This malady later surfaced when over and over they unsuccessfully attempted to repair the air conditioning in the mission office.

During our second assignment to Quito, Ecuador, it became necessary to change mission presidents. The old president had been called from Guayaquil and his three year time of service was ending, so the Lord called President Tim Sloan from Salt Lake City to replace the native Spanish speaking president. President Sloan and I met during our first assignment to Quito when I was assigned to the Employment Resource Center, and he was called upon to organize and implement a comprehensive Employment Resource plan that eventually would be implemented throughout the church. He was an excellent administrator and I looked forward to his arrival.

In Quito, the mission president lived in a church owned condo that sat on the side of a mountain and had a beautiful view of the entire Quito valley, and while the location was excellent, the home and all furnishings were old and in disrepair. The same could be said of the mission president's office that had been thrown together by young Elders many years ago and never updated. The furniture was old, the carpet had holes and the lighting was inadequate. For most president's this was adequate, but because of the problems encountered with the president being replaced by Sloan, Elder Carl Pratt, a member of the Area Presidency and General Authority decided to tour the mission concentrating not only on the outgoing president, but also on the physical facilities and especially the home and office that President Sloan would occupy. What he found was appalling.

He immediately required that the mission president's private residence be renovated, top to bottom. Nothing was overlooked, not the walls, ceilings, floors, furniture or appliances. Everything was replaced with new and operational items. He then advised the physical facilities department in Quito to do the same for the mission president's personal mission office.

When he began to examine the residence, he was pleased with the efforts but kept a hands-on approach. When a kitchen appliance did not work, it was instantly replaced. When it came time to tour the newly renovated mission president's office, it failed to pass muster. Again, the cheapest and least expensive furnishings were used, some, although new, looked like they could have been purchased at a yard sale. Elder Pratt was furious, and having been born in the Colonies and been a General Authority who served most of his time in Mexico, Central and South America, he knew what it was like to be away from family and not living in the best of conditions. His approach with the physical facilities department was simple. They were told that mission presidents sacrificed greatly and they should have only the best living and working conditions. Therefore, the mission president's office was gutted and furnished as though it were to be occupied by a General Authority.

My role was simple. When the physical reconfiguration of the mission office began, I was given responsibility to guarantee that the work was completed properly and the offices arranged so that they would provide the greatest effectiveness and efficiency.

One day as I stood in my Perpetual Education Fund office, Elder Pratt walked in wanting to talk. I had great respect for him and loved his no nonsense way of approaching the work of building the Kingdom of God. As we talked, he asked me a question about our numerous mission assignments in the states and now abroad. I responded, "Elder Pratt, it is my desire to wear myself out in the service of the Lord."

He smiled, "Very commendable, Elder Whitaker. I am sure you will."

As years passed, assignments mounted and my health declined, I came to realize the prophetic nature of that statement and the fact that the Lord allowed my desire to become a reality.

Often during the six months we spent in Montevideo, I only could shake my head as I watched what should have been easily resolved go without resolution. It was sad to know what could be done, but that they who had the ability to make key corrections by giving guidance from the physical facilities office in Montevideo and the Area office in Buenos Aires failed to do so. The problem of incompetence in repairing the many issues only impacted us for six months, while the mission president and his wife lived with the problem for as long as they remained in country.

Cheryle's Near Fatal Fall

We had been in Uruguay for six days. Without transportation or a firm understanding of our assignment, we decided to spend the morning in the mission home. When I walked into the front room, Cheryle walked upstairs to visit with the mission president's wife.

I had not been seated on the couch for more than five minutes when I heard a number of successive loud banging noises coming from the stairs located in the hallway just outside the living room. Immediately it registered: someone had fallen down the flight of seventeen hardwood stairs. I jumped up and ran to the doorway, and saw Cheryle on the floor at the bottom of the stairs trying to get up.

Before I could reach her, she was on her feet, swaying slightly. I looked into her face and noted that she was white as a sheet, her eyes having difficulty focusing and when she spoke, her speech was jumbled, slurred and awkward.

"Are you all right?" I asked, knowing the answer before she was able to form her words.

Silence.

She reached out, grabbed the railing and steadied herself.

Then in a slow deliberate voice she whispered, "I guess I'm all right."

CHERYLE'S NEAR FATAL FALL

The noise brought the president's wife running from upstairs to the top of the landing while the president ran from his office into the hallway. As I steadied Cheryle, the president and I walked her into his office and sat her down in a chair.

When I asked her where she hurt, she pointed to the back of her head. I reached back, parted her hair and gently felt a knot the size of a golf ball. What was interesting was the fact that although the fall was severe, the scalp had not been lacerated, so there was no blood, just a huge bump. I began to question her as to what happened.

"I was in my nylons and when I stepped onto the first wooden step, my foot slipped out from under me and I lost my balance. I tried to grab the handrail but couldn't. Then I bounced down the steps hitting the back of my head and also hitting the small of my back."

It should be noted that her explanation was far more convoluted than the above sentence indicates, but for writing purposes, I have placed the words in the correct order. In reality, some of her words came out garbled and she would stumble and repeat some words during the explanation.

While Cheryle sat in the chair, the president's wife went to the kitchen for some ice while I stepped out into the hallway to examine the stairwell. I counted seventeen stairs, of which her head struck at least fourteen, snapping her neck with each hit and bruising her lower spine and her lower back. We debated the need to take her to a hospital, but after reviewing her condition and the medical options presented in Uruguay, which were not very good, we decided to keep her under observation in the mission home. A priesthood blessing was given and then began my serious observations of her speech and ability to walk.

While some would wonder about that decision, after three mission assignments to South America, neither of us had much faith in the medical system in any of the counties in which we lived. The same was true for Uruguay, and as time passed and the health of the mission president's wife deteriorated following her being mugged after only six weeks in country, our decision proved wise.

The bottom-line was that doctors in South America, unless trained in the United States, hesitated to diagnose any illness affecting a North American for fear of being second-guessed and proven wrong by American doctors, hence, they feared losing face. Therefore, instead of making a diagnosis or recommending a treatment, many of the medical professionals in Latin America often would say that they were unable to identify the problem and would pass the patient on to another doctor, and so on. It was a vicious cycle.

As time went by, and we watched the mission president's wife suffer as she was passed from one doctor to another, Cheryle and I agreed that we would monitor her health, and if it deteriorated, we would end the assignment and return to the United States.

When I stepped back to the staircase and examined the stairs, and realized how hard she fell and where she struck her head and lower spine, I knew that she should have broken her neck and her back. Even in traumatic situations, like this, the angels of heaven were there to help, as they were in this situation.

The next day, on at least three occasions, her sentences were incoherent and her words were garbled. On occasion, as late as November 6, the impact of the fall still was very visible. While others noted the impaired speech pattern, she usually was not aware of the problem, thinking she was speaking fine.

At times she would attend a meeting one day and forget she had attended. Additionally, immediately following the fall, she began to experience dizzy spells, often three to four times a day causing her to take a seat or fall as she did some weeks later while at a transfer conference. She also experienced headaches she did not have before the fall, and she was not sleeping at night due to the pain in the top of her neck, spine and lower back. She also experienced periods where she was weepy, which again was not part of her nature. All this, coupled with the lack of motor coordination, was making each day a challenge.

I continued to monitor her very closely.

Cheryle was not one to complain or quit anything, however I was concerned. She was also the target of the giant mosquitos that were a part of daily life on the coast. The bites were so severe that her right arm swelled greatly. Yet, she continued to push forward.

Unfortunately, her self-diagnosis that all was fine was far from correct, and in a six month period, her health deteriorated to the point that it would end our mission. The concussion that was a result of the fall would not heal for another two years, but the fall was only the beginning to our misadventures in Uruguay.

Finding an Apartment

Searching for an apartment in Montevideo was difficult. In two weeks, we, along with the wife of the mission president and a real-estate person, looked at more than twenty apartments. Some were on the beach. Some were dives. Some had no furnishings, others had old furniture. None had the equipment to wash or dry clothes. In South America, many used the sink for washing and the sun for drying, and during the winter months when there was no sun, only rain and fog from the nearby ocean, everyone wore cold, damp clothing. Not in my world! My requirements for an apartment were very concise, and since the mission had never had a couple assigned to the office, we were plowing new ground, so on and on we searched.

Finally we hit pay dirt. The interesting part was that another senior couple was living in the complex and loved it. Ironically, it had been recommended to us when we first arrived, but in my zeal to check things out, I opted to search, and search and search, only to be drawn back to the original complex. Coming back to where we probably should have begun reminded me of a particular line from *Secret of the Andes,* a classic book for children that takes place in a beautiful mountain valley hidden away from the world high in the Andes. Cusi, a young Indian boy lives with an old Inca Llama herder, Chuto, and helps him care for the llamas. It's not until Cusi leaves the valley to go down to the world of people in order to search for his heart's desire that he comes to understand the ancient Incan saying, "Grieve not if you're searching circles."

We had taken two weeks to circle back to where we should have started. Our relief kept us from grieving. The complex was very nice and had three towers, each housing six apartments on each of the five floors. It also had up-to-date conveniences and a separate wash room with washers and dryers. For me, this was a must since Cheryle deserved all the conveniences available as she served so far from home and family. We checked out a vacant apartment on the second floor, and although in Quito and Lima I refused to live below the fifth floor because of security reasons, and since this was the only one bedroom available and the only apartment we could afford, and though it was small, we took it.

Looking back, we had little choice, but lacking time before we left the next day on a three day mission tour to Northern Uruguay, I failed to completely check out apartment security. And I failed to examine the two large sliding glass doors that opened onto to a small outside porch that also provided access to the ground. That would prove to be a mistake; a lesson learned and in the overall scheme of things, a blessing provided.

Travel into the Interior

During the first week of October, after about eleven days in country, the travel began. On October 8, the mission president and I travelled to Maldonado where a zone conference was held, and where he conducted personal interviews with the missionaries assigned to the zone.

The next week, with only three weeks in country, we were asked by the president to accompany him and his wife on a three day mission tour which would take us from Montevideo to the northern reaches of Uruguay just south of the Brazilian border. The focus of the trip was to provide the president the opportunity to hold zone conferences in the cities of Trienta Tres and Melo, then speak at a mission fireside in Minas, one of the cities to which he was assigned as a young missionary.

The country of Uruguay is far different than Ecuador. While Ecuador has the Andean mountain range with its towering peaks and volcanoes, and Peru has the Andes and is considered to be the land of the Inca, Uruguay is a country surrounded by ocean at the bottom and rolling hills and green plains and pastures in the interior.

After traveling nearly 750 miles from the bottom to the top, I am still looking for a mountain; hills yes, mountains no. As we traveled to the interior, I was impressed with the well-constructed and beautifully maintained highway system.

We traveled roads that did not have the famous potholes of Ecuador or horrendous traffic of Peru. It was a system that had little traffic, which made travel rather relaxing. And unlike Ecuador and other countries, Uruguay had full-service gas stations on the highways which offered not only gas, but also the all-important restrooms. There were no gas stations, thus no restrooms, outside of the cities in Ecuador and Peru. One only could pray for a big rock or hearty bush should the need of a bathroom arise.

Additionally, in Uruguay there were some roads with two lanes each way, others only a single lane cut through the green and lush landscape. Toll booths were located at determined distances, and the charge for a single car was around $2.40. When traveling on a long trip, we usually could count on four toll-booths going, and the same four upon our return.

Large ranches dotted the country-side. Some had cattle, others horses, some sheep, and a few contained all of the above. Watching the country side as we traveled, I often would see a large hacienda far in the distance which frequently was surrounded by ten miles or more of fields and grazing land. The land was beautiful, however, I will admit, I missed the Andes.

One other interesting item was that in both Ecuador and Peru, each country had a deep cultural history created by a blend of the native cultures and Spanish influence.

In Uruguay, they had no distinct culture. No music, no art, basically nothing that would reflect who populated the area prior to the arrival of the Europeans. When the area was first populated, the Europeans killed all the Indians, hence eliminating their culture. What was left for the future was a blend of European cultures with a smattering of Spanish and a small Catholic influence.

Our Apartment Burglarized

We moved into our new apartment, and after spending only one night in our own bed, we left the next day for a three day mission tour. The tour went well and we enjoyed the companionship of the president and his wife. All was going well until our return to Montevideo and I opened the front door to our apartment where I was met by the lights on, and the curtain in front of the large sliding glass patio doors blowing in the wind. I immediately knew that we had a problem.

I quickly looked at the dining table where I had left my new Dell laptop; it was gone. Then I pulled back the curtains and saw that the sliding glass door was open. Cheryle walked into the ransacked bedroom, the drawers opened and items thrown across the bed. My first reaction was anger. Then I looked in a hidden location to verify that our passports and cash were still there. Nothing had been touched.

When the damage was calculated, we lost our laptop, a camera and all of Cheryle's jewelry. Close to $2000 worth of items. Fortunately, the jewelry was not costly, but losing all the information on the laptop did make me angry. Since things had been difficult the first three weeks, and now compounded with the burglary, all I could say was, "I'm out of here!" That comment was met by Cheryle saying, "You're kidding me!"

We called the police, and it was learned that our apartment was one of four in our complex burglarized and another four in a building across the way also were hit. They got into ours by standing on a planter below our patio and climbing up and over the small patio wall. Then they entered through the sliding glass doors. I later learned that the doors could not be locked, even if you threw the lock into a closed position because management had removed the springs that snapped the locks shut, because too many residents in their moments of drunken revelry, locked themselves out of their apartments while partying on the patio. Security became tired of having to get them back in, so, unbeknownst to us, we left an unsecured apartment—a great lawsuit in the United States, but down here, don't bother.

I also was convinced that it was an inside job, and that feeling was reinforced after I complained loudly enough and they fired all of the security officers. They also replaced the locking mechanisms in the sliding doors, placed screws in the sliders so the doors could not be opened, and placed bright security lights in the grounds below our apartment building.

In an apartment across the yard, the thieves entered one apartment where the elderly residents were home. They beat the man and ransacked the apartment.

Before we arrived in Montevideo, thieves burglarized an apartment and were armed. When the police arrived, a gun battle broke out. Welcome to Uruguay! And to think that we were advised upon receiving the assignment, that Montevideo was far safer than Quito or Lima, which turned out to be untrue. Our problems were mounting: first, Cheryle's fall, and now this. Things were not going well, and unfortunately, conditions during our stay would only continue to deteriorate.

I had to laugh at the "investigation." A young, arrogant cop showed up. It was obvious that he was irritated at having to take a report. I guess he thought it was below him. When I identified myself as a retired Detective from the Los Angeles Police Department, his attitude worsened. He stood in our hallway, asked what was taken and never asked for descriptions or serial numbers; he never looked at the point of entry or the bedroom, and put all victims from the apartments on a small single sheet of paper. That was it. He had no idea how to conduct an investigation. Again, welcome back to South America! As my frustration with his incompetence increased, it showed in my attitude. You can take a tough cop off the street, but you never can eliminate the many lessons that a tough street cop learned.

Some told me it was best we were not in the apartment at the time of the burglary, for they knew of my past and my ability to react with aggressiveness to a violent situation. That probably would have been the case had we been home, and since losing a physical confrontation was not an option, someone would have been seriously injured; and I would have done my best to insure it was not me. So, another of the

Lord's tender mercies was extended to us, for had I defended us and our possessions, I would now be in jail.

The Work

After two months, my responsibilities started to become clear. I served as a third counselor in the mission presidency, mission president's confidant, chauffeur and conducted all the President's Exceptions Interviews for investigators who had past transgressions that needed to be addressed by the proper priesthood authority.

At first, I thought that it would be very similar to the position I had for five years in the Nevada Las Vegas Mission. However, it was not the same, and while my talents were not fully used, I was committed to do what the mission president wanted in the manner comfortable to his management style.

After talking to many General Authorities, I was comfortable stating that at that time, I was probably one of the most experienced mission counselors serving in the church. However, that failed to help with this assignment. While the president and I tried to work closely together, we never did develop that oneness that allowed me to make my observations and recommendations with candidness. More often than not, my observations and recommendations fell on deaf ears.

In my last assignment to Lima, Peru, my companion was an Area Seventy, and I had the responsibility to work with 208 stake presidents and nearly 1400 bishops in five countries. While this mission was not falling into place as I expected, I tried to keep myself busy basically by supporting the president as his "Jack of all trades, master of none." As time passed, my frustration mounted.

While I thought that I would be involved in helping to train the missionaries because of my experience, the president decided that my training and management style did not fit into the structure he wanted for the mission. He made this clear on an occasion early into the assignment. It was after I sat in a zone training meeting where I made recommendations to the Elders in order to assist and help them in their role playing activities that I felt would increase their effectiveness. I stopped when it was obvious that the water was not getting to the end of the row.

"Elder's," I said, "in my opinion you could be working much harder and be far more effective. The work is just not getting done the way the Lord desires."

My words were followed by dead silence.

A few days later the president pulled me aside and said, "Elder Whitaker, my missionaries have complained that you were too hard on them during and after their training, so in the future, I don't want you to talk to, or in any way train the Elders and Sisters. Basically, they are not in your lane."

So there it was. It was felt that I was too direct and blunt.

That conversation ended my participation in the mission.

While I continued to have no place to sit or work, and my responsibilities were all but nonexistent, Cheryle was doing well in her areas of responsibility. Although she did have a chair and a spot at the desk in the area with the office staff, her computer was obsolete and again, no support came from either the regional office in Montevideo, or the Area office in Buenos Aires.

Finally, after months of waiting and me being fairly vociferous about the lack of functional equipment and support, a new computer was delivered for Cheryle. The only problem was that it was designed to play only video games and could not be used for the Microsoft Office applications that were needed. My only comment was, "You have got to be kidding me."

I have shared before how proud I was of Cheryle's accomplishments, for she was one of a very few Sisters in the church who had filled four full-time assignments to South America and could speak the language. Many of the other senior Sisters, including the wives of mission president's, never tried to learn Spanish, some going three years using only English. Cheryle was different. She never hesitated to jump in, learn the language and develop the skills that allowed her to magnify her callings. She was loved by all she contacted, and the women in South America, whether members of the church or not, loved her companionship and ever present smile, optimistic attitude and cheerfulness. She is truly one of the noble and great of Father's earthly daughters.

During the weeks of November 5-9 and 12-16, we had five mission conferences. This required the transporting of 185 missionaries to the chapel on their assigned day. Each conference was an all-day event. With some missionaries, it required them to get on a bus at 3:00 a.m. to guarantee that they arrived by the 7:00 a.m. cut off. Then they went through a temple session, and following the session, returned for training by the mission president. After an hour of training, they were fed lunch and then more training followed which involved scenarios applicable to how and what to teach. Cheryle and I were involved in the lunch, set-up and when it was over, I put on my sanitation engineer hat, or in everyday terms, I became the trash collector and lugged the garbage to the dumpster. One finds early on that in the mission field, one wears many hats.

After completing those tasks, I listened to the missionaries practice their role playing, and since I was forbidden to make recommendations, I reluctantly, and only when asked, very cautiously shared with the president my few observations and recommendations. It soon became clear that these also were not wanted, so I became quiet; my abilities not used, each day growing longer and Cheryle's health continuing to decline.

Each day was difficult, and I don't say this to discourage anyone from serving, rather I mention this because I believe that we should enter these assignments not wearing rose colored glasses. Each country in South America is different. The customs, the Spanish language, the rate of money exchange, the food, the weather, housing, and the people and mission presidents, but what usually made it wonderful were the people. As in the past, we were treated very well by the people of Uruguay. Much of it had to do with the fact that we spoke the language. This effort was appreciated in each of the countries in which we served.

We were blessed to have a car, and quickly became aware that in Uruguay, as in other countries where we served, traffic laws didn't exist. Well, that wasn't totally true. There were three laws in Uruguay that were set in stone. The first law required you always to have your headlights on.

Driving without lights, even in the day, immediately would bring the police down on a driver. The next law was that under no circumstance could a right hand turn be made on a red light. And finally, many intersections did not allow for left hand turns, so drivers needed to think quickly and plan ahead if they wanted to go left.

Most streets did not have street signs, not even stop signs, so when we came up to one of these intersections, the best we could do was cast a quick glance left, then one right, offer a short prayer, slam the pedal to the metal and go. Fortunately, it always worked for me, but from the amount of broken glass and shredded plastic tail light lenses I saw strewn across the asphalt, it appeared that many might have forgotten the prayer part!

It also was required that if living in the country, within three months we needed to secure a Uruguayan driver's license. This required that the regional church office take the paperwork submitted to them, compile it, and then return it to you, so you could travel three hours to secure the license. We waited six months for this process to be completed, which never was done. That paperwork, and our papers required to secure our Uruguayan residency cards, sat on the desk of an administrative assistant for six months and never was processed. We virtually were being ignored, and it was becoming more evident each day that in the minds of those with whom we labored, it would have been better had we ended the assignment and returned to the states. From start to finish, nothing ever fell into place.

If one could come up with a saying for this experience, it would be: "While serving in Uruguay, or in any of the countries of South America, always try to anticipate the unanticipated. And even if you try to do so, you probably will be wrong 99% of the time!"

Bikers as our New Neighbors

On Monday, November 19, the empty apartment across the hall was rented. In our building and on our floor, we had two elevators and six apartments. Everything inside, as well as outside the apartments had hardwood flooring or tile floors, a combination that only increased, not reduced the noise. With the quiet of the evening shattered, the new tenant began to move in. His staff of movers were three drunken bikers, and he made number four. *Oh how lovely was the morning!*

The day was filled with them leaving the apartment door open and doing what many do when they have friends help them move. He supplied them with beer, whiskey and cigarettes. Needless to say, it was not a dull, nor a quiet afternoon, and as our apartment quickly filled with cigarette smoke, it reminded me of the old days when I was on the police department dealing with the raucous bars, rowdy apartments and booze fueled parties. Unfortunately, this was now, and within fifteen feet of our front door.

The loud laughter and louder talk began about seven in the morning and lasted until 12:30 a.m. the next morning. Then all was quiet, but not for long. At 5:30 a.m., an alarm went off in the apartment, and as if the conductor raised his baton and hit the downbeat, the noise erupted again. I came to find out that they drank all night and were all very, very drunk.

BIKERS AS OUR NEW NEIGHBORS

I dressed for an eight o'clock meeting, and when I opened our apartment door, the noise, the laughter, the heavy smoke and the raucous voices blared and boomed into the hallway from their open apartment door. Calmly, I pulled out one of my Los Angeles Police Department business cards, wrote down my cellular number on the back, and pounded on their open door. I was in my usual attire of black suit, briefcase in hand, and wearing my trademark dark, aviator sunglasses.

A man in his late thirties with disheveled hair and appearing very drunk stumbled to the door.

"Good morning," I said. "I am your neighbor and would like to welcome you to the neighborhood!"

With eyes that were bloodshot and glassy, he shook my extended hand. I smiled, and he invited me in. When I entered the front room, I saw three of his drinking buddies sitting around a small table filled with empty beer bottles, half-filled whiskey bottles and an innumerable amount of crushed cigarette packs. Apparently I was wrong in my assessment that they had taken a break to rest; they hadn't. They drank all night and all of them were three-sheets to the wind. Boy did this bring back a flood of memories! While other missionaries probably would feel uncomfortable in this situation, in a flash, my mind was carried back to days long past when I served on the police department where I frequently dealt with situations such as this, so I actually felt quite at ease and knew what to do. I introduced myself to each man, and then I handed my new neighbor my business card with the cell number face up. He took it, smiled, and then turned it over. "A Detective," he exclaimed! "Los Angeles Police Department!"

"Retired," I said.

But that comment appeared not to sink in. All they understood was that I was a cop. The others in the room suddenly became quiet. "It was many years ago," I added. "My wife and I now are serving as missionaries for the Church of Jesus Christ of Latter-day Saints, the Mormons."

Slowly the blood returned to their faces. Two of the three seated around the table smiled, and in broken English, we talked. "This is going to be our party house," one exclaimed. *Not if I can help it,* I thought. The fourth man who was seated across the table remained silent. It was obvious that my presence upset him, and my past profession caused him some anxiety.

The plan was working.

I told my new neighbor that should an emergency arise and he needed to contact someone in the building, he now had my number. I did not tell him that the Chief of Police for the entire country of Uruguay, Julio Guarteche, was a friend and a member of the LDS church. Long ago I was taught not to tell all I knew.

"Would you like some whiskey?" my neighbor asked.

"No thank you, I don't drink."

A look of disbelief crossed his face.

We talked for a few minutes, and one asked me what I thought about Obama. I explained that I supported my leaders, and ended the conversation with that. The last thing I needed was to get into a political discussion with a drunk, especially while the mission president sat outside our building patiently waiting to pick me up. I thanked each man for his time, told them it was a pleasure to have met them and that I hoped to see them again in the future. For those who know President Bob McKee, this was a real McKee moment. I smiled as I briefly talked about our assignments as missionaries. I was kind in my approach and gracious as I welcomed them. Then, as I turned to leave, I said, "I have a small favor."

"What is it, Richard," the new tenant asked.

"Without causing you or your friends any problems, would it be possible to tone down the noise, especially early in the morning and late at night? It would be appreciated."

Each apologized for any discomfort caused. They all smiled, we shook hands again, my business card was passed around the room for the second time, and smiling, I left, shutting the door behind me.

Upon my return home that evening, I wrote the apartment administrator and explained the situation. Not long afterward, Cheryle saw Carlos, the complex manager, at the front door of our new friend. He was explaining the noise regulation while pointing to the specific paragraph in the contract and advised him that he would be evicted if the rules were not followed; so ended the day.

During the next ten days, the noise diminished significantly, but not completely.

The noise from the apartment wasn't the only challenge we had with our neighbor. I had to laugh to myself each time I heard him start up his Harley Davidson which was parked in the underground parking lot immediately beneath our unit. The entire building would shake and rumble as that very familiar sound would override the sweet singing of the many birds in our backyard that were welcoming the morning with their sweet, cheerful songs.

After my visit, and what appeared to be some complaints from additional residents, the Harley was moved to the front of the building and onto the parking area adjacent to the street.

Some weeks later at about 8:30 p.m., music suddenly started in their apartment and again rocked the building, echoed through the halls, and bounced off the tile and hardwood paneled walls. Since the doors to each apartment lacked any type of weather-stripping or seals, when their wooden front door was closed, the noise still filtered under the door, as did the cigarette smoke. While we did bundle up a towel and stuff it under our front door when we were at home, the noise and smoke still seeped its way into our apartment.

As the music blasted, I waited a few minutes, then went outside and pounded on the door. No answer. I then walked down stairs, stepped out front and looked up into the apartment. The drapes were pulled, the lights were off and it was obvious that no one was home. The radio had gone off by itself at full volume. Very calmly—I am learning—I went back into our apartment and on the back of one of my Los Angeles Police Department business cards, I told our neighbor what had happened and asked him to check his radio. Then I taped the card to his door. After about an hour, the radio automatically shut off and later that evening I heard our neighbor return home. The next morning, I saw that the card was gone. It now gets better.

For some time the apartment had been quiet. Cheryle believed that the occupant decided to move because he didn't want to deal with the noise restrictions and the numerous complaints coming from a number of tenants, as well as the fact that his friends refused to visit because he had a cop for a neighbor. We found out that he did indeed move. Later I saw him enter another apartment at the front of the complex. I also learned that the apartments were rented on a monthly basis to summer party animals; hence, the noise.

Cheryle is Assaulted and Robbed

During my meeting with the mission president and the manager of the physical facilities in Uruguay, Cheryle went shopping with our nurse, Sister Barney. As she walked out of the store, she physically was assaulted and robbed. Two street thugs watched Cheryle and Hermana Barney walk into the store. One was on a motorcycle, while the other stood partially hidden behind a tree. The suspects then waited.

When Cheryle walked around the front of the car holding her wallet in her hand, the suspect on the motorcycle started the bike and the other one moved forward. As Cheryle reached for the car door, the criminal on foot grabbed her arm and pulled her toward the street. She struggled with the man in an effort to maintain control of her wallet, but she was overpowered. He was able to rip the wallet from her grasp just as the second thug on the motorcycle drove up. In seconds, the first suspect was on the back of the bike, grinning at Sister Barney as they sped off. During the scuffle, Cheryle was thrown off balance into the traffic lane. As she turned, she watched a bus slam on his brakes, narrowly missing her.

In the process of composing herself, a young woman approached Cheryle and handed her a piece of paper with the motorcycle license number on it that she was able to write down. Immediately, Sister Barney said they should go to the police station down the street, but Cheryle was prompted to come back to the mission home. They drove back to the house and relayed what had happened.

Since she wasn't injured, I began mentally to make an inventory of the contents of the wallet, while the mission president called Chief of Police Guarteche. The president left a message, and almost immediately received a telephone call.

It was the Chief.

Hermano Guarteche told the president that he would send his bodyguard and head of security to the mission home to pick up Cheryle and Sister Barney, and then he personally would escort them to the police station.

As I began the calls to the banks to cancel all credit cards, the president, Cheryle and Sister Barney walked out front and were met by Alfredo, the bodyguard to the Chief. When Cheryle walked to the rear car door and opened it, she was met with the sight of an H&K machine gun on the seat. "Oh my," she said. Alfredo, having already been briefed by Hermano Guarteche on my background and realizing that guns were nothing new to Cheryle, smiled, picked up the weapon and placed it on the front passenger floorboard, just under the feet of the president. Then off they went in his black SUV with the heavily tinted windows.

At the police station, it became apparent that were it not for the fact that Hermano Guarteche had made a call, and his personal bodyguard was present, Cheryle would have been in line a long time. In minutes, everything came to a stop so that the norteamericana who was a friend of The Chief could be helped. As information was gathered and placed in the computer, Cheryle knew there was a problem. Suddenly, the computer crashed and all the information was erased. A second and third attempt saw the same results. Finally, it was accomplished after they decided that the report would be handwritten. Alfredo then drove the trio back to the president's home. Cheryle had calmed down by the time they returned.

"You need to go outside and meet Alfredo," she said. "He wants to meet you." Setting the phone down on the table, I walked out the front door to the waiting SUV. Suddenly, the driver's door opened and Alfredo emerged.

From around the front of the car stepped a huge man. He stood about six foot three and weighed close to two hundred and seventy pounds. And there was not an ounce of fat on his body. With a huge grin on his face, we shook hands and then I found myself in a powerful bear hug. The man was solid muscle! We talked and I thanked him for his help. He smiled and opened the front passenger door to show me his H&K.

"Would you like to go shooting sometime?" he asked.

"I would love to," I answered, "but wouldn't there be a problem getting me onto the range?"

"No problem," he answered with the same grin. "You are a friend of the Chief and I am the firearms instructor for the country!" I gave him one of my LAPD business cards, and he was thrilled. I thanked him again and we parted, each knowing that he had just met a brother-in-arms.

When I first saw Alfredo, I knew that he probably came from Russian stock. I was right. He had the look of a Russian soldier which was verified when I found out that both sets of grandparents had fled Russia during the Second World War and had settled in Uruguay.

As to the license plate on the suspect's motorcycle, it appeared that it was stolen since we never heard anything further on the matter.

Not long after the incident, I received a poignant e-mail from Ron Kaski who was one of the Assistants to the President when I served in the Nevada Las Vegas Mission presidency. Allow me to share it:

From Elder Ron Kaski

Pres & Sister Whitaker,

Hope you are both doing well after your harrowing experience last week. You've been in our thoughts and prayers.

Truth be told - I was a little nervous for the well-being and safety of the mugger, who I assumed Sister Whitaker chased down, grabbed, and yelled, "What's in the bag, kid?" That, coupled with the voice of you, President, saying "Unlock the shotgun," and then engaging in a foot-chase through the back streets.

Well, perhaps it's my own little fiction, but I can only assume that's the way it went down, based upon your history.

I know the Lord is watching out for both of you. I miss you both and think of you often. After all, I was in your home on the first day of my mission - where President (then brother) Whitaker ripped Elder Kay "up one side, across the top, and down the other," and at the mission home with you on my last day. My memories are filled with fondness and the bond that only this type of service can create.

Alright - enough of my memory lane. Hope you're both well.

Sincerely,

Ron

The Meek Shall Inherit the Earth

While serving in foreign lands, I have learned to understand the importance of the doctrine that stresses humility and meekness. There has been no greater lesson of this than when I traveled to the districts and wards located in the interiors of Ecuador, Peru and Uruguay.

On one special occasion, I traveled with the president to the interior city of Pando, Uruguay. Our destination was a small district located deep in the interior. Being a district meant that the church unit was smaller than a ward and instead of a bishop, it had a district president who presided over the members. The mission president had been requested to speak to the members in Pando, hence our attendance.

When we arrived, we were treated with great respect. The president took his place on the stand while I sat on the back row of the chapel. Although I was invited to sit on the stand, I declined because I had been taught that he who held the keys not only spoke, but also should be the only person in a mission presidency recognized by his place on the stand. Long ago, I decided that I did not need the recognition or praise for serving or doing my duty. That belonged to the president, so I graciously declined the invitation to sit on the stand. Little did I know that this decision not only would hurt the feelings of those who presided, but also it offended the members who always put great store in being in the presence of the leaders sent from the United States.

Before the meeting began, I noted that the attendance was good, especially for a branch, and they had a pianist, something that often was not found in this type of unit. Then the prelude music began. For those of you who are not musicians, when one plays the piano, the right hand plays the melody while the left hand plays the bass cleft and the accompaniment. Both hands are usually moving with the left hand making regular chord changes.

Today, I heard something different. As the music played, I heard something that I had never heard before in a church meeting. While the right hand picked out the melody, the left hand never changed keys or chords. It played a solid beat, probably in the key of C, and no matter what chords the left hand should have played, the key never changed. Then the meeting began, and during each hymn, the method of playing never changed. As a musician, I marveled at two things. First, even though the congregation sang off key, they sang with loud and vibrant voices. And although the president and I sang louder than everyone else in order to try and get them on key, or close to the right pitch, our efforts were in vain.

Strong off key voices enthusiastically belted out hymns of the Restoration and praise of the Savior. As the cacophony of many different notes filled the chapel, the piano never stopped playing, hitting most of the correct notes with the right hand, and missing entire chord changes with the left. They truly were making a "joyful noise to the Lord," and I realized that with this humble display of devotion, there was not an absence of the Spirit, but an increase that filled the chapel the same as if the hymns were sung by the Mormon Tabernacle Choir. The humble faith of these Saints and their love for the Savior transcended the need for perfect pitch and perfection at the piano. Their faith was demonstrated as they did the best they could with what they had, and it was a testimony to me that in that chapel were those whom the Lord referred to when He said, "The meek shall inherit the earth."

Invasion of the Insect Hordes!

The thunder rolled while lightening cracked across the sky. Brutal winds howled through the trees as violent storms moved in from the Atlantic and brought torrential rains to the eastern coast and interior of Uruguay. Sounds like winter, right? Wrong. This was the precursor to summer coming to the Southern Hemisphere.

Some days we were awakened to brilliant sunshine, but it never lasted very long. As afternoon approached, dark ominous rain clouds would rush across the sky, just waiting to unload their cargo of moisture on the already saturated land. The storms came and went very quickly. Then the sun would break forth and the landscape would be warmed and dried. As that cycle of moisture and heat reoccurred over and over, another element was added to the cycle: monstrous mosquitoes!

I never had lived where mosquitoes were a problem. In Los Angeles, they were not a factor, nor were they in Henderson, Nevada. When we served in Quito, we lived at 10,000 feet and although it rained daily, the altitude and weather conditions were not conducive to the breeding of the little pests. Then in Lima, although on the Pacific Ocean, the city did not have the many stand-alone lakes and bodies of water found in Montevideo.

Not living with the threat of bites and dengue fever, I failed to realize how painful the attacks could be, nor did I realize that these little buggers, who seemed large enough to wear saddles, could penetrate right through a white dress shirt or suit pants. One day while I was sitting in the president's office at a small table in the corner of the room, I suddenly felt a stabbing pain on my right thigh. Looking down, there he was, saddle and all. The large mosquito had penetrated my suit pants and began his feast. Suddenly, my mind turned from the calm Elder Whitaker to a man who had only one thought on his mind: homicide.

In one fluid motion, my right hand slapped down and killed my adversary. However, I was too late to stop the attack. The damage had been done. He had pierced my skin. Then I felt another stabbing pain on the top of my right hand. The homicidal feeling returned! I was lucky in that after this second attacker finished his bloody work, he was so full of my blood that he could not fly. *Oh, no you don't, you are mine,* I thought. Then I saw him. He was resting on my sleeve. Smash! He died instantly, spewing bright red fluid onto my white sleeve.

When the day was over, I realized that I not only had been attacked by vicious blood suckers, but fleas also had made a meal of me. So, there I stood in the bathroom with flea bites surrounding my knees and the back of my legs, and mosquito bites on my legs, arms and the back of my hands. All the scratching in the world would not relieve the pain, but when I pinched each bite, I was able to release much of the poison. Then I hatched a plan.

The next day, I would spray my body with OFF, followed by a rub down with an anti-itching solvent. I did that, and although I still itched like the devil, I didn't have any new bites!

I have mentioned that in front of our apartment building we had a moat usually filled with stagnant water. So, right in front of our building we bred mosquitoes. It was so bad that we could not open any windows nor use the beautiful porch and landing attached to the rear of our unit for fear of becoming the victim of a horrific invasion, and since they did not have any screens covering windows, we relied on the air conditioner for ventilation.

So there I sat, fighting back the best I could, never knowing when the attacks would come, and praying that the OFF and other insect fighting materials worked. It promised to be a very long, painful summer!

Life is Hard in Uruguay

On January 28th, the president and I travelled to Las Piedras to take two mattresses to a Sister missionary companionship and also pick up two Elders who had completed their missions and were scheduled to fly home the next day.

We arrived at the apartment building where the sister missionaries lived. The president grabbed one mattress and I the other. Then we began our climb up the narrow stairwell. We trudged up the first floor and then the second. By the time I reached the fourth floor, some hallway flowers and a few planters had become the victims of the wobbling mattress. Standing on the narrow stoop of the fourth floor, I looked down at some of the carnage. *Not bad,* I thought considering the labor was cheap, the stairwells only three feet wide and the curves sharp. Then I looked up and saw that there were another ten floors to the top. My rubbery legs regained full strength when I realized that I would not need to climb any further. Then, I stopped and looked up and down the stairwell. The building, as most in South America, did not have an elevator.

Once inside, the president and I maneuvered the mattresses into the bedroom and plopped them onto the wooden framed beds that had hemp rope crisscrossed to support the mattress instead of metal springs.

All in all, the apartment was not bad. When it stormed, rain poured through the windows that did not shut securely. A long rope was extended across the living room and used to hang clothes for drying. In the kitchen, they had a microwave, but had run out of propane and did not know who to contact to get a refill. We remedied this, and they were delighted.

Since it was a long drive to Las Piedras, I asked to use the restroom. As I closed the door, one of the Sisters shouted, "Elder Whitaker.....wait!"

When I opened the door, she and her companion stood with huge sheepish grins crossing their faces.

"We need to tell you something about the bathroom!"

"I guess now would be a good time, Sisters."

"The toilet has no running water!"

"No running water?" I repeated.

"That's right."

"Then how does it work?"

Sister Ahern, the junior companion stepped forward to offer the explanation.

"Well, first you walk over to the shower, and you will see a large bucket. Fill the bucket with water and carry it over to the toilet. After you use the toilet, pour the water from the bucket into the toilet bowl. Look up and you will find a hole chipped out of the concrete block wall. Reach into this hole and you will find the flushing mechanism. Pull down. This will flush the toilet. But be careful, Elder Whitaker, that you don't fill the toilet bowl too full, or you will have a mess to clean up!"

With that explanation, both Sisters began to chuckle as I shut the door and readied myself for a new adventure. Basically, all worked as planned, but in five years living in South America, this was a first!

After we delivered the mattresses, and my education into the unique sanitary conditions in Las Piedras were completed, we drove to another part of the city to pick-up the two Elders.

As we arrived on the street where the Elders lived, I noted a disheveled man sitting on a root stump in front of a store. He wore no shirt, his skin was a dark ebony and he wore a ratted afro. He was barefoot and his movements and general demeanor indicated that while the lights were on, there were times that nobody was home. Getting up from his stool, he would walk short distances and carry on intricate conversations with people only he could see. The conversations only stopped as pedestrians walked past. Then he would stop, approach each individual and ask for some money. When denied, he would bid them a good day, smile a large smile that was accentuated by beautiful straight white teeth, and then rapidly move on to the next person.

What was the most remarkable thing about this man was not his ebony skin, slender body or large afro, but his eyes. They were the most beautiful blue; light in color, almost to the point of being iridescent and deeply penetrating. It was the first time in my life that I had ever seen this, and I was in awe at their brilliance. Although his skin was black, his features were very fine. What an interesting genealogy this wonderful citizen of the street would have. I could not help but be fascinated by the man who had no care in the world, knew everyone, including our missionaries, and would talk to anyone about anything. It was quite a show, but when I thought that the curtain had closed, the third and final act began.

When asked where he lived, he pointed to different spots on the sidewalk or doorways which he used in order to avoid the elements. I watched from behind the darkened windows of the SUV as he looked up and down the street, and believing that he was alone, he abruptly sat down on his small circular log which was located next to a small hole in the block wall which was covered by an aluminum door with a latch. After a few more furtive glances up and down the street, he reached over to the hole, slipped the clasp on the door and opened it. He then reached into his personal safe, removed a white cylindrical tube about four inches in length and removed the top. He then proceeded to apply his personal deodorant stick under both arms. I was in a state of shock. Never before had I seen a homeless person worry about their personal hygiene, but this man did.

After applying a goodly amount to both underarms, he slipped the top back on, looked around to make sure no one was looking and placed his treasure back into its hiding spot. He closed the door and slipped the clasp securing his treasures. He then stood, waved his arms in circles to allow the antiperspirant to dry, broke into a large smile while running his fingers though his afro and shaking his head vigorously to guarantee that he again was ready for the day. When all was completed, he threw his shoulders back, tossed his chin into the air and headed out to begin the afternoon as the best looking and most pampered panhandler in the neighborhood!

Pickin' and Grinnin' with Some Very Drunk Neighbor's

I always have enjoyed the company of non-members of the church, as well as those members who are less active. Unlike many church members, I can relate to both, and I find that they, each in their own way, bring much to the table. I have lived a fascinating life which has included selling women's shoes; making donuts; being a salesman in a stationary department; stock boy; lifeguard and swimming instructor; lead singer in rock and roll bands; police officer/detective; work in the top secret black world of aerospace; casino security in the eye-in-the-sky at a major Las Vegas casino; published author of two books, and then a priesthood leader and missionary for the Church of Jesus Christ of Latter-day Saints. To say that I have had many memorable experiences different than most members of the church would be an understatement.

But I have found that what draws me closer to many is my love for music and the ability to sit down at a piano and play rock and roll or pick up a guitar and play many of the folk songs of the 1950's and 1960's.

This talent again surfaced one Saturday morning as I was awakened at about 7:00 when my senses were bombarded by a drunken party of young adults in an apartment just across the hall. Someone was playing a guitar while others were drunkenly screaming every American rock and roll song they

PICKIN' AND GRINNIN'
WITH SOME VERY DRUNK NEIGHBOR'S

knew. It was horrible. It sounded like a group of cats trying to escape an electronic cage. This was a different apartment than the one occupied by the four drunk bikers. Of the six apartments on our floor, we had two occupied by drunken revilers.

Calmly, I got up, slipped on my Levi's and a tee-shirt and threw on my LAPD (Los Angeles Police Department) baseball hat. Now ready to face a new experience, I opened my door where all of my senses were bombarded by the smell of booze, cigarette smoke and loud music, which came sliding out from under their door. I walked over to the apartment and knocked on the door. Suddenly, there was silence. Then the door opened and a blast of smoke engulfed me.

At first all eyes were on me and what I would say. Softly, and very politely I asked the group to tone it down. I saw that the small room was occupied by four young men and three attractive young ladies. All appeared to be college age. While the guys obviously had been drinking, the girls were cold-stone-sober. Then I saw the guitar and one guy playing a Beatles song. *Here is my chance,* I thought.

Invited into the smoke filled room, I was offered coffee, alcohol, and food. I declined all, but when the guitar was set down, I asked if they minded if I played a little. Their eyes lit up, and smiles crossed each face. They literally were flabbergasted that an old, sober norteamericano wearing a LAPD hat would knock on their door at 7:00 a.m. and want to sit in and jam with them. Someone asked why I was in Montevideo. This was my chance to explain who I represented, and when they heard Mormon Church, each had a positive thing to say, and even shared with me the members of the church they knew and how they respected them.

The entire experience brought back many memories from fifty years ago when I would sit with my high school buddies and we would play and sing into the early morning hours.

As I sat in the world of my neighbors, I was treated with the greatest respect which only grew with each song I played. I even taught them the background to some of the Doo-wop songs. They loved it, and although I would at times need to ask them not to scream, but sing, they were in awe.

Then, the young man sitting on the couch next to me shared that he was from Uruguay, but had just graduated from college in the United States. As his questions about the church increased, and I noted that he was quite sober considering the atmosphere, I was able to teach him the First Discussion. All listened while I taught and still played. Not bad for an old guy! After about thirty minutes, I thanked them and we shared abrazos, or hugs, and then I left. This was just another sweet and amazing experience where I was allowed to share the Gospel message through my knowledge of music.

The Beginning of the End

I already have related that on our sixth day in Uruguay, Cheryle fell down a flight of seventeen stairs striking her head at least fourteen times. While we pushed forward, her condition only worsened.

After her second stumble in late December during a missionary conference, the Mission Medical in Salt Lake was advised of Cheryle's condition. They decided that she immediately should return to the United States for medical treatment.

We were advised that our assignment would be terminated on Tuesday, February 26 with our flight back to the United States scheduled to depart late Monday night, February 25. So if the question is asked: "Elder Whitaker, did you complete the assignment the Lord sent you on?"

My answer would be a resounding, "Yes!"

While some would comment that we did not complete the time, the Lord has taught me, and it has been evident in each of my mission assignments, that the completion of a difficult assignment is more important to the Savior than time filled. We did our best and were leaving this assignment knowing that we went where we were asked to go; we did what we were ask to do, and completed our assignment under some very difficult circumstances.

Since Cheryle still was suffering from forgetfulness, dizzy spells, lack of motor coordination, the dropping of items, and pain in her neck and lower back, I knew we must return to the states. We had pushed as far as we could. Nothing more was possible. Her health issues coupled with my neck and headache problems sealed the deal. We were leaving.

In four assignments to South America, one mission to the Addiction Recovery Program in Las Vegas, coupled with my five years serving in three mission presidency's in Las Vegas, we knew that during each assignment we had given our all and had laid our sacrifice upon the alter and worn ourselves out in the service of the Lord. As we both were suffering from medical issues, there was nothing more to do but return to the United States, recover, and then provide what future service the Lord requested.

Our assignment to Uruguay had not only been a difficult and challenging experience for both of us, but also one we would not change. Cheryle was able to help organize and run a mission office that lacked her preciseness and skills, and I had it impressed on me by the Spirit that my service to the president was not unlike the service Hyrum Smith provided to his brother, Joseph. I was his friend, counselor, confidant and brother in the gospel. I was able to take twenty years of missionary experience and share it in a way that was of great help and assistance to my priesthood leader. While I was not called upon to use many of the missionary skills learned from prior experiences, when all was said and done, I had been a friend to the president and this was what the Lord desired. My frustration was washed away when I understood that simple concept. While I was there for the president, Cheryle was there for his wife and we both were there for their family which included a beautiful eighteen year old daughter who suffered for her parents as much as is humanly possible.

As the time approached for our departure, my feelings of frustration abated. While I had struggled for six months trying to determine my role, it finally was made clear, and when that happened, I was at peace not only with our leaving, but also in my review with the Lord as to what I had accomplished.

While I did not fill the assignment as planned, I was always there for the president as we spent time together and were able to talk and share feelings from the depths of our heart. I was able to evaluate and make observations that led to recommendations, always knowing that this wonderful man would listen and go to the Lord for confirmation, and then make those decisions the Savior would make if He were here personally managing this mission. When the Spirit approved what we had accomplished and approved our departure, I was satisfied. With peace in my soul, I continued making the final arrangements for our departure.

Departing Uruguay

After the decision was made to terminate our assignment in Uruguay and seek medical help for Cheryle in the United States, the next step was to secure the required paperwork to get us out of the country. In all reality, after our first three months in country, the regional office in Montevideo should have provided us with the paperwork that would have changed our status from Tourist to Resident, but as we entered our fifth month, we had not received anything and had it not been for my insistence, that process at the beginning of the sixth month never would have begun. My disappointment in the administrative capabilities of the Montevideo Regional Office continued.

This incompetence was just another of the many irritants that plagued this assignment, and bothered me greatly, considering the fact that our tourist status had expired at the end of our third month. Legally, and technically….we were illegal! Again, the administrative incompetence experienced during this mission whether it emanated from Buenos Aires or Montevideo, never ceased to amaze me.

Regularly, I attempted to secure our residency papers, but to no avail. First, we were told that our papers and the file had been lost. Then they were found on the desk of the individual who had this assignment. It appeared that she had piled a stack of other papers on top of ours, so when it came time for us to leave the country, the mission was required to pay a fine which secured us a temporary extension on our Visa. Nearly six months had passed. Finally, a stake president working for the church stepped in and our exit papers were completed.

Five days before our flight, we had our exit paperwork in hand. The next obstacle was to make the flight arrangements.

After living in South America for five years, we learned a little about the travel process and became familiar with the staff in Missionary Travel. So after the president advised Salt Lake that we were leaving and gave them our departure date, Missionary Travel stepped in and began to make our flight plans. The Sisters working in Travel were all wonderful, especially Norma Olivas and Julianne Given.

For our departure plans, we again would be working with Sister Given.

Because of the damage from the fall to Cheryle's neck and back, I opted for the first time in our married life to request a seating upgrade. I just could not see her sitting for nearly sixteen hours in a small, economy seat, so, I paid out of pocket for the upgrade, realizing that it would take some time to pay off the debt, but felt that it was worth the expenditure.

I advised Sister Given of my desire to upgrade and she said I could put it on my credit card. I gave her the necessary information, and assumed that all would go smoothly. It did not. The next day she sent me an e-mail advising me that our

Master Card had been blocked and could not be used. This was the first I had heard of the problem, so while I began the process of determining why the card was blocked, I gave Sister Given our Visa Card information. Within hours she got back to me and told me that the card was invalid. There we were, six thousand miles away from home, living closer to Antarctica than the Equator, and other than some cash I brought for an emergency, we had no means of making any major purchases. The challenges continued.

After some research, I was able to determine two things. First, the Master Card was blocked because of a missed payment that just slipped through the cracks of our busy missionary lives. I paid the late fee, and the card was activated. This information was forwarded to Sister Given, who then was able to make the flight arrangements. We were booked in First Class. A once in a lifetime experience!

The second item was the Visa Card. I was told by Visa that the card was old. It appeared that when a replacement card was sent, we already had left for Uruguay, therefore, the new card was not activated. We scuttled using the Visa.

On the evening of Monday, February 25, the president and his daughter drove us to the airport. The office Elders transported our luggage using the mission truck. So far it was smooth sailing!

At 7:00 p.m. the airport was not busy and check-in went as planned. We secured our tickets, checked our luggage, sailed through customs and passed through the final door leading to the passenger area. Ironically, this last door is referred to by the missionaries as the "Veil."

Prior to stepping into the passenger waiting area, we said our brief goodbyes. I am not one for small talk and long goodbyes. When called, I accept an assignment, serve and when it is time to go, I leave. No parties, no fanfare, few goodbyes. Here today, gone tomorrow.

No one in Montevideo except the president and the office Elders knew we were leaving, and because of my silence and manner of serving my president, many did not even know that I spoke Spanish. I was quiet in the meetings on Sunday and unless assigned to speak or involved in a courteous conversation, I was silent.

The upgrade for our flight was well worth the additional cost. We were seated toward the front and it was the first time I ever had been on an airplane in a full reclining seat. While Cheryle was able to sleep through much of the nine hour journey from Montevideo to Miami, I was still on an airplane, and no matter how hard I tried, I just couldn't find a comfortable position.

The weather was rough, and we hit a strong headwind which caused us to land in Miami nearly thirty minutes behind schedule. When we exited the plane at 6:15, I knew that we were in trouble. Our connecting flight was scheduled to leave at seven.

Bolting from the plane, we ran to the carousel area, and as in times past, I looked for a Sky Cap.

I shot a quick glance to the left and then the right.

Being so early in the morning, the place was deserted.

Then, suddenly from around a corner shuffled an elderly man wearing a gray uniform topped off with a hat that identified him as Jose, the Sky Cap!

"Jose, my dear friend, we need your help!"

His face broke into a large grin as if he knew what was needed before the words were spoken.

Standing in the deserted concourse, I explained our predicament, and advised him I would make it worth his while if he would get us through Customs and Security before our flight left. He smiled, looked at my missionary tag, then at his watch.

"Elder Whitaker, you *are* in trouble!"

"I know we are," I said, "but that is why I have you!"

As the luggage came off the plane, we were fortunate that ours were some of the first bags unloaded. I marveled as Jose, a seventy-two year old Cuban, grabbed our bags and effortlessly threw them onto his cart.

"Hurry, hurry, hurry," he shouted as the carousel area filled. Waving his arms, he pointed to a door over which was a sign that read: *Diplomats.*

"Through there!" he shouted. "Run! Run!"

We broke into a run and followed him as he gracefully jogged behind the full luggage cart.

As we hurried through a sliding glass door, the attendant asked, "Are you with Jose?

"Yes," I responded.

"Into this line."

I looked up.

The sign read, "Diplomats Only."

We were the only ones in the line and in no time we were on our way to Customs.

I looked at my watch. 6:25 a.m.

Within minutes, our Passports had been stamped, papers collected and we hurried to Security.

6:30 a.m.

Jose hurried to my side. "Your luggage is on the way, good luck and God bless you!"

I paid Jose $40.00 and thanked him. That was one of the best investments we had made in years.

Now, we needed more than luck. My petition for angels to attend continued for I knew that the plane was boarding.

Hundreds now crammed themselves into two lines that serpentined into the Security Checkpoint.

This is not going to work, I thought.

"Oh ye of little faith," I heard softly whispered in my ear. I turned to see who had made the comment. I was alone.

Then I looked to my right. Another small line with two passengers had formed just the other side of our restraining line.

"Excuse me," I asked a woman I had observed was a passenger on our plane. "Is your line for First Class?"

"No," she said, "it is for those who will miss their connection at seven.

I glanced down at my watch.

It was now 6:38.

Quickly, I removed the restraining line and pushed Cheryle and the carry-ons through.

No guts, no glory, I thought.

I looked to the right. Another line was also feeding into this line, but we were next.

My watch read, 6:40.

Then we were motioned forward.

We quickly passed through the checkpoint. Now I had to get the carry-ons and computers onto the belt.

Time was running.

I set off the alarm as I walked through the scanner.

Okay, a wand search. No problem. Let's just get going!

6:45.

Although we were through Security, we now had to make it to our plane. Our next challenge: the Sky Rail!

Up a set of escalators we rushed. Cheryle fell behind and a kind young man grabbed her carry-on as I struggled with mine that had slid down some of the escalator stairs. Seconds before the twisted strap to my computer bag disappeared between the grinding steps, I bent down and snatched the bag.

After throwing it across my shoulder, the stair locked into another and I stepped onto the main concourse.

"That was close," I whispered.

On we raced to the Sky Rail. The waiting area was packed with humanity. A crowd had formed at the doors and I felt like I was in the middle of an ant colony.

A sign above the Sky Rail read, "Next Train, three minutes." That was going to be a long three minutes.

The tram pulled up.

Pushing and sliding in between other passengers, I maneuvered myself to the front, next to the door. As the doors opened, a mass of humanity surged forward with me in the middle. I felt like I was in a Japanese travel documentary. I turned my head and looked for Cheryle.

She was standing alone on the concourse.

The doors began to slide shut!

"Get in!" I shouted.

"I can't get in," she whispered. "The car is full!"

While she was correct in that assessment, I was determined to make room for one more.

Like a boxer throwing a quick right cross, my arm bolted forward between the closing doors and I grabbed her jacket.

"Come on! I shouted as I jerked her into the car to the dismay of the others in the car.

"If they can jam people in Sky Rail cars in China and Japan, I could do it here," I mumbled under my breath.

Just as I pulled her close to me, and before I could grab a pole, the doors slid shut and the car jumped forward. With the jerking forward momentum, I stumbled and lunged forward. As I struggled to stay on my feet and maintain my balance, my right arm shot forward and my hand made a fist. Unfortunately, my clenched fist caught the man directly in front of me in the groin. With an audible gasp and ear piercing moan, he doubled over in pain!

"Sorry," I said while I struggled to regain my balance. His face flushed, and then went white.

His mouth now opened but no words exited. As his eyes began to roll back and he grimaced in pain, I knew that he was not happy.

While I felt bad, anyone who travels knows that in crowded airports and trams, it quickly becomes survival of the fittest. I looked at Cheryle. She stood just inside the car, her skirt caught in the door. She couldn't move. But at least, she was onboard.

I looked back at my victim. With my aviator glasses, my silver hair and dressed in a dark suit, I must have appeared to be a formidable opponent for he said nothing as his eyes watered. Again, I said I was sorry.

I now was talking to stone.

The tram raced down the track and around a turn. Then as suddenly as it began, it ended. The doors flew open and in a massive surge, we literally were blasted out onto the concourse. Hurriedly, we stepped to the first Arrival and Departure board we could find.

I looked at the board. We had five gates to go. I then looked down at my watch.

6:50.

"Run, Cheryle, run," I shouted!

I sprinted ahead in an effort to get to the plane before the doors closed. Cheryle was just behind me. For all she had been through in the past six months, she still was pushing forward.

As we slid up to the counter, the attendant smiled and said, "The Whitakers?"

"Yes," I answered as I gasped for breath.

With great calmness and professionalism, the agent looked at us and said, "I was hoping it was you. I saw that your plane was delayed. Boarding is around the corner through the large door."

We hurried to the door that provided access to the walkway allowing entrance to the plane.

6:55.

I jerked on the closed door, but it was locked!

The pilots were ready to depart! The blocks were being removed and the hook to tow the plane was being fastened into place.

"No," I pleaded under my breath, "Wait!"

I raced back around the corner to the counter. "The doors are locked!" I shouted.

An attendant appeared, slid her identification through the pad and opened the door.

6:58.

Running down the hall we stepped into the plane. It was 7:00 a.m. straight up!

The plane was full and fortunately, we had the first two seats, First Class, on the left just behind the bulkhead that divided the cabin from the flight crew. Quickly, I threw open an overhead bin. It was empty. What a blessing.

We seated ourselves and took a deep breath as a flight attendant stepped over to our seats.

"I am glad you made it," she said. "Normally, the pilots don't wait this long. They only waited because you were in First Class and we were notified that your plane from Montevideo was delayed."

"I am glad they waited," I said.

Had I not changed our seats from Economy to First Class, we still could be standing in that airport; well, not really, but it would have been a real mess to have missed that plane.

I offered a silent prayer, and looked at Cheryle and whispered, "Angels attend."

She smiled.

The plane began to roll back.

We were finally on our way home.

After we settled into our seats and were in the air, I started to look around the cabin. Across the aisle, and to my immediate right was an off-duty American Airlines pilot. He was involved in a very animated conversation with another passenger. I leaned forward and smiled. My eyes saw a young black woman who busily was trying to convince the pilot that she was a swim suit model. She even had her IPAD out showing him photographs of herself in every swimsuit pose imaginable, and a few that I am convinced never would have made it through the Sports Illustrated Swim Suit Edition! With each photograph, our "model" provided a detailed description. He was caught in the web. When she pulled her crotch length knitted dress up to allow him a glance at one of her very long legs, I laughed. She's working all right, but not as a swim suit model!

During the flight, she consumed one drink of wine after another. I stopped counting at five, then it was time for her to use the restroom.

When she stood, I was embarrassed, so I turned and looked at Cheryle who followed her with her eyes as the model made the short trip to the restroom.

"You are missing quite a show," was her only comment.

"I'll pass."

While she used the restroom, the off-duty pilot walked into the galley area and began talking with the two flight attendants who serviced the First Class passengers. When our "model" exited the restroom, the off-duty pilot asked a flight attendant to take some photos of him with his new friend.

Your wife will love those, I thought.

In moments, the front galley became a photo studio filled with laughter.

I focused my gaze on the bulkhead. Unfortunately, it was not wide enough so I turned, looked at Cheryle, and hoped that the young lady soon would return to her seat. When the photo op ended, she found her seat and became very quiet as the effects of the wine began taking effect, much to the dismay of the young pilot.

Well into the flight, I watched as a male flight attendant stepped from the rear of the plane and stood next to the cockpit door. Once he was in position, another flight attendant removed a rolling cart from beneath a counter and jammed it into the narrow aisle that separated the main cabin from the galley and cockpit area. Since there was only one aisle on the plane, this blocked all traffic into the Galley and sealed off the restroom area. Then the male flight attendant picked up a wall mounted phone, spoke into it briefly and then hung it up. In moments, the door to the cockpit opened and out stepped one of the two pilots. Without hesitation, the male flight attendant stepped into the cockpit and quickly closed the door. The pilot then stepped into the restroom. When finished, the pilot exited the restroom and used the wall mounted phone to make contact with the cockpit. It was obvious from the conversation that he and the other pilot had worked out a code that would allow for proper identification.

Suddenly, the cockpit door opened and the flight attendant exited. Once the door was closed and secured, a flight attendant removed the rolling cart from the aisle and slid it back under the counter.

I sat in my seat and reflected upon what I had just observed.

Smooth, I thought. *Very, very smooth.*

After that, the remainder of the flight was exactly what we wanted from a cross country journey; smooth flying with the wind at our back!

We landed in Las Vegas as scheduled and made our way down to the baggage carousel where our dear friend Don McClelland was waiting. The young woman from our flight, who professed to be a model, stood across from Don. She watched the carousel carefully, and when she saw her small bag, she snatched it up and walked toward the exit where she was escorted out the door by her chauffer.

Only in Vegas, I thought.

It felt good to be home, especially considering the events that had transpired during the past six months.

On Sunday evening, President David Gates of the Anthem Stake released us from our assignment. We expressed our gratitude for the opportunity to serve, and Cheryle and I bore a strong testimony to the fact that we had been able to accomplish what the Lord sent us to do. President Gates agreed. I then shared with him my testimony that during the past twenty years that I had been involved in the missionary effort of the church, it was the completion of the assignment, not the filling of time that was most important.

Many continued to show their concern for Cheryle and asked about her health. We had scheduled an MRI which would be reviewed by a neurologist. She appeared to have weathered the worst of the storm, and aside from being tired; the dizzy spells decreased as did the headaches and pain to the back of her lower spine. There remained some pain and discomfort to the neck area, but I was confident that after the medical evaluations, and some time, she would be as good as new….or almost! While the concussion was severe and the fall could have been fatal, she definitely was on the mend. We were told that because of the severity of the concussion, it would require approximately two years for the effects to disappear. And so it was. Nearly two years to the day after the accident, she was back to her normal self.

When we arrived home and were standing in our living room, I told her that I believed that four mission assignments and living in South America for five years were sufficient. Any further missions would be in the states. She smiled and said, "I certainly hope so!"

End...

Made in the USA
Middletown, DE
11 March 2023